MEMOIRS

Illustrating the

HISTORY OF JACOBINISM

written in French by

AUGUSTIN BARRUEL

and translated into English by

THE HON. ROBERT CLIFFORD, F.R.S. AND A.S.

*Princes and nations shall disappear from
the face of the earth . . . and this* REVOLUTION
shall be the WORK OF SECRET SOCIETIES.
—Adam Weishaupt's *Discourse for the Mysteries*

Part I

THE ANTICHRISTIAN CONSPIRACY

London
Spradabach Publishing
2021

SPRADABACH PUBLISHING
BM Box Spradabach
London WC1N 3XX

Memoirs Illustrating the History of Jacobinism,
Part I: The Antichristian Conspiracy
originally published in English in 1798
© Spradabach Publishing 2021

First Spradabach edition published 2021

ISBN 978-1-9993573-1-3

British Library Cataloguing-in-Publication Data:
A catalogue record for this book is available from the British Library.

Table of Contents.

ADEPTS AND PROTECTORS.

Note on This Edition.

ugustin Barruel's *Memoirs Illustrating the History of Jacobinism* is an extensive work of half a million words, which some modern publishers have compressed into a single, hefty volume. This has been accomplished through an unreasonable reduction of font size, which has turned the end product into a daunting, eye-taxing chore. Other publishers have simply churned out a straight scan of the original, and packaged it with generic and often ugly covers, which look exactly the same across their entire catalogue, except for the titles and the names of the authors. Rather than reduce costs either at the expense of readability or through laziness, the choice was made here to reproduce the work in four volumes, as originally intended, but reformatted for improved readability and with a focus on aesthetics. The assumption is that readers who choose this edition will prioritise these two elements over economy, while not having to spend ten times more on an antique or a boutique edition that is only for display and will never be read; after all, a book is neither just text nor just an ornament: it is, when done well, a functional, poly-faceted source of pleasure and instruction.

The text herein presented is based primarily on the revised and corrected second edition of Robert Clifford's translation of the *Memoirs*, published by T. Burton, in London, in 1798. Other English editions or reprints of the period, as well as the original French text, have been examined. Said text appears as in the original—including spelling, punctuation, and Italics—except that the archaic long 's', which was already on the way out at the end of the 18th century, has been replaced by the modern 's' throughout; where applicable, since it sometimes and inconsistently appears as Lewis, the name of the king of France has been untranslated back to Louis, followed by whatever numeral applies, as per convention, including the period used at the time to indicate an ordinal; the name of Frederick the Great, or II, has been spelt with the 'k', as in the 1799 edition; the marginal signposts, which evince minor differences in wording depending on the edition, have followed the wordings of the first

and second (corrected) 1798 editions, whichever
was deemed optimal; the translator's prefaces, ab-
sent in some versions, have been taken from where
they could be found; names of members of Adam
Weishaupt's Illuminati (dealt with in the third and
fourth volumes) as well as other names that were
found incorrectly spelt, were left as they appeared
in the original, but with a footnote indicating the
correct spelling; the capitalisation of titles in French
has been brought into conformity with French convention; geographical names bearing the names of
saints have been rendered as in French; inconsistently spelt names have been homogenised; the titles
of written works mentioned in Roman type have
been Italicised; long quoted passages have been set
as block quotes; commas have substituted periods
in bibliographical footnotes where volume, letter,
and / or page were given, and capitalisation has
bee adjusted accordingly; and a number of minor
spelling errors or obviously missing punctuation
marks have been silently corrected. The long notes
at the end of some chapters, such as Chapter IV and
Chapter IX in this volume, have been restored to
their status of footnotes, following the French edition; but On the other hand, exclamation marks,
sometimes multiple, added by the translator, but
not appearing in the French, were left in the text,
as this is how English-speaking readers would have
experienced it when it was first published. Editorial
footnotes have been added and identified as such,
to distinguish them from Barruel's own. And, final-

ly, comprehensive indexes for each volume have been created for the first time.

Preface of the Translator.

In the work laid before you, you are not to expect the beauties of imagination; truth alone is the object of this research. History has always been considered as the school in which the statesman is to learn the art of government; the citizen to read with awe of those disastrous days of blood and rapine, expressed by the term *Revolution*. This work will lay open the most terrible and perhaps the most astonishing concatenation of intrigue, that has ever entered the mind of man, to bring about the dreadful revolution, with which all Europe has been convulsed.

The First Part will contain, THE ANTICHRISTIAN CONSPIRACY, or that of the *Sophisters of Impiety* against the God of Christianity, and against every religion and every Altar, whether Protestant or Catholic, Lutheran or Calvinist, provided it be but Christian.

The Second Part will show, the ANTIMONARCHI-CAL CONSPIRACY, or that of the *Sophisters of Impiety*, coalescing with those of *Rebellion* against kings.

The Third Part will demonstrate THE ANTISO-CIAL CONSPIRACY, or that of the *Sophisters of Impiety* coalescing with those of *Anarchy* against every religion, against every government, without even excepting the republican, against all civil society and all property whatever.

The first of these conspiracies was that of those men called Philosophers. The second that of the Philosophers united with the Occult Lodges of the Freemasons.[1] The third was that of the Philosophers and the Occult-Masons coalescent with the Illuminées, who generated the Jacobins.

It is with confidence that we present the first volume to the public, after the approbation which

---

1   We say OCCULT LODGES as the Freemasons in general were far from being acquainted with the conspiracies of the Occult Lodges; and indeed many were not people to be tampered with. It might be objected, that all lodges were occult; with regard to the public they were so; but besides the common lodges, there existed others which were hidden from the generality of the Freemasons. It is those which the author styles ARRIÈRES LOGES, and that we have translated by OCCULT LODGES.

one of the most distinguished authors of the age, both for his political knowledge, and the noble ardour he has shown in his writings to subdue the growing evil, was pleased to express, when he read the first volume of the French original. He was flattering enough to say, in writing to the author,

> The whole of the wonderful narrative is supported by documents and proofs, with the most juridical regularity and exactness. The reflexions and reasonings are interspersed with infinite judgment, and in their most proper places, for leading the sentiments of the reader and preventing the force of plausible objections. The tendency of the whole is admirable in every point of view, political, religious, and philosophical.[2]

After such a decided opinion on the French original, the translator cannot but think it *a duty he has fulfilled* in laying such a work open to those of his countrymen who may not be sufficiently versed in the French language; and if in so critical a moment, he can by this means, serve his country, he is willing to take upon himself all those inaccuracies of style, which are too frequent in translation, especially when done in haste. That the reader may be instructed in these dreadful plots, and be ac-

---

2   Edmund Burke to Abbé Barruel, May 1, 1797, in Thomas W. Copeland, ed., *The Correspondence of Edmund Burke*, 10 Vols. (Chicago and Cambridge, 1958–1978), 9: 319–320. —Ed.

quainted with the whole and nothing but the truth, is the sincere wish of the

TRANSLATOR.

It would be useless to add, that in all quotations the most literal exactness has been observed.

Preliminary Discourse.

At an early period of the French Revolution, there appeared a Sect calling itself JACOBIN, and teaching *that all men were equal and free!*[1] In the name of their Equality and disorganizing Liberty, they trampled under foot the Altar and the throne; they stimulated all nations to rebellion, and aimed at plunging them ultimately into the horrors of anarchy.

At its first appearance, this Sect counted 300,000 adepts; and it was supported by two millions of men, scattered through France, armed

The Jacobins appear.

---

1 The exclamation mark doesn't appear in the French. —Ed.

with torches and pikes, and all the fire-brands of revolution.

It was under the auspices of this Sect, and by their intrigues, influence, and impulse, that France beheld itself a prey to every crime; that its soil was stained with the blood of its pontiffs and priests, of its rich men and nobles; with the blood of every class of its citizens, without regard to rank, age, or sex! These were the men who, after having made the unfortunate Louis XVI., his Queen and Sister, drink to the very dregs the cup of outrage and ignominy during a long confinement, solemnly murdered them on a scaffold, proudly menacing the sovereigns of the earth with a similar fate! These are the men who have made the French revolution a scourge to all Europe, a terror to its Rulers, who in vain combine to stop the progress of their revolutionary armies, more numerous and more destructive than the inundations of the Vandals.

Whence originated these men, who seem to arise from the bowels of the earth, who start into existence with their plans and their projects, their tenets and their thunders, their insidious means and ferocious resolves? Whence, I say, this devouring Sect? Whence this swarm of adepts, these systems, this frantic rage against the Altar and the throne, against every institution, civil and religious, so much respected by our ancestors? Can their primogeniture in the order of the revolution give them this tremendous power, or were they not anterior? Is it not their own work? Where then was their hiding place, their schools, their masters, where shall we find these, and who will dive into their future projects? This French revolution ended, will they cease to desolate the earth, to murder its kings, or to fanaticise its people?

These certainly are questions that cannot be indifferent to nations or their rulers, or to those who watch for the happiness and preservation of society; and these are the questions which I will attempt to answer. I will draw their solution from the very annals of the Sect, whence I will show their plans and systems, their plots and their means. Such, reader, will be the object of the following Memoirs. *Importance of their History*

Had I seen the conspiracies of the Jacobins end with the disasters they produced; had I even seen the cloud of our misfortunes dissipated with the French Revolution, still should I have remained convinced of the importance and necessity of disclosing to the world the dark recesses from which it burst into being.

When with aweful astonishment we read of plagues and other scourges that have desolated the earth, though the danger be passed, they are not to be considered as objects of mere curiosity. In the history of poisons we find the antidotes; in the history of monsters we learn by what weapons they were destroyed. When former calamities reappear, or are to be apprehended, is it not our duty to explore the causes which first promoted their destructive influence, the means by which they might have been opposed, and the errors whereby *to posterity;*

they may again be produced? The present generation is instructed by the misfortunes of the past; be then the future instructed by the history of ours.

to the present generation.

But we have evils yet more pressing to encounter: the present generation has been deluded; and such delusions must be done away as may double our misfortunes in the instant when we think ourselves most secure. We have seen men obstinately blind to the causes of the French Revolution: we have seen men who wished to persuade themselves that this conspiring and revolutionary Sect had no existence anterior to the Revolution. In their minds the long series of miseries which have befallen France, to the terror of all Europe, were merely the offspring of that concourse of unforeseen events inseparable from the times. In their conceptions, it is in vain to seek conspirators or conspiracies, and as vain to search for the hand that directs the horrid course. The man who rules today, knows not the plans of his predecessor; and he that shall follow will, in their opinions, be equally ignorant of those of the present ruler.

1st error. On the cause of the revolution.

Prepossessed with such erroneous notions, and acting under so dangerous a prejudice, these superficial observers would willingly make all nations believe, that the French Revolution ought to be to them no cause of alarm; that it was a volcano rapidly venting itself on the unfortunate country that gave it existence, while its focus and its origin remain unfathomable. "Causes unknown (they will say) but peculiar to your climate; elements less subject to ferment; laws more analogous to your character; the public fortune better balanced; these and such as these are reasons sufficient to make you regardless of the fate of France. But, alas! should such be your impending fate, vain will be your efforts to avert the threatening blow. The concourse and fatality of circumstances will drag you toward it; the very ramparts which you shall build against it will fall back upon you, and perhaps level the space that now divides you from the horrid scene of anarchy and desolation."

Who would conceive, that I have heard this very language fall from the mouth of those whom the unfortunate Louis XVI. had called near his person to ward off the blows perpetually aimed at him by the Revolution! a language better calculated to lull all nations into that fatal security which portends destruction?—I have now before me the memorial of an ex-minister, consulted on the causes of this infernal Revolution, and particularly as to the chief conspirators (whom he should have better known) and on the plan of the conspiracy. I hear this man answer, that it would be useless to seek either a man or any set of men conspiring against the Altar and the throne, or to suppose that any plan had been framed for that purpose. Unfortunate monarch! Are those who ought to watch for the safety of your person, for the security of your people, ignorant of the names, nay even of the very existence of your enemies! If then we behold both you and your people falling victims to their plots, can we or ought we to be astonished?

Truths combating this error.

Strong in the facts, and armed with the proofs produced in the following Memoirs, we shall hold a very different language. We shall show what it is incumbent on all nations and their chiefs to be informed of: we shall demonstrate that, even to the most horrid deeds perpetrated during the French Revolution, every thing was foreseen and resolved on, was premeditated and combined:—that they were the offspring of deep-thought villany, since they had been prepared and were produced by men, who alone held the clue of those plots and conspiracies, lurking in the secret meetings where they had been conceived, and only watching the favourable moment of bursting forth. Though the events of each day may not appear to have been combined, there nevertheless existed a secret agent and a secret cause, giving rise to each event, and turning each circumstance to the long-desired end. Though circumstances may often have afforded the pretence or the occasion, yet the grand cause of the revolution, its leading features, its atrocious crimes, will still be found one continued chain of deep-laid and premeditated villany.

2nd. error. On the nature of the revolution.

In revealing the object, and showing the extent of these plots, I meet a second error, more dangerous than the first. There are men who, though they hesitate not to believe that the French Revolution was premeditated, yet think that the intentions of the first authors were pure, and that they only sought the happiness and regeneration of empires; that if great misfortunes have since happened, they arose from the obstacles thrown in their way; that a great people cannot be regenerated without commotion, but that the tempest will subside, and a calm succeed the swelling billow; that then nations, astonished at the apprehensions they had entertained of the French Revolution, and true only to its principles, will be happy in imitation.

This error is the favourite theme of the *Jacobin missionaries*; it was this that gained them their first instruments of rebellion; that cohort of constitutionalists, who still look on their decrees of the RIGHTS OF MAN as the summit of legislative perfection, and still impatiently wait the fatal day when the world shall impetuously move in the sphere of their political rhapsody. It was this that gained them that prodigious number of votaries more blind than wicked, and who might have been mistaken for honest, if virtue could have associated with ferocity in search of happier days. It was this that gained them those men whose well-meant, though stupid credulity, misled them to believe in the necessity of the carnage of the 10th of August and of the horrid butcheries of the 2d of September; in a word, all those men who, in the murder of 3 or 400,000 fellow-creatures, in the extermination of millions of victims by famine, the sword, or the guillotine, seek consolation, in spite of this depopulating scourge, in the empty hope that this dreadful chain of horrors may be productive of happier days.

Truths combating this error.

To confound these hopes, and to show the fallacy of these pretended good intentions, I will oppose the real views of this revolutionary Sect, their true projects, their conspiracies, and their means of execution. I will show them undisguised, for they must be divulged, the proofs being acquired. The French Revolution has been a true child to its parent Sect; its crimes have been its filial duty; and those black deeds and atrocious acts the natural consequences of the principles and systems that gave it birth. Moreover I will show that, so far from seeking future prosperity, the French Revolution is but a sportive essay of its strength, while the whole universe is its aim. If elsewhere the same crimes are necessary, they will be committed; if equal ferocity be requisite they will be equally ferocious; *and it will unavoidably extend wheresoever its errors shall be received.*

True consequences deduced from these truths.

The reflecting reader will conclude, then, that either this Jacobin Sect must be crushed, or society overthrown; that all governments must give place to those massacres, those convulsive disorders, and to that infernal anarchy which rages in France. Indeed there is no other alternative, but universal destruction or extinction of the Sect. Let it however be remembered, that to crush a Sect is not to imitate the fury of its apostles, intoxicated with its sanguinary rage and propense to enthusiastic murder; it is not to massacre and immolate its adepts, or retort on them the thunders they had hurled. To crush a Sect, is to attack it in its schools, to reveal its imposture, and show to the world the absurdity of its principles, the atrocity of its means, and above all the profound wickedness of its teachers. Yes; strike the Jacobin, but spare the man; the Sect is a Sect of opinion, and its destruction will be doubly complete on the day when it shall be deserted by its disciples, to return to the true principles of reason and social order.

The Sect, I grant, is monstrous, but all its disciples are not monsters. Its care in hiding its latter projects, the extreme precaution with which it initiated the chosen of the elect, shews how much it feared the desertion of the multitude of its disciples, and its consequent destruction, had the horror of its mysteries been surmised. For my part, I never doubted, how depraved soever the Jacobins may have been, that the greatest part would have deserted the Sect could they have foreseen whither and by what means they were led. Could the French people have followed such chiefs, had it been possible to make them conceive to what lengths the plans and plots of the conspirators would carry them?

Though France were, like hell, a bottomless pit, impenetrable to every voice but that of the fiends of the Revolution, still it is not too late to acquaint other nations of their danger. They have heard of the crimes and horrors of that Revolution, let them contemplate the lot that awaits them should Jacobinism prevail; let them learn that they are not less within the grand revolutionary circle than

To know the plots of the Jacobins, the interest of all nations,

France itself; that all those crimes, the anarchical and bloody scenes which have followed the dissolution of the French empire, equally await all other nations; let them learn that their altars and their thrones, their pontiffs and their kings, are doomed to the same fate with those of France: all are comprehended within the grand conspiracy.

and of all governments.

When a phantom of peace shall seem to terminate the present war between the Jacobins and the combined powers, it certainly will be the interest of all governments to ascertain how far such a peace can be relied on. At that period, more than at any other, will it be necessary to study the secret history of that Sect, which sends forth its legions rather to shiver the sceptre than to fight the power; which has not promised to its adepts the crowns of princes, kings and emperors, but has required and bound those adepts by an oath to destroy them all. At that period we must recollect, that it is not in the field of Mars that the war against Sects is the most dangerous; when rebellion and anarchy are in the very tenets of the sectary, the hand may be disarmed, but war glows warmly in the heart.—The Sect, being weakened, may slumber for a time, but such a sleep is the calm preceding the irruption of the volcano. It no longer sends forth its curling flames; but the subterraneous fire winds its course, penetrates, and preparing many vents, suddenly bursts forth and carries misery and devastation wherever its fiery torrent rolls.

It is not the object of these Memoirs to treat of that state of war or of peace commenced between one power and another. In such cases it often happens that, all resources being exhausted, the sword must be sheathed, though the original grievances still subsist. Let the rulers of the people discuss the means of force; but we know there exists another sort of war, which a confidence in treaties only serves to render more fatal; we mean a war of plots and conspiracies, against which public treaties can never avail. Woe to that Power which shall have made peace without knowing why its enemy had declared war against it. What the Sect had done before it first burst forth, it will do again to prepare a second eruption. In darkness it will conspire anew, and calamities still more disastrous will teach all nations that the French Revolution was only the first step towards the universal dissolution which has so long been meditating and contriving by the Sect.

Such were the reasons by which I was impelled to investigate the plots and wishes, the tortuous means and nefarious nature of this Sect. We have witnessed the frantic rage and the ferocity of its legions; we have known them as the agents of the French Revolution, as the perpetrators of all its atrocious crimes and devastations; but few are acquainted with the schools that have formed them. Posterity, alas! will feel for many generations their dire effects. To trace their ravages, it will only have to cast its eyes around. The ruins of the palaces

Object of these Memoirs.

and the temples, the fallen cities, the mansions destroyed throughout the provinces, will paint in glowing colours the devastations of the modern Vandals. The lists of proscription, fatal to the prince and to so many of his subjects, the deserted villages, all, in a word, will long be the vouchers of those fatal lamp-posts, of that insatiable guillotine, of those legislative executioners supported by bands of assassins.

Circumstances so painful and so humiliating to human nature will not require to be recorded in these memoirs. It is not to shew what a Marat or a Robespierre has done, but to expose the schools, the systems, the conspiracies, and the masters that have formed a Philippe d'Orléans, a Sieyès,[2] a Condorcet, or a Pétion, and who at this very time are forming in all nations men that would rival Marat and Robespierre in their cruelties. Our object is, that, the Sect of the Jacobins and their conspiracies once known, their crimes shall be no longer matter of surprise; that their propensity to the effusion of blood, their blasphemies against Christ and his altars, their frantic rage against the throne, and their cruelties against their fellow-citizens, shall be as clearly understood as the ravages of the plague. And may nations in future as sedulously guard against the one, as they shun the other!

---

2   Barruel uses the alternative spelling Syeyes throughout. I have changed it to the conventional spelling to avoid it being a distraction. —Ed.

It was to attain this important object that all our researches into the Sect have been directed at its chiefs, its origin, its plots, its plans, and its progress; more desirous of investigating the means it employed to bring about the revolution, than to describe its conduct during that revolution.

The result of our inquiries, corroborated by proofs drawn from the records of the Jacobins, and of their first masters, has been, that this Sect with all its conspiracies is in itself no other than the coalition of a triple Sect, of a triple conspiracy, in which, long before the Revolution, the overthrow of the Altar, the ruin of the throne, and the dissolution of all civil society had been debated and resolved on.

A triple conspiracy to the denounced.

1st. Many years before the French Revolution men who styled themselves Philosophers conspired against the God of the Gospel, against Christianity, without distinction of worship, whether Protestant or Catholic, Anglican or Presbyterian. The grand object of this conspiracy was to overturn every Altar where Christ was adored. It was the conspiracy of the *Sophisters of Impiety*, or the ANTICHRISTIAN CONSPIRACY.

2dly. This school of impiety soon formed the *Sophisters of Rebellion*: these latter, combining their conspiracy against kings with that of the Sophisters of Impiety, coalesce with that ancient Sect whose tenets constituted the whole secret of the Occult Lodges of Free-masonry, which long since, imposing on the credulity of its most distinguished adepts, only initiated the chosen of the elect into the secret of their unrelenting hatred for Christ and kings.

3dly. From the Sophisters of Impiety and Rebellion, arose the *Sophisters of Impiety and Anarchy*. These latter conspire not only against Christ and his altars, but against every religion natural or revealed: not only against kings, but against every government, against all civil society, even against all property whatsoever.

This third Sect, known by the name of *Illuminées*, coalesced with the Sophisters conspiring against Christ, and with the Sophisters who, with the Occult Masons, conspired against both Christ and kings. It was the coalition of the adepts of *impiety*, or the adepts of *rebellion*, and the adepts of *anarchy*, which formed the CLUB *of the* JACOBINS. Under this name, common to the triple Sect (originating from the name of the Order whose convent they had seized upon to hold their sittings), we shall see the adepts following up their triple conspiracy against God, the King, and Society. Such was the origin, such the progress of that Sect, since become so dreadfully famous under the name of Jacobin.

In the present Memoirs each of these three conspiracies shall be treated separately; their authors unmasked, the object, means, coalition, and progress of the adepts shall be laid open.

Proofs of the most pointed nature are necessary, when such horrid plots are denounced to all nations; and it is to give these proofs the greater authenticity, that the title of Memoirs has been prefixed to this work. To have written the simple history of the Jacobins might have sufficed for many; but these Memoirs are intended for the historian, who will find a collection of proofs, both numerous and convincing, all extracted from the records and avowals of the conspirators themselves. Strong in these proofs, we shall not fear to proclaim to all nations, 'that whatever their religion or their government may be, to whatever rank they may belong in civil society, if Jacobinism triumphs, all will be overthrown; that should the plans and wishes of the Jacobins be accomplished, their religion with its pontiffs, their government with its laws, their magistrates and their property, all would be swept away in one common mass of ruin! Their riches and their fields, their houses and their cottages, their very wives and children would be torn from them. You have looked upon the Jacobinical faction as exhausting itself in France, when it was only making a sportive essay of its strength. Their wishes and their oaths extend throughout Europe; nor are England or Germany, Italy or Spain, strangers to their intrigues.'

Consequences of this conspiracy.

Let not the Reader take this for the language of enthusiasm or fanaticism; far be such passions either from myself or my readers. Let them decide on the proofs adduced, with the same coolness and impartiality which has been necessary to collect and digest them. The order observed in the investigation of these conspiracies shall be exactly that in which they were generated. We shall therefore begin with the conspiracy against the whole religion of the Gospel, and which we have styled the ANTICHRISTIAN CONSPIRACY.[3]

---

3   In lower case in the French original. —Ed.

CHAPTER I.

Of the Principal Actors in the Conspiracy.

bout the middle of this century appeared three men who were leagued in the most inveterate hatred against Christianity. These were Voltaire, d'Alembert, and Frederick II, King of Prussia. Voltaire hated Religion because he was jealous of its Author, and of all those whom it had rendered illustrious; d'Alembert because his frigid heart was incapable of affection; and Frederick because he had never seen it but through the medium of its enemies.

Chiefs of the conspiracy.

To these a fourth must be added, and this was Diderot. Hating religion because he doated on nature, and enthusiastically wedded to the chaos of his own ideas, he chose rather to build a system on chimeras and form mysteries of his own, than submit to the light of the Gospel. Numerous adepts were afterwards drawn into this Conspiracy, and these were generally stupid admirers or secondary agents. Voltaire was the chief, d'Alembert the most subtle agent, Frederick the protector and often the adviser, and Diderot the forlorn hope.

Voltaire.

Mary Francis Arouet[1] was born at Paris, February 20, 1694, the son of an ancient notary of the Chatelet. Through vanity he changed his name to that of Voltaire, which he deemed more noble, more sonorous, and better suited to the celebrity at which he aimed: and never had there appeared a man with such versatile talents, and such a thirst of dominion over the literary world. Gravity of manners, a contemplative mind, or a genius for discussion or deep research, unfortunately were not among the gifts which Nature had lavished on him; and, more unfortunately still, in his heart were engendered all those baleful passions which render abilities dangerous. From his youth he seemed to direct them all at the overthrow of religion.

While only a student of rhetoric, in the college of Louis le Grand, he drew on himself the following rebuke from his professor, the Jesuit Le Jay. *Unfortunate young man, at some future day you*

---

1   Voltaire's name was François-Marie Arouet. —Ed.

will come to be the standard-bearer of Infidelity.[2]
Never was oracle more literally fulfilled.

On leaving college, he neither sought nor loved any other society than that of men whose profligate morals could strengthen his infidelity. He was particularly intimate with Chaulieu, the poet of voluptuousness, the Anacreon of his day; and with a few Epicureans who held their meetings at the Hotel de Vendôme. His first essays were in satire which gave offence to government, and in tragedy, in which we should have seen the rival of Corneille, Racine, and Crébillon, had he not at the same time emulated Celsus and Porphyrius, with all the other enemies of religion. At a time when licentiousness in opinion still met with obstacles in France, he sought an asylum in England. He there found men whom the writings of Shaftesbury, commented on by Bolingbroke, had trained up to Deism. He mistook them for philosophers, and was persuaded that they alone were esteemed by the English. If he was not then mistaken, opinions are since greatly changed. All those Sophisters whom Voltaire extols as the glory of Great Britain, if not forgotten, are more despised than read. Collins and Hobbes, when remembered, are classed with Tom Paine; an Englishman's good sense does not allow him to hate religion, nor make an ostentatious display of impiety. With him nothing is less philosophical, notwithstanding his toleration and variety of creeds,

---

2   *Life of Voltaire*, edit. of Kell, and Feller's *Hist. Dict.*

than that affected hatred to Christianity which marks our Sophisters, and which more particularly characterizes their plans to overthrow it.

Philosophism is said to have originated in England. I deny the fact. Philosophism is the error of every man who, judging of all things by the standard of his own reason, rejects in religious matters every authority that is not derived from the light of nature. It is the error of every man who denies the possibility of any mystery beyond the limits of his reason, of every one who, discarding revelation in defence of the pretended Rights of reason, Equality, and Liberty, seeks to subvert the whole fabric of the Christian religion.

Such an error may constitute a Sect. The history of ancient Jacobinism demonstrates that the Sect existed long since; but it was shrunk back to its dark abodes at the time when Voltaire appeared.

Such an error may be that of a few individuals. Many of the same sort had been broached during the two last centuries. Numerous were the Sects which had sprung from Luther and Calvin, each making its partial assault on the ancient tenets of Christianity; when at length there arose a set of men who attacked them all and would believe nothing. These were at first styled Libertines, the only denomination they deserved.

Voltaire might every where have met with some of these men, but more particularly at Paris under the Regency of the Duke of Orléans, who, though himself a monster of libertinism, yet, feeling the necessity of religion to the state, would not suffer it to be impugned in their publications.

It was in England, it is true, where, under their Collins and their Hobbes, the libertines first styled themselves Philosophers, and assumed the character of deep-thinkers, supported probably by some impious productions, which in any other part of Christendom would neither have enjoyed equal publicity nor even impunity. But it may be certainly concluded, that Voltaire would every where have been what he became in England; he would have been so, at least, wherever, from the lenity of the laws, he could cherish his insatiable appetite for the dominion over the empire of science or of literature.

It was in vain for him to aspire at the reputation of a Bossuet or a Pascal, or to affect the blaze of genius which had shone forth in defence of religion; but, hating their cause, and envying their glory, he dared to be jealous of their God: at his empire, therefore, he levelled his blows, and would be foremost in the ranks of the Philosophists.—He succeeded; but, to keep his pre-eminence, blushed not to blend Philosophy with impiety, and deliberately to contrive means for the overthrow of religion. England was the place where he first conceived a possibility of success. Condorcet, his adept, his confidant, his hisstorian, and his panegyrist, asserts this in positive terms: *There it was* (in England) *that Voltaire swore to dedicate his life to the accomplishment of that project; and he has kept his word.*[3]

---

3   *Life of Voltaire*, edit. of Kell.

On his return to Paris about the year 1730, he made so little a secret of his design, he had published so many writings against Christianity, and was so sanguine in his hopes, that Mr. Hérault, the Lieutenant of Police, upbraided him one day with his impiety, and added, *You may do or write what you please, but will never be able to destroy the Christian religion.* Voltaire without hesitation answered. *We shall see that.*[4]

Stimulated by the obstacles he met with, and perceiving much glory in his enterprize, he would not willingly have shared it with any body. "I am weary," he would say, "of hearing people repeat that twelve men were sufficient to establish Christianity, and I will prove that one may suffice to overthrow it."[5] When he uttered these words, his malignity seemed to blind him to such a degree, as to hide from him the immense distance between the genius that creates, and the petty cunning of the mischievous monkey that destroys. The Sophister may conjure the clouds, or veil the world in darkness, but does not by that approach the God of truth. The virtues, the miracles, and all the divine knowledge of the apostles, were necessary to teach man the true path of life.

Although in his outset Voltaire flattered himself that he should enjoy alone the glory of destroying the Christian religion, which was his sole object, he nevertheless soon found that associates would

---

4   *Ibid.*
5   *Ibid.*

be necessary. He even began to fear the noise of his undertaking, and hence resolved to move in the surer though humbler sphere of a Conspirator.— Already his numerous writings, either impious or obscene, had gained him many admirers and disciples, who, under the name of Philosophers, prided themselves in the hatred they bore to Christianity. From these he chose d'Alembert as the most proper person to second him in his new plan of attack; and he could not have chosen better.

Among the Sophisters we should compare Voltaire to Agamemnon, and d'Alembert to Ulysses. If the comparison be too noble, see the latter cunning, cringing, and even yelping like the fox.— Born of Fontenelle according to some, of Astruc the physician according to others, his birth was always a mystery to him. His mother Claudina Alexandrina Guérin de Tencin,[6] an apostate nun from the convent of Montfleury in Dauphiny,[7] was at the head of one of those societies of men of letters which were common in Paris, and she used to style them her *beasts*. Whether designed to conceal his

D'Alembert.

---

6   D'Alembert's father was Louis-Camus Destouches (1668 - 1726), an artillery General in the French Royal Army. —Ed.

7   The youngest of five children, Alexandrine (1682 - 1749) was placed in a convent at the age of eight and forced by her parents to take the veil in 1698. Wilful my nature—she's been referred to as an Amazon in an age of men—she tenaciously petitioned for her secularisation, although she'd have to wait until the death of her father and the ailing health of her mother to overcome their resistance; in 1712, Pope Clement XI formally rescinded her vows. —Ed.

birth or not, is unknown; but certain it is, that in the night between the 16th and 17th of November 1717, he was found, wrapped in swaddling cloaths, in the portico of the small church of St. John; and hence obtained the name of *Jean le Rond* at the Foundling Hospital whither he was carried and in which he was bred.

While yet a youth he enlisted under the banners of infidelity, thereby repaying with ingratitude the church that had charitably reared him. With the small sums given him for his education, he bought, like many other young men, all the profligate works written against a religion from whose proofs they impatiently flee, as wicked boys calumniate the kind master who thwarts their evil dispositions.

Both his heart and mind led him to be a disciple of Voltaire; and even their diversity of character and the immense difference of talents were soon confounded in their mutual bias to infidelity, and confirmed hatred to Christianity.

Voltaire was fiery, passionate and impetuous; d'Alembert cold, reserved, prudent and crafty.—Voltaire was fond of show, d'Alembert almost feared to be seen. The one, like the chief who is obliged to mask his battery, reluctantly used dissimulation while he wished to wage open war with Christianity, *and die on a heap of Christians*, whom he terms Bigots, *immolated at his feet.*[8]— The other, by instinct a dissembler, waged war like the partizan who, from behind a bush, smiles to

---

8   To d'Alembert, 20 April 1761, vol. 68, let. 85, p. 164.

see his enemy fall into the snares he has laid.[9] Voltaire, transcendent in polite literature, was but superficial in mathematicks. In the latter d'Alembert was profound, indeed he owed all his reputation to them; for in everything else he was a dry, finical, and confused writer; sometimes as mean and vulgar as Voltaire is noble, easy, and elegant, he would plod to turn a bad epigram, while the latter would have wittily filled whole volumes.

Voltaire, impudently daring, whether for or against, would quote the Scriptures, history, or the holy fathers, affirming, inventing, or traducing the passage as he wanted; for to wound was his only aim. D'Alembert carefully guards against the reply that may expose him; his steps mysterious and indirect conceal his design; shrinking from refutation, if attacked he flies, suppressing the fight lest he should proclaim his defeat. Voltaire on the contrary, seeks his enemies, and loudly calls to them; though a hundred times defeated, he returns to the charge; though his error be refuted, he will incessantly repeat it. It is not in defeat but in flight alone that he sees disgrace; and thus after a war of sixty years we still see him ranging on the field of battle. D'Alembert seeks the smile of every little assembly; and the applause of forty men in an academical circle constitutes his greatest triumph; while all the world, from London to St. Petersburg, from Sweden to America, to please Voltaire, must sound his fame.

---

9   From d'Alembert, 4 May 1762, vol. 68, let. 100, p. 199.

D'Alembert enlists from around him the secondary adepts; he trains and initiates them, directs their missions, and holds petty correspondences. Voltaire will conjure kings, emperors, ministers and princes against his God; all must do homage to the sultan of infidelity. Among these latter personages history must distinguish that Frederick, which as yet it has only known by titles glorious to monarchs, whether conquerors or rulers.

Fred-
erick II.

In this Frederick II., the Solomon of the North according to the Sophisters, we see two distinct men. First that King of Prussia, that hero less worthy of our admiration displaying his vast military talents in the field of victory, than as the father of his people, giving life to agriculture and energy to commerce, protecting the arts, and counterpoising in some sort, by the justice and wisdom of his administration, exploits perhaps more brilliant than just. In the second (so beneath a monarch) we see the Sophister, the philosophic pedant, the conspirator of infidelity; less cruel and enthusiastic indeed than Julian the apostate, but much more artful and perfidious.

It is painful to disclose the dark mysteries of this impious prince; but history must be true, and herein especially. To trace the conspiracy against their thrones, kings must know what share their colleagues have had in the conspiracy against the Altar.

Frederick, born with a mind worthy of a Celsus or his school, had not the help of a Justin or a Tertullian to guide his steps in religion, and unfortunately was surrounded by its calumniators. While only Prince-royal he was in correspondence with Voltaire, chiefly on religion or metaphysics; and even at that early age it appears he deemed himself a Philosopher; for he says—

> To speak with my usual freedom, I must confess to you, that whatever regards the God made man displeases me in the mouth of a Philosopher, who should be above popular error. Leave *to the great Corneille, when doating and falling back to childhood*, the insipid talk of versifying the *Imitation of Christ*; and whatever you may give us, let it be your own. We may speak of fables, but merely as fables; and a profound silence in my opinion should be kept concerning those fables of the Christians which have been sanctified by time and the credulity of the absurd and stupid.[10]

Even in his first letters we find, with the ridiculous pride of a pedantic king, all the versatility and hypocrisy of a Sophister. Frederick denies, when Voltaire supports liberty.[11] With Voltaire, man is a pure machine; Frederick then maintains that man is free. In one place we are free, precisely because we can form a clear idea of freedom.[12] In another, man is all matter; yet one can

---

10   From Frederick, May, 1738, vol. 64, let. 53, p. 275.

11   Their Letters in 1737, vol. 64.

12   From Frederick, 16 Sept. 1771, vol. 66, let. 12, p. 30.

hardly form, though it were with Frederick's own versatility, to a more absurd idea, than that of matter thinking, free, or arguing, though it were with Frederick's own versatility.[13] He upbraids Voltaire with the praises that he had bestowed on Christ, and three years after is not ashamed to write—

> For my part, I own that, whatever people may enlist under the banners of Fanaticism, I never shall. I may indeed compose a few Psalms to raise a good opinion of my orthodoxy. Socrates incensed the household Gods, so did Cicero, and he was not credulous. We must give way to the fancies of a frivolous people, in order to avoid blame and persecution; for, after all, what is most desirable in the world is to live in peace; let us then live foolishly with fools, that we may live quietly.[14]

The same Frederick had written, that the Christian religion yielded none but poisonous weeds; [15] and Voltaire had congratulated him, *as having above all Princes fortitude of soul, with sufficient perspicacity to see that for the seventeen hundred years past the* CHRISTIAN SECT *had never done any thing but harm,*[16] though we afterward find him the opponent of that work of Philosophic in-

---

13   From Frederick, 4 Dec. 1775, vol. 66, let. 100, p. 237.

14   From Frederick, 6 Jan. 1740, vol. 64, let. 107, p. 471.

15   From Frederick, 8 Jan. 1766, vol. 65, let. 143, p. 334.

16   To Frederick, 5 April, 1767, vol. 65, let. 159, p. 374.

sight, or rather of infamous profligacy, the *System of Nature*. "One might be tempted," he says,

> to acuse its author of want of sense and skill when, calumniating the Christian religion, he imputes to it failings that it has not. How can he with truth assert that religion can be the cause of the misfortunes of mankind! He would have been more correct, had he simply said, that men from ambition and self-interest, concealed under the veil of religion, had sought to disturb the world and gratify their passions. What is there reprehensible in the morals of the commandments? Were there in the whole Gospel but this single precept, *Do as thou wouldst be done by*, we should be obliged to confess, that those few words contained the whole quintessence of morality:—The forgiveness of injuries, charity, and humanity—were not these preached by Jesus in his excellent sermon on the mount?[17]

When he wrote thus, how much had Frederick lost of that perspicacity which had so lately distinguished him from other princes! But, strange to say, after having viewed religion in so clear a light, he compliments Voltaire on being its scourge,[18] he still communicates plans for its destruction,[19] and foresees, that should it be preserved and protected in France, *the fine arts*

---

17 *Examination of the System of Nature*, by Frederick, King of Prussia.

18 From Frederickkk, 12 Aug. 1773, vol. 66, let. 40, p. 94.

19 From Frederick, 29 July, 1775, vol. 66, let. 93, p. 216.

and higher sciences must fall, and that the rust of superstition will completely destroy a people, otherwise amiable and born for society.[20]

Had this sophistical monarch really foreseen events, he would have seen that people, *otherwise amiable* and *born for society*, when it had lost its religion, terrifying all Europe with its horrid deeds. But, like Voltaire, he was to be the sport of his pretended wisdom, as he was of his philosophy; and, though we shall often see him judging shrewdly of the adepts, we shall always find him conspiring with them against the religion of Christ.

The correspondence that so clearly developes the two characters of the royal adept and of his idol Voltaire begins in 1736; and it was uninterrupted during their lives, some few years of the latter's disgrace excepted. It is in this correspondence that we must contemplate him. Incredulous and impious, divesting himself of his royal insignia, he is more emulous of the Philosophist than he was jealous of the Cæsars, and to rival Voltaire becomes his servile copyist. A poet beneath mediocrity, a metaphysician on the lower form, he excels in but two things, his admiration for Voltaire and his impiety; in the latter he often outgoes his master.

In consideration of this zeal and homage, Voltaire overlooked his caprice, and the rough usage he sometimes met with, even to the correction of

20   From Frederick, 30 July, 1774, vol. 66, let. 59, p. 137.

14

the cane inflicted on him by a major at Frankfurt by order of the despotic Sophister. It was too essential that the Sect should secure at any expence the support of a royal adept, and we shall see how very much he served them. But first, in order to asecertain the extent of their mutual hatred to Christianity, let us attend to the vast obstacles they overcame; let us hear Voltaire pathetically describing his sufferings at Berlin a few years after his arrival, in a letter to Mad. Denis, his niece and confidant. He says,

> La Métherie may in his Prefaces extol his extreme felicity in being with a great king who sometimes reads his poetry to him; yet in private he weeps with me; he would willingly return, though it were on foot. But why am I here? I will astonish you. This La Métherie, a man of no consequence, chats familiarly with the king when their readings are over. He speaks to me with confidence. He declared to me that talking to the king a few days ago of my supposed favour with his majesty, and of the jealousy it excited, the king had answered, *I shall certainly not want him above a twelvemonth longer; we squeeze the orange and then throw away the rind* . . . . . I made him repeat these consolatory words; I questioned him again and again, but he only reiterated his declaration.—I have done my utmost not to believe La Métherie; and yet, in reading over the king's verses I found an epistle to one of his painters called Père, which begins thus:

Quel spectacle étonnant vient de /rap-
per mes yeux?
Cher Pere, ton pinceau, t'égale an rang
des dieux.
Tell me, what sight has struck my
wond'ring eyes?
Thy skill, dear Pere, with gods immortal
vies.

Now this Père is a fellow of whom he takes no
notice, and yet he is the *dear Père, he is a God*;
he may perhaps see me in the same light, and
that is not saying much.—You may easily guess
what reflexions, what a recoil upon myself, and
what perplexity, nay what anxiety this declaration of La Méterie's has created within me.[21]

This first letter was sometime after succeeded
by a second, as follows:

My sole views at present are, to desert in a gen-
teel manner, to take care of my health, to see you
again, and forget this three years dream. I plainly
perceive the orange has been squeezed, and must
think of saving the rind. For my own instruction
I will compile a dictionary for the use of kings:
My friend, signifies my slave; my dear friend, is
as much as to say, you are to me more than in-
different: you are to understand by I will make
you happy, I will bear with you as long as I shall
have need for you; sup with me to-night, means
I will make game of you to-night. This dictionary might be carried on to great length, and be
not unworthy a place in the Encyclopædia.

---

21   To Mad. Denis, 2 Sept. 1751, vol. 54, let. 208, p. 352.

Seriously this distresses me. Can there be truth in what I have seen? What! delight in making mischief among those that five with him! To say every thing that is kind to a person, and write pamphlets against him! To lure a man from his country by the most endearing expressions and solemn promises, and treat him with the blackest malice! What contrasts! And this is the man who wrote in such a philosophic strain, that I mistook him for a Philosopher, and styled him the *Solomon of the North!* Do you remember that fine letter, which never pleased you? You are a Philosopher (said he) and so am I. Upon my word, Sire, as to Philosophers we are neither of us so.[22]

Voltaire never spoke more truly; neither Frederick nor he could pretend to Philosophy in its true acceptation; but they were eminently so in the sense of the conspirators, with whom impiety and hatred to Christianity constituted its sole essence.

It was soon after writing this last letter, that Voltaire stole away from the court of his disciple, and received at Frankfurt that corporal *correction* which made him the laughing-stock of all Europe. Established however at Ferney, he soon forgot the bastinado; Frederick was once more the *Solomon of the North*, and returned the compliment by saluting Voltaire as the Father of Philosophy. Though not in friendship, they were soon united in mutual hatred to Christianity; and though they never met again,

---

22   To Mad. Denis, 18 Dec. 1752, vol. 54, let. 227, p. 518.

their plans were more easily formed, and intelligently conducted, in their future correspondence.

Diderot.

As to Diderot, he flew spontaneously toward the conspirators. A heated brain; an enthusiastic rage for that Philosophism of which Voltaire had set the fashion; a confusion of ideas, the more evident as both his speech and pen followed all the explosions of his brain, pointed him out to d'Alembert as a man essential to the conspiracy, and who would say, or could be made to say, such things as he dared not speak himself. They were both, until death, as truly attached to Voltaire as the latter was to Frederick.

Uncertainty of the chiefs in their philosophical opinions.

Had any thing but chaos been to have succeeded to Christianity, had any doctrine whatsoever been to have been taught, never were four men less fitted for such an undertaking.

Voltaire leaned to Deism, and seemed for some time to have adopted it; but, insensibly falling into Spinoza's systems, he knew not what to believe. Consulting at one time d'Alembert, at another Frederick, he was, during the remainder of his life, a prey to remorse, if doubts and anguish of mind void of repentance can be so called. At nearly fourscore he expresses himself in the following manner;

> Doubts encompass us round, *and doubting is a disagreeable state.* Is there a God such as he is said to be? A soul such as is imagined? Analogies such as are laid down? Is there any thing to be hoped for after this life? Was Gilimer in the

right to laugh, though stripped of his dominions, when brought before Justinian; or Cato in preferring suicide to the sight of Cæsar? Is glory then but an illusion? Shall Mustapha, in the effeminacy of his harem, beaten, ignorant, proud, and committing every folly, be happier, provided he digests well, than the Philosopher who digests ill? Are all men equal before the Great Being that animates nature? In that case, could the soul of Ravaillac be equal to that of Henry IV., or had neither of them a soul? Let the heroic philosophers unravel all this; for my part I can make nothing of it.[23]

D'Alembert and Frederick, being alternately pressed by these questions, answered each after his own way. Unable to fix his own opinion, the former frankly confesses he has not the gift of solving them: "I own to you," says he,

> that concerning the existence of God, the Author of the *System of Nature* seems too warm and dogmatic; and on this subject Scepticism seems the most rational. What do we know about it? is with me an answer to most metaphysical questions; and the natural reflection must be, that since we know nothing of the matter, it is, doubtless, unnecessary that we should know more.[24]

This remark on the unimportance of these questions was added, lest Voltaire, wearied out by the anxiety of his mind, should forsake a Philos-

---

23   To Frederick, 12 Oct. 1770, vol. 65, let. 179, p. 426.

24   From d'Alembert, 25 July, 1770, vol. 69, let. 36, p. 68.

ophy unable to solve his doubts on questions by no means, in his opinion, indifferent to the happiness of man. Voltaire still insists; but d'Alembert, continuing in the same style, says, "*No*, in metaphysics, appears to me not much wiser than yes; and *non liquet* (it is not clear) is generally the only rational answer."[25]

Frederick was as averse to doubts as Voltaire; and, perpetually wishing to stifle them, he was at length persuaded that he had succeeded.—"A philosopher of my acquaintance," says he,

> a man pretty bold in his opinions, thinks that we have a sufficient degree of probability to constitute a certainty that *post mortem nihil est* (or, that death is an eternal sleep). He maintains that man is not twofold, but is only matter animated by motion; and this strange man says, that there exists no relation between *animals* and the supreme *intelligence*.[26]

This resolute Philosopher, this strange man, was Frederick himself; and a few years after he makes no secret of it, for he more decidedly writes, "I am well convinced that I am not twofold; hence, I consider myself as a single being. I know that I am an animal organised, and that thinks; hence, I conclude that matter can think, as well as that it has the property of being electric."[27]

---

25 From d'Alembert, 4 Aug. 1770, vol. 69, let. 38, p. 72.

26 From Frederick, 30 Oct. 1770, vol. 65, let. 180, p. 429.

27 From Frederick, 4 Dec. 1775, vol. 66, let. 100, p. 237.

Verging toward his grave, but wishing to inspire Voltaire with confidence, he writes again: "The gout has successively run over all my body.— Our frail machine must needs be destroyed by time, which consumes every thing; my foundations are undermined; but all this gives me very little concern."[28]

As to the fourth hero of the Conspiracy, the famous Diderot, he is the very person whose decisions against God d'Alembert has found too warm and dogmatic; though oftentimes, in the same work, we find him, after deciding against the Deist, arguing in the same peremptory manner for or against the Sceptic and the Atheist. But whether writing for or against a God he always appears free from doubts or anxieties. He fairly wrote what he thought at the moment, whether *he crushed the Atheists with the weight of the universe,* and asserted that *the eye of a mite, the wing of a butterfly,* was sufficient to defeat them,[29] or declared that *glorious display did not give him even the most distant idea of any thing divine,*[30] and that *this universe was but the fortuitous result of motion and matter,*[31] whether, when the existence of God was to be left in doubt, *Scepticism at all times and in all places could alone preserve us from the two opposite excesses,*[32] or *he prays God for the Scep-*

---

28 From Frederick, 8 April, 1776, vol. 66, let. 108, p. 257.

29 Philosophical Thoughts, No. 20.

30 The Code of Nature.

31 Philosophical Thoughts, No. 21.

32 *Idem.* No. 33.

tics, because he sees *they all want light;*[33] wheth-er, in short, to form a sceptic, *it was necesssary to have a head as well organised as that of Montaigne the philosopher.*[34]

Never was a man more peremptory when affirming or denying any point, more perfectly void of constraint or care, or more impervious to remorse; for he was a perfect stranger to them even when asserting positively, that *between him and his dog he knows of no other difference but their dress.*[35]

With these extravagancies in their religious opinions, we find Voltaire impious and tormented by his doubts and ignorance; d'Alembert impious, but calm in his; while Frederick, impious and triumphant (or thinking he had triumphed) over his ignorance, left God in heaven, provided there were no souls on earth; and Diderot, by turns Atheist, Materialist, Deist, and Sceptic, but ever impious, ever frantic, was the better fitted for the various parts he was doomed to act.

Such were the men whose characters and whose errors were necessary to be known, in order to ascertain the Conspiracy of which they were the chiefs, of the existence of which we shall give undeniable proof, define its precise object, and unfold its means and progress.

---

33 *Idem.* No. 22.
34 *Idem.* No. 28.
35 *Life of Seneca*, Page 377.

CHAPTER II.

Of the Existence, Object, and Extent of the Antichristian Conspiracy.

T o say that there existed against the Christian religion a Conspiracy, of which Voltaire, d'Alembert, Frederick II., King of Prussia, and Diderot, were the prime authors and instigators, is not merely saying, that each of them individually was an enemy, and that their writings tended to the destruction of the religion of Christ; for, both before and after them, we have seen enemies of this same religion seeking to diffuse, by their writings, the venom of infidelity. France has had her Bayle and her Montesquieu; the first a true Sophister, undecided in his principles, and

The characteristics of a conspiracy.

supporting the pro and con with equal facility; but destitute of that hatred which constitutes the Conspirator, and leads him to seek accomplices: the latter was but a youth when he wrote his *Persian Letters*, and had no fixed principle against that faith, to which he was one day to do homage, by declaring that he always respected religion, and that he looked on the Gospel *as the fairest gift that God had bestowed on man.*[1]

England has seen her Hobbes, her Wollastons, and her Collins, with many other disciples of infidelity; but each of these Sophisters was impious in his own way; they sought not to league together, though Voltaire and Condorcet strongly assert the contrary. Each made his partial attack on Christianity from his own heated brain, and that is not sufficient to constitute a Conspiracy.

In order to prove a real Conspiracy against Christianity, we must not only point out the wish to destroy, but also the secret union and correspondence in the means employed to attack, debase, or annihilate it. When, therefore, I name Voltaire and Frederick, Diderot and d'Alembert, as the chiefs of this Antichristian Conspiracy, I not only mean to shew that each individual had impiously written against Christianity, but that they had formed the wish, and had secretly concurred in that wish, to destroy the religion of Christ; that they had acted in concert, sparing no political nor impious art to effectuate that de-

---

1   *Vid.* Montesquieu, Feller's *Hist. Dict.*

struction; that they were the instigators and conductors of those secondary agents whom they had misled; and followed up their plans and projects with all that ardor and constancy which denotes the most accomplished Conspirators. My proofs shall be drawn from what we may very properly term the records of the conspiracy, I mean from their most intimate correspondence, a long time secret, or from their own assertions contained in their various writings.

When Beaumarchais gave us a complete edition of Voltaire's works, with all the magnificence of the Baskerville type, either the adepts, dazzled by their success, were persuaded that the publicity of this monstrous conspiracy could only give new lustre to its chief; or the Editors themselves were ignorant of the fact; or concluded that, being scattered and dispersed through forty large volumes of letters to all sorts of persons, and on all sorts of subjects, no man could at once seize the thread of a conspiracy, the work of many long years.—But whatever may have been their intentions, how great soever their art in suppressing parts of the correspondence, they have not effectually done away all means of discovery. Never should I have undertaken a work of such labour, so painful and so disgusting, had I not seen the possibility and the necessity of proving from the very records of the conspirators the reality of their plots; of denouncing to all nations, with proof in hand, the men who wished to mislead them, and sought to overturn every Altar

The true archives of the conspiring Sophisters.

Their
object.

provided it was Christian. With them the altars of London or Geneva, of Stockholm or Petersburg, were to share the same fate with those of Paris or Madrid, of Vienna or Rome; thus adding, by their fall, a new though tardy proof of the universality of this conspiracy. Such then are their black and obscure crimes. Behold them conspiring against your God, in order to undermine your sovereign and your laws! Behold them seeking to overthrow all civil society, and to extend universally the evils of the French revolution.

Their
watch-
word.

I know that the importance of the charge requires strong evidence and clear proofs to justify it; if then my proofs should appear too numerous let the reader reflect on the magnitude of the charge.

In all conspiracies we find a secret language, or a watchword, which, though unintelligible to the vulgar, perpetually recalls the object to the mind of the conspirator. The words chosen by Voltaire must have been dictated by some fiend of hatred or of frantic rage: And what words! *Crush the wretch!* (*ecrasez l'infame!*) What a signification is attached to these three words in the mouths of Voltaire, of d'Alembert, of Frederick, and of their disciples! They mean *Crush Christ, crush the religion of Christ, crush every religion that adores Christ.* Oh readers! restrain your indignation till you have seen the proof!

Its true
sense as
under-
stood by
Voltaire.

When Voltaire complains that the adepts are not sufficiently united in the war which they wage against *the wretch*, and wishes to revive their zeal, he recalls to their minds the hopes and projects he had conceived so early as 1730, when the lieutenant of the police of Paris warned him that he would not succeed in overturning the Christian religion, and when he daringly answered, *We shall see that.*[2]

When exulting in the success of the war and progress of the conspiracy against the wretch, he triumphs in the idea "that in Geneva, Calvin's own town, there are but a few beggarly fellows who believe in the consubstantial."[3]

When he wishes, during this war against *the wretch*, to give his reasons for tolerating the Socinians, it is, he says, *because Julian would have favoured them, and he hates what Julian hated, and despises what he* (Julian) *despised.*[4]

What (let us ask) is this hatred, common to the Socinians and to Julian the apostate, if not their hatred to the divinity of Christ? What is meant by the consubstantial fallen into disrepute, if not Christ? Or, how can the word *wretch* be otherwise interpreted in the mouth of him that has said, "I am weary of hearing people repeat that twelve men have been sufficient to establish Christianity, and I will prove that one may suffice to overthrow it;"[5] in the mouth of a man who, in his intrigues against *the wretch*, exclaims, "Could not five or six men

---

2   To d'Alembert, 20 June, 1760, vol. 68, let. 66, p. 118.

3   To d'Alembert, 28 Sept. 1763, vol. 68, let. 119, p. 253.

4   To Frederick, 8 Nov. 1773, vol. 66, let. 46, p. 112.

5   *Life of Voltaire* by Condoret.

of talents, and who rightly understood each other, succeed after the example of twelve scoundrels who have already succeeded?"[6]

In the mouth of this frantic infidel can we misconceive the sense of these words? The twelve apostles are called *twelve scoundrels!* and their divine master a *wretch!* I may dwell too long on the proofs, but the charges are too heinous to pass them over lightly.

All the men so much extolled by Voltaire for their ardor in *crushing the wretch*, are precisely those who attacked Christianity without the least decorum or decency; such as Diderot, Condorcet, Helvétius, Fréret, Boulanger, Dumarsais, and other such infidels; and those whom he particularly wishes d'Alembert to rally, the more effectually to crush the wretch, are the Atheists, the Deists and Spinosists.[7]

Against whom then will the Atheist, the Deist, and the Spinosist coalesce, but against the God of the Gospel?

Voltaire proceeds to direct the zeal of the conspirators against the holy fathers, and against those modern authors who have written in defense of Christianity and of the divinity of Christ; both of these he wishes to see treated with the utmost contempt; and he thus writes to his adepts:

---

6   To d'Alembert, 24 July, 1760, vol. 68, let. 70, p. 127.

7   To d'Alembert, 27 July, 1770, vol. 69, let. 37, p. 70.

Victory is declaring for us on all sides; and I can assure you, that in a short time none but the rabble will follow the standard of our enemies; and that rabble we equally contemn whether for or against us. We are a corps of brave knights, defenders of the truth, and admit none among us but men of education. Courage brave Diderot, intrepid d'Alembert! Form with my dear Damilaville, and rash forward on those fanatics and knaves. Pity poor Pascal, but despise Houtville and Abbadie as much as if they were *fathers of the church*.[8]

Here then is clearly shewn, what Voltaire means *by crushing the wretch*. It is to undo what the apostles have done; to hate what Julian the apostate hated; to attack those whom the Deists, Atheists, and Spinosists always attacked. It is, in short, to rash on the holy fathers, or on any man who dares to defend the religion of Christ.

The sense of this atrocious watchword is equally clear in the mouth of Frederick. With this royal Sophister, as with Voltaire, *Christianity, the Christian Sect, the Christicole superstion* (*La superstition Christicole*), and *the wretch*, are all synonymous terms. With him, as with Voltaire, *the wretch yielded none but poisonous weeds*; the best writings against *the wretch* are precisely the most impious, and if any in particular deserve his highest esteem, it is, that since Celsus, *nothing so striking had been published* against Christianity.

By Frederick.

---

8   To Damilaville, 19 Nov. 1765, vol. 59, let. 123, p. 216.

The fact is, that Boulanger, unfortunately more known by his impiety than by his conversion, *is still superior to Celsus himself.*[9]

By d'Alembert.

As to d'Alembert, we may see, that though he seldom uses this shocking word, he was well acquainted with its meaning. This is evident by his answers to Voltaire, by the means he suggests, and by the writings he approves and seeks to circulate as fittest to *crush the wretch*; which writings are precisely those that most directly tend to eradicate religion from the minds of the people. We may see, when, wishing to shew his zeal for the progress of the conspiracy against *the wretch*, he professes his eagerness to support Voltaire, and his sorrow that from local circumstances he cannot speak with the same freedom against Christianity. His expressions and the numberless letters hereafter quoted, will leave no more doubt of him than of Voltaire or Frederick.[10]

Extent of the conspiracy.

Such was the general acceptation of the watchword among all the conspirators. Condorcet, indeed, laying aside the word wretch, positively asserts that Voltaire had sworn *to crush Christianity*;[11] and Mercier says, *to crush Christ.*[12]

That the views of the conspirators were to crush Christ, is not too strong an expression. In the ex-

---

9   See let. of the King of Prussia, No. 143, 145, 153, anno 1767, et passim vol. 65.

10   See d'Alembert's Letters, 100, 102, 151, vol. 68.

11   *Life of Voltaire.*

12   Mercier's let. No. 60, of M. Pelletier.

tent of their projects no shadow of his worship was to remain: it is true, that among the Christians they honoured the church of Rome with their chief hatred. But Luther and Calvin, the Churches of England and of Geneva, though separated from Rome, had retained their belief of Christ, and were therefore to share the fate of the former.

The whole Gospel of Calvin is ridiculed by Voltaire as *the fooleries of Jean Chauvin;*[13] and it is of these fooleries that he speaks when, writing to d'Alembert, he says, *in Calvin's own town* (Geneva) *there were but a few beggarly fellows who believed in the consubstantial,* that is to say, *who believed in Christ.* He particularly exults in the approaching fall of the Church of England when he extols the *English truths,*[14] that is, the impieties of Hume; and when he thought himself authorized to write, that *in London Christ was spurned.*[15]

Those disciples who paid him the homage of their philosophic science, adopting his style, write thus: "I don't like Calvin, he was intolerant and poor. Servetus[16] fell a victim to him; and it

13 To Damilaville 18 Aug. 1766, vol. 59, let. 239, p. 424.

14 To the M. d'Argence de Dirac, 28 Apr. 1760. vol. 56. let. 133, p. 276.

15 To d'Alembert, 28 Sept. 1763, vol. 68, let. 119, p. 254.

16 Michael Servetus (Spanish: Miguel Serveto, French: Michel Servet; 1509 or 1511 - 1553). Already author of several controversial religious works, after finishing his studies in medicine in 1539 he entered into correspondence with John Calvin; their theological disagreements caused their correspondence to grow heated, thanks in part to Servetus' tone. Eventually, he

is a fact, that he is no more spoken of at Geneva than if he had never existed. As to Luther, though he had not much wit, as is easily perceived in his writings, he did not persecute; he only loved wine and women."[17]

It is observable, that for a considerable time the conspiring sophisters found particular satisfaction in their successes against the Protestant churches. With what excessive joy would Voltaire write, that England and Switzerland were over-run with men *who hated and despised Christianity* as *Julian* the apostate *hated and despised it*;[18] and that *from Geneva to Berne not a Christian was to be found.*[19] Frederick, on his side, writes with equal joy, *In our protestant countries we go on much brisker.*[20]

Such was the extent of this conspiracy; it was to overturn every Altar where Christ was adored. A superficial historian might have been misled by seeing the adepts solicit, more than once, the recal of the Protestants into France; but at the very time that Voltaire is expressing how much he laments to see the petition made by the minister Choiseul rejected, he hastens to add (fearing that his dis-

---

was denounced as a heretic by Guillaume de Trie, a friend of Calvin, and by Calvin humself, who later had him prosecuted, leading to his imprisonment and execution. —Ed.

17 From the Landgrave of Hesse, 9 Sept. 1766, vol. 66, let. 64, p. 410.

18 To d'Alembert, 8 Feb. 1776, vol. 69, let. 151, p. 257.

19 From Frederick, 8 Nov. 1773, vol. 66, let. 46, p. 112.

20 From Frederick 8 Jan. 1766, vol. 65, let. 143, p. 334.

ciples might imagine he wished to spare the Huguenot more than the Catholic) that the Huguenots and the Calvinists *are not less mad than the Sorbonists or the Catholics*; that they were even *raving mad*;[21] nay, sometimes he saw *nothing more atrabilarious and ferocious than the Huguenots.*[22]

All this pretended zeal of the conspirators to calvinize France, was but a preparatory step to unchristianize it with the greater ease and expedition. We may trace the ground of their intended progress in the following words of d'Alembert to Voltaire: "For my part I see every thing in the brightest colours; already I behold toleration established; *the Protestants recalled*, the Priests married, confession abolished, and fanaticism crushed, *without its being perceived.*"[23] *Fanaticism* and *wretch* in d'Alembert's mouth are synonymous, the latter is even made use of in the same letter, both meaning *Christ* or *his whole religion crushed.*

There is however an exception often made by Voltaire, which might have left to Christ some few worshippers among the rabble. He seems little jealous of that conquest when he writes to d'Alembert,

> Both you and Damilaville must be well pleased to see the contempt into which *the wretch* is

---

21 To Marmontel, 2 Dec 1767, vol. 60, let. 200, p. 336.

22 To the M. d'Argence de Dirac, 2 March 1763, vol. 58, let. 36, p. 74.

23 From d'Alembert, 4 May 1762, vol. 68, let. 100, p. 201.

fallen among the better sort of people throughout Europe; they are all we wished for or that
were necessary; we never pretended to enlight-
en *house-maids and shoemakers*; we leave
them to the apostles.[24]

Again, he writes to Diderot, "Whatever you do,
have your eye on *the wretch*. It must be destroyed
among the better sort; but we may *leave it to the
rabble* for whom *it* was made;"[25] or when, in fine,
he writes to Damilaville, "I can assure you, that
in a short time none but the rabble will follow the
standard of our enemies; and that rabble we equally despise whether for or against us."[26]

Voltaire, despairing of more enlarged success,
would sometimes except *the clergy and the great
chamber of Parliament*. But in the sequel of these
memoirs we shall see the conspirators actively extending their principles, and instilling their hatred
against Christianity into every class of men from
the cottage to the throne, and not even excepting
their so-much-despised rabble.

---

24 To d'Alembert, 2 Sept. 1768, vol. 68, let. 234, p. 486.
25 To Diderot, 25 Sept. 1762, vol. 57, let. 242, p. 475.
26 To Damilaville, 19 Nov. 1765, vol. 59, let. 123, p. 216.

The Secrecy, the Union and the Epoch of the Conspiracy.

I n conspiracies it is not enough for the agents to have a particular watchword, or formula, in order to conceal their common object; but they must also have peculiar names, by which they distinguish each other, but which are wholly unintelligible to the public. They always carefully conceal their correspondence; but if they apprehend discovery, they then use these precautions lest their names, or the object of the plot, be exposed.

Such means were not neglected by Voltaire or d'Alembert. In their correspondence Frederick is

Assumed names of the conspirators.

often called *Luc*,[1] d'Alembert *Protagoras*,[2] though he often styles himself *Bertrand*. Both were well applied to him, the former to denote the infidel, the latter to typify the means of his impiety by the shifts of *Bertrand* in Fontaine's fable of the Monkey and the Cat: when d'Alembert is *Bertrand* (the monkey), Voltaire is *Raton*[3] (the cat). Diderot personates *Plato* or *Tonpla*;[4] and the general term for the conspirators is *Cacouac*.[5] They say he is a good Cacouac when he can be perfectly depended upon. They are often too, and particularly Voltaire, called brothers, as in Masonry. They also give peculiar imports to entire phrases of their enigmatical language; for example, *the vine of Truth is well cultivated*; is tantamount to saying, we make rapid progress against religion.[6]

Their secret language.

Of this secret language they particularly made use when they suspected that their letters were opened or stopped, a suspicion which often gave Voltaire and d'Alembert great uneasiness. It was for this reason that many of their letters were directed to fictitious persons, to merchants, or to some clerk in office who was in the secret. It does

---

1   From d'Alembert, 17 Nov. 1760, vol. 68, let. 77, p. 145.

2   To Thiriot, 26 Jan. 1762, vol. 57, let. 157, p. 320.

3   From d'Alembert, 22 March 1774, vol. 69, let. 128, p. 216.

4   To Damilaville, 11 Aug. 1766, vol. 59, let. 237, p. 420. In French Plato is spelled Platon, the anagram of which is Tonpla; hence Plato and Tonpla are to be looked upon as synonymous.

5   From d'Alembert, 18 Oct. 1760, vol. 68, let. 76, p. 141.

6   To d'Alembert, 17 Nov. 1760, ut supra.

its in other respects; but especially on those who laboured for or wrote in defense of religion.

But, openly as the Conspirators expressed themselves to each other, secrecy was strictly recommended to them with respect to the public; and Voltaire perpetually apprizes the adepts of its importance. "The mysteries of Mytra (he would make d'Alembert write to the adepts) are not to be divulged; . . . . the *monster* (religion) must fall, pierced by a hundred invisible hands; yes, let it fall beneath a thousand repeated blows."[9]

This secrecy, however, was not to be so much with respect to the object of the conspiracy, as the names of the Conspirators, and the means they employed; for it was impossible for the rancorous hatred of Voltaire to disguise the wish of annihilating Christianity; but he had to fear on one side the severity of the laws, and on the other the contempt and infamy which would certainly attach to himself and his disciples, for the impudence of their falsehoods and the effrontery of their calumnies, had it ever been possible to trace their authors and abettors.

It is not the fault of history if it be obliged to represent the Chief of the conspiracy as at once the most daring and most unrelenting in his hatred to Christ, yet the most desirous of concealing his attacks. Voltaire secretly conspiring and masking his means, is the same man as when bold and blaspheming. He is the same Sophister, whether openly

Their secresy.

---

9   To d'Alembert, 1 May 1768, vol. 68, let. 229, p. 478.

attacking the altars of his God, veiling the hand that strikes, and seeking in the dark to undermine the temple. It is hatred that fires his rage, and the same hatred that leads him through the tortuous ways of the Conspirator. To unmask this dissimulating man shall be a leading object in the following Memoirs.

In his character of Chief, the mysteries of Mytra, as well as the intrigues of the Conspirators, could be of no small concern to him; and the following were his secret instructions: "Confound *the wretch* to the utmost of your power; speak your mind boldly; but when you strike conceal your hand. You may be known; I am willing to believe there are people sufficiently keen-scented, but they will not be able to convict you."[10]

"The Nile is said to spread around its fertilizing waters, though it conceals its head; do you the same, and you will secredy enjoy your triumph. I recommend *the wretch to you.*[11] We embrace the worthy knight, and exhort him to conceal his march from the enemy."[12]

No precept is oftener repeated by Voltaire than this, *strike, but conceal the hand*; and if by indiscretion any adept occasioned discovery, he would complain most bitterly, he would even deny works that were the most notoriously his.

---

10 To d'Alembert, 20 April and 8 May, 1761, vol. 68, Lett. 85-6, p. 164-6.

11 To Helvétius, 11 May, 1761, vol. 57, let. 53, p. 110.

12 To Mr. de Villevielle, 26 April, 1767, vol. 60, let. 102, p. 180.

I know not (says he) why people are so obstinately bent on believing me the author of the *Philosophical Dictionary*. The greatest service you can do me is to assert (though you even pledge your share in Paradise) that I had no hand in that hellish work. There are three or four people who perpetually repeat that I have supported the good cause, and that I fight mortally against the wild beasts. *It is betraying one's Brethren to praise them on such an occasion; those good souls bless me, but they also ruin me . . . . .* It is certainly his, they say; it is his style and manner. Ah, my Brethren, what fatal words! you should on the contrary cry out in the public streets, It is not he; *for the monster must fall pierced by a hundred invisible hands; yes, let it fall beneath a thousand repeated blows.*[13]

It was in this art of secrecy, and the skill of concealing his steps, that d'Alembert so much excelled. Him it was that Voltaire recommended to the Brethren for imitation, *as the hope of the flock.* "He is daring (would he say to them), but not rash; he will make hypocrites (that is, religious men) tremble, without giving any hold against himself."[14]

Frederick not only approved of this secrecy,[15] but we shall see him playing off all the artifices of a dark policy to ensure the success of the conspiracy.

In every plot union is as essential to the conspirator as secrecy to the cause, and therefore it is of- Their union.

---

13 To d'Alembert, 1 May 1768, vol. 68, let. 229, p. 178.

14 To Thiriot, 19 Nov. 1760, vol. 56, let. 228, p. 453.

15 From Frederick, 29 Juin, 1771, vol. 66, let. 10, p. 26.

ten and particularly recommended. Among others, we find the following instructions:

> Oh, my Philosophers, we should march closed, as did the Macedonian phalanx, which was only vanquished when it opened. Let the real Philosophers unite in a brotherhood like the Freemasons; let them assemble and support each other, and let them be faithful to the association. Such an academy will be far superior to that of Athens, and to all those of Paris.[16]

If any dissension, by chance, happened among the Conspirators, the Chief immediately wrote to appease them: "Ah, my poor Brethren (he would say), the primitive Christians behaved themselves much better than we do. Have patience; do not let us lose courage; God will help us, provided we remain united;" and when he wished to insist more particularly on the object of that union, he would repeat his answer to Hérault, *We'll see whether it be true, that the Christian religion cannot be destroyed.*[17]

Most of these dissensions arose from the difference of opinion in the Conspirators, and the discordancy of their Sophisms against Christianity, which often made them thwart each other. Voltaire, aware of the advantage it gave to religious writers, immediately enjoined d'Alembert to seek, if possible, a reconciliation with the Athe-

16   To d'Alembert, 20 April, 1761, vol. 68, let. 85, p. 162.

17   To d'Alembert, 20 Juin, 1760, vol. 68, let. 66, P., 118.

ists, Deists, and Spinosists. "The two parties (says he) must necessarily coalesce. I wish you would undertake that reconciliation; say to them, *if you will omit the emetic, I will overlook the bleeding.*"[18]

This Premier Chief, always fearful lest their ardor should subside, and wishing to animate their zeal, would write to the other chiefs,

Their ardor and constancy.

> I fear you are not sufficiently zealous; you bury your talents; you seem only to contemn while you should abhor and destroy the monster. Could not you *crush* him in a few pages, while you modestly hide from him that he falls by your pen? It was given to Meleager to kill the boar. *Hurl the javelin, but hide your hand.* Comfort me in my old age.[19]

He would write to a young adept, who might be dejected through ill success, *Courage! do not suffer yourself to be dejected.*[20] Again, to bind them by the strongest ties of interest, he would tell them, through the medium of d'Alembert, "Such is our state, that we shall be the execration of mankind if we have not the better sort of people on our side. We must therefore gain them, cost what it will; labour then in the vineyard, *and crush the wretch; oh, crush the wretch.*"[21]

---

18   To d'Alembert, 27 July, 1770, vol. 69, let. 37, p. 70.

19   To d'Alembert, 28 Sept. 1763, vol. 68, let. 119, p. 253.

20   To Damilaville, 15 Juin, 1761, vol. 57, let. 70, p. 143.

21   To d'Alembert, 13 Feb. 1764, vol. 68, let. 129, p. 282.

Thus clearly is every distinctive mark of the conspirator, as enigmatical language, a common and secret wish, union, ardor and perseverance, to be seen in these first authors of the war against Christianity. Hence the historian is authorised to represent this coalition of Sophisters as a real conspiracy against the Altar. At length Voltaire not only avows it, but wishes every adept to understand, that the war of which he was the chief was a true plot, and that each individual was to act the part of a conspirator. When he feared an excess in their zeal, he would write himself, or through d'Alembert, that in the war which they waged, *they were to act as conspirators, and not as zealots.*[22]

When the chief of these infidels makes so formal a declaration, when we find him so clearly ordering them to *act as conspirators*, it would be absurd to seek farther proofs as to the existence of the conspiracy. I fear they have already been too numerous for the reader; but in a matter of such importance, I was to presume him equally rigid as myself with respect to its demonstration. Now as nobody, unless blind to conviction, will deny this to have been a real conspiracy of the Sophisters against Christ and his Church, I will, before I close this Chapter, try to ascertain its origin and epoch.

If this conspiracy were to be dated from the day on which Voltaire consecrated his life to the annihilation of Christianity, we should look back to the year 1728, that being the time of his return from

Open avowal of Voltaire.

Epoch of the conspiracy.

---

22   To d'Alembert, 19 Sept. 1764, vol. 68, let. 142, p. 316.

London to France; and his most faithful disciples inform us, that he made his determination when in England.[23] But Voltaire lived many years ruminating alone his hatred against Christ.—It is true, he was already the officious defender of every impious work that had the same tendency; but these were only the isolated productions of Sophisters, writing singly, without any of the appurtenances of the conspirator. To form adepts, and to instil his hatred into them, must be the work of time; and his efforts, unfortunately crowned with success, have greatly augmented their number, when, in 1750, he, by the express desire of the King of Prussia, took his departure for Berlin. Of all the disciples whom he left in Paris, the most zealous were d'Alembert and Diderot; and it is to these two men that the coalition against Christ can be traced. Though it might not then have acquired all its strength, it certainly existed when the plan of the Encyclopedia was decided on; that is to say, the very year that Voltaire left Paris for Berlin. Voltaire had formed his disciples; but d'Alembert and Diderot united them in one body to make that famous compilation, which may truly be styled the grand arsenal of impiety, whence all their sophisticated arms were to be directed against Christianity.

Voltaire, who alone was worth a host of infidels, labouring apart in the war against Christianity, left the Encyclopedists for some time to their

---

23 *Life of Voltaire*, edit. of Kell.

own schemes; but though his disciples had been able to form the coalition, they were incapable of carrying it on. Their difficulties augmenting, they sought a man able to remove them, and without hesitation fixed on Voltaire, or rather, to use the words of his historian, *Voltaire, by his age, his reputation, and his genius, naturally became their chief.*

At his return from Prussia, about the year 1752, he found the conspiracy complete. Its precise object was the destruction of Christianity; the chief had first sworn it; the secondary chiefs, such as d'Alembert, Diderot, and even Frederick, notwithstanding his quarrels with the premier, were ever after leagued with him in the same bonds. At this period, the adepts were all that Voltaire could number as his disciples: but from the day of the coalition between the premier, the secondary chiefs, and the adepts' agents or protectors, from the day that the object of this coalition to crush Christ, under the appellation of *wretch*, and his religion, had been decreed, until the grand object of the coalition was to be consummated by the proscriptions and horrid massacres of the Jacobins, near half a century was to elapse; for so much time was necessary for the harbinger of blood and corruption to prepare the way for the Philosophist of destruction and murder. During this long period of time, we shall see this sophistical Sect, that had sworn to *crush*, naturally coalescing with the Sect, which, under the name of *Jacobin*, really does *crush* and masssacre.

46

Where then is the difference between the so-phistical Sect under Voltaire and d'Alembert, anticipating the murders of the French revolution by their wishes and their conspiracies, and those Sophisters who, under the name of *Jacobins*, overthrow the Altar and imbue its steps with the blood of its priests and pontifs? Do not they proscribe the religion of the same Christ, of the same God, whom Voltaire, d'Alembert, Frederick, and all that impious clan of adepts, have sworn to crush and abhor? Will any one tell us that there is any difference between the sophisms of the former and the pretexts of the latter, between the school of Voltaire and the maxims of the Jacobinical den?

The Jacobins will one day declare that all men are free, that all men are equal; and as a consequence of this Equality and Liberty they will conclude that every man must be left to the light of reason. That every religion subjecting man's reason to mysteries, or to the authorities of any revelation speaking in God's name, is a religion of slavery and constraint; that as such it should be annihilated, in order to re-establish the indefeasible rights of Equality and Liberty, as to the belief or disbelief of all that the reason of man approves or disapproves: and they will call this Equality and Liberty the reign of reason and the empire of Philosophy. Can the intelligent reader believe, that this Equality and Liberty is not apposite to the war carried on by Voltaire against Christianity? Had ever the chiefs or adepts any other view, than that

The Sophisters and the Jacobins compared.

of establishing their pretended empire of Philosophy, or their reign of reason, on that self-same Equality and Liberty applied to revelation and the mysteries in perpetual opposition to Christ and his Church?

Did not Voltaire hate the church and its pastors because they opposed that Equality and Liberty applied to our belief, because nothing was *so contemptible and so miserable in his eyes*, as to see one man have recourse to another in matters of faith, or to ask what he ought to believe?[24] *Reason, Liberty*, and *Philosophy*, were as constantly in the mouths of Voltaire and d'Alembert, as a means of overthrowing Revelation and the Gospel, as they are at this day in the mouths of the Jacobins.[25] When the adepts wish to extol the glory of their chiefs, they will represent them as *perpetually reclaiming the independence of Reason*, and devoutly expecting those days when the *sun shall no longer shine but upon free men acknowledging no other master but their own reason.*[26]

When therefore, on the ruins of the temple, the Jacobins shall have erected the idol of their Reason, their Liberty, or their Philosophy, will they have fulfilled any other wish, confirmed any other oath, than that sworn by Voltaire and his adepts?

When the Jacobins shall apply the axe to the foundations of the temples, whether Protestant or

---

24 To Duke d'Ufez, 19 Nov. 1760, vol. 56, let. 226, p. 450.

25 See the whole of their correspondence.

26 Condorcet's *Progress of Reason*, 9th Epoch.

Catholic, or indeed of any Sect acknowledging the God of the Christians, will they have more widely extended their systems of destruction, than Voltaire did conspiring against the Altars of London or Geneva equally as against those of Rome?

When their grand club shall be filled with every infidel that the French revolution can produce, whether Atheist, Deist, or Sceptic, will their revolutionary cohorts be differently formed from those which d'Alembert was to quicken and stir up against the God of Christianity?

In short, when one day these legions sallying from this den of impiety, from the grand club of the Jacobins, shall triumphantly carry to the Pantheon the ashes of Voltaire, will not that be the consummation of the Antichristian Conspiracy, will not that be the revolution so long planned by Voltaire? The means may differ; but the object, the spirit, and the extent of the conspiracy will remain. We shall see that the very means employed, the revolution that destroys the Altar, that plunders and massacres its priests by the hand of the Jacobin, were not foreign to the wishes or intentions of the first adepts. The most dreadful and disgusting parts of this irreligious revolution only differs from their plans by a difference in terms; *one* WISHED *to crush, the other* DID *crush.* The means were such as the times suggested, both were not equally powerful.—We will now proceed to tear the veil from those dark intrigues successively employed by the Sophisters during the half century which preceded and prepared such scenes of blood and confusion.

CHAPTER IV.

First Means of the Conspirators.— The Encyclopedia.

o *crush the wretch* in the sense of Voltaire, or to attain the destruction of the altars of that God whose worship had been taught by the Apostles, nothing less could suffice than the total subjection of the public opinion, and the annihilation of the faith of all Christian nations. To extirpate it by force was above the strength of the rising coalition. Force was only to be resorted to when, by a revolution in all religious ideas, things had been brought to that state in which our Jacobin legislators found them; or when, by infidelity, the courts, the senates, the armies, in short, men of all descriptions, had been gained over to a blind confidence in and submission to their Sophistry. Indeed the necessary growth of impiety and corruption supposed too long a period for Frederick or Voltaire ever to flatter themselves with the hope of seeing it.[1] It was then too early for them to grasp the falchion of the butchering Jacobin; nor must we expect, in the following pages, to read of guillotines, or forced requisitions in battle array against the altars of Christianity.

In the beginning their intrigues are hidden and silent, slow and tortuous; but more insidious from their secrecy, more certain from their slowness; the public opinion was to perish, as it were, by inanition, before they dared lay the axe to the Altar. This mode of proceeding, we find, is perfectly understood by Frederick when he writes to Voltaire, *that to undermine the edifice in silence is to oblige it to fall of itself*;[2] and still better understood by d'Alembert, when, upbraiding Voltaire with being too hasty, he says, *If mankind grow enlightened, it is because we have used the caution to enlighten them by degrees*,[3] Convinced of the necessity of this gradation, d'Alembert bethought himself of the Encyclopedia, as the grand means of philosophising mankind, and of *crushing the wretch*. His project is no sooner conceived, than it is enthusiastically adopted by Diderot; and Voltaire more than once animated

The Encyclopedia projected.

---

1   From Frederick, 5 May, 1767, vol. 65, let. 160, p. 377.

2   From Frederick, 13 Aug. 1775, vol. 66, let. 95, p. 222.

3   From d'Alembert, 31 July, 1762, vol. 68, let. 102, p. 207.

their drooping courage, by his constant attention to the undertaking.

To judge of what prodigious importance the success of this famous dictionary was to conspiring chiefs, we must be acquainted with its plan, the method of its execution, and how it was to become the infallible agent of infidelity, and its most powerful weapon in perverting the public opinion, and overturning all the principles of Christianity. *It supposed object.*

The Encyclopedia is at first ushered into the world as the aggregate, the complete treasure of all human arts and sciences, of Religion, Divinity, Physics, History, Geography, Astronomy, and Commerce; in a word, of whatever can constitute a Science: of Poetry, Oratory, Grammar, Painting, Architecture, Manufactures, and whatever can be the object of useful or pleasing arts. This great work was to comprehend the very minutiae of different trades, from the manufacturer to the labourer; it was to be of itself an immense library, and to supply the place of one. It was to be the work of scientific men, the most profound in every branch that France could produce. The discourse in which it was announced by d'Alembert to all Europe was written with so much art, and had been so profoundly meditated and so nicely weighed; the concatenation of the sciences and the progress of the human mind appeared so properly delineated; whatever he had borrowed from Bacon or Chambers on the filiation of ideas so completely disguised; in short, the plagiary Sophister had so perfectly decked himself in the plumage of others, that the prospectus of the Encyclopedia was looked upon as a masterpiece, and its author, of course, considered as the most proper person to preside over so stupendous a work.

It real object.

Such were their mighty promises, but these were never intended to be fulfilled; while, on the other side, they had their secret object, which they were determined to accomplish. This was, to convert the Encyclopedia into a vast emporium of all the sophisms, errors, or calumnies, which had ever been invented against religion, from the first schools of impiety, to the day of their enterprize, and these were to be so artfully concealed, that the reader should insensibly imbibe the poison without the least suspicion. To prevent discovery, the error was never to be found where it might be supposed. Religion was not only to be respected, but even advocated in all direct discussions; though sometimes the discussion is so handled, that the objection they seem to refute is more forcibly impressed on the mind of the reader. The more to impose on the unthinking, d'Alembert and Diderot artfully engaged several men of unblemished character to partake in this vast and laborious undertaking. Such was Mr. de Jeaucourt, a man of great learning and probity, who has furnished a number of articles to the Encyclopedia: his name alone might have been thought a sufficient guarantee against all the art and perfidy of its principles; and it was further declared, that all points of religion were to be discussed by divines well known for their learning and orthodoxy.

All this might have been true, and yet the work only prove the more perfidious; for d'Alembert and Diderot had reserved to themselves a three-fold resource for forwarding their Antichristian Conspiracy.

Their first resource was that of insinuating error and infidelity into those articles that might be deemed the least susceptible of them; such, for example, as History or Natural Philosophy, and even into Chemistry and Geography, where such danger could not have been surmised. The second was that of references, a precious art, by which, after having placed some religious truth under the reader's eye, he is tempted to seek further information in articles of a quite different cast. Sometimes the mere reference was an epigram or a sarcasm; they would, for instance, after having treated a religious subject with all possible respect, simply add, *See the art.* PREJUDICE, or SUPERSTITION, or FANATI-CISM. Lastly, when our referring Sophisters feared this shift could not avail them, they would not hesitate at altering and falsifying the discussion of a virtuous co-operator or at adding an article of their own, whose apparent object was to defend, while its real intention was to refute what had already been written on the subject. In fine, impiety was to be sufficiently veiled to make it attractive; but at the same time to leave place for excuse and subterfuge. This was the peculiar art of our barking Sophister d'Alembert. Diderot, more daring, was at first countenanced in the mad flights of his im-

Its means and devices.

piety; but in cooler moments his articles were to be revised; he was then to add some apparent restriction in favour of religion, some of those high-sounding and reverential words, but which left the whole of the impiety to subsist. If he was above that care, d'Alembert as supervisor-general took it upon himself.

Peculiar care was to be taken in the compiling of the first volumes, lest the clergy, those men of prejudice, as they were called, should take the alarm. As they proceeded in the work they were to grow more bold; and if circumstances did not favour them, nor allow them to say all they wished to say, they were to resort to supplements, and to foreign editions, which would at the same time render this dangerous work more common and less costly to the generality of readers.

The Encyclopedia, perpetually recommended and cried up by the adepts, was to be a standing book in all libraries; and insensibly the learned was to be converted into the Antichristian world. If this project was well conceived, it was impossible to see one more faithfully executed.

Proofs

as to the fact,

It is now our duty to lay before the reader the proofs, first as to the fact, secondly as to the intention. For the first it will be sufficient to cast the eye on divers articles of this immense collection, especially where the principal tenets of Christianity, or even of natural religion, are treated, and to follow them through the divers references which the Sophisters have prepared for the reader. We shall find the existence of God, free agency, and the spirituality of the soul, treated in the style of a Christian Philosopher; but a *vide* DEMONSTRA-TION, or a *vide* CORRUPTION, will be added to pervert all that had been said; and the article to which d'Alembert and Diderot more particularly refer the reader, are exactly those where the doctrine of the Sceptic or the Spinosist, of the Fatalist or the Materialist, is chiefly inculcated. (*See note.*)[4]

---

4   Look for the article GOD (Geneva edition), and you will find very sound notions, together with the direct, physical, and metaphysical demonstration of his existence; and indeed under such an article it would have been too bold to have broached any thing even bordering on Atheism, Spinosism, or Epicurism; but the reader is *referred* to the article DEMONSTRATION, and there all the physical and metaphysical cogent arguments for the existence of a God disappear. We are there taught, that all direct demonstrations *suppose the idea of infinitude, and that such an idea cannot be very clear either to the Naturalist or the Metaphysician.* This, in a word, destroys all confidence the reader had placed in the proofs adduced of the existence of God. There again they are pleased to tell you, that a single insect, in the eyes of the Philosopher, more forcibly proves the existence of a God, than all the metaphysical arguments whatever (*Ibid.*); but you are then *referred* to CORRUPTION, where you learn how cautious you must be of asserting in a positive manner that corruption can never beget animated bodies; that such a production of animated bodies by corruption seems to be countenanced by *daily experiments'*, and it is precisely from these experiments that the Atheists conclude the existence of God to be unnecessary, either for the creation of man or animals. Prepossessed by these *references*, against the existence of God, let the reader turn to the articles of ENCYCLOPE-DIA and EPICURISM. In the former he will be told, *that there is no being in nature that can be called the first or last, and that a machine infinite in every way must necessarily be the Deity.*

In the latter the atom is to be the Deity. It will be the primary cause of all things, by whom and of whom every thing is active, essentially of itself, alone unalterable, alone eternal, alone immutable; and thus the reader will be insensibly led from the God of the Gospel to the heathenish fictions of an Epicurus or a Spinoza.

The same cunning is to be found in the article of the SOUL. When the Sophisters treat directly of its essence they give the ordinary proofs of its *spirituality and of its immortality.* They will even add in the article BRUTE, that the soul cannot be supposed material, nor can *the brute be reduced to the quality of a mere machine, without running the hazard of making man an Automaton.* And under NATURAL LAW we read, that if the determinations of man, or even his oscillations, arise from any thing *material, and extraneous to his soul, there will be neither good nor evil, neither just nor unjust, neither obligation nor right.* Then *referred* to the article LOCKE, in order to do away all this consequence, we are told that it is of no importance *whether matter thinks or not; for what is that to justice or injustice, to the immortality of the soul and to all the truths of the system, whether political or religious*; the reader, enjoying the Equality and Liberty of his reason, is left in doubt with regard to the spirituality, and no longer knows whether he should not think himself all matter. But he will decide when, under the article ANIMAL, he finds that life and animation are only physical properties of matter, and lest he should think himself debased by his resembling a plant or an animal, to console him in his fall, they will tell him, article ENCYCLOPEDIA and ANIMAL, *that the only difference between certrain vegetables, and animals such as us, is, that they sleep and that we wake, that we are animals that feel, and that they are animals that feel not*; and still further in the article ANIMAL, that the sole *difference between a stock and a man is, that the one ever falls, while the latter never falls, after the same manner.* After perusing these articles *bona fide*, the reader must be insensibly drawn into the vortex of Materialism.

In treating of Liberty or free agency we find the same artifice. When they treat of it directly, they will say, "Take away

Liberty, all human nature is overthrown, and there will be no trace of order in society—Recompense will be ridiculous, and chastisement unjust.—The ruin of Liberty carries with it that of all order and of police, and legitimates the most monstrous crimes.—So monstrous a doctrine is not to be debated in the schools, but punished by the magistrates, &c. *Oh Liberty! they exclaim. Oh Liberty, gift of heaven! Oh, Liberty of action! Oh, Liberty of thought! thou alone art capable of great things."* [*See articles* AUTHORITY *and the* PRELIMINARY DISCOURSE.] But at the article CHANCE (*fortuit*) all this liberty of action and of thought is only *a power that cannot be exercised, that cannot be known by actual exercise*: and Diderot in the article EVIDENCE, pretending to support Liberty, will very properly say, "This concatenation of causes and effects supposed by the Philosophers, in order to form ideas representing the mechanism of the Universe, is as fabulous as the Tritons and the Naiads;" but both he and d'Alembert will descant again on that concatenation, and, returning to CHANCE (*fortuit*), will tell us "That though it is *imperceptible*, it is not the less real; that it connects all things in nature, and that *all events depend on it*; just as the wheels of the watch, as to their motion, depend on each other; that from the first moment of our existence, we are by *no means masters of our motions*; that were there a thousand worlds similar to this, simultaneously existing, and governed by the same laws, every thing in them would be done in the same way; and that *man, in virtue of these same laws, would perform at the same instants of time the same actions* in each one of these worlds." This will naturally convince the uninformed reader of the chimera of such a Liberty or free agency, which cannot be exercised. Not content with this, Diderot in the article FATALITY, after a long dissertation on this *concatenation of causes*, ends by saying, that it *cannot be contested either in the physical world*, or *in the moral and intellectual world*. Then what becomes of that Liberty without which there no longer exists *just or unjust, obligation or right*.

These examples will suffice to convince the reader of the truth of what we have asserted, as to the artful policy with which the Encyclopedia had been digested; they will show

This cunning could not escape those authors who wrote in the defence of religion.[5] But Voltaire, resorting to calumny in order to defend their Encylopedia, would represent these authors as enemies of the state, and bad citizens.[6] Such, indeed, were his usual weapons; and had he perfectly succeeded in deceiving people, it would have been sufficient to have examined his confidential correspondence with the very authors of the work, to be convinced of the wickedness of their intentions.

as to the intention.

At a hundred leagues from Paris, and not thwarted by the obstacles which d'Alembert had to combat, he often complains, that the attacks are not sufficiendy direct. He is often ruffled by certain restrictions usual to d'Alembert, and at length he breaks out on those which are visible in the article Bayle. d'Alembert answers,

> This is an idle quarrel indeed on Bayle's Dictionary. In the first place, I did not say, *happy would it have been had he shown more reverence to religion and morality.* My phrase is much more modest: and beside, in a cursed country like this where we are writing, who does not know that such sentences are but a mere matter of form, and only a cloak to the

with what cunning its authors sought to spread the principles of Atheism, Materialism, and Fatalism, in short, to plant every error incompatible with that religion for which at their outset they professed so great a reverence.

5   See *Religion Vindicated, the Writings of Gauchat,* of Bergier, our *Helvian Letters,* &c.

6   To d'Alembert, 16 Jan. 1757, vol. 68, let. 18, p. 31.

truths additionally conveyed? Every one is aware of that.[7]

During the time that Voltaire was busied with the articles he so frequently sent to d'Alembert for the Encyclopedia, he often complained of his shackles, and was unable to dissemble how much he desired to attack religion openly. He writes, "All that I am told about the articles of Divinity and Metaphysics grieves me to the heart; *O how cruel it is to print the very reverse of what one thinks.*"[8] But d'Alembert, more adroit, sensible of the necessity of these palliatives, *lest he should be looked upon as a madman by those whom he wished to convert,* foresaw the day when he could triumphantly answer, "If mankind is so much enlightened to-day, it is only because we have used the precaution, or had the good fortune, *to enlighten them by degrees.*"[9]

When Voltaire had sent certain violent articles, under the name of the priest of Lausanne, d'Alembert would immediately write, "We shall always receive with gratitude whatever comes from the same hand. We only pray our heretic to draw in his claws a little, as in certain places he has shown his fangs a little too much. This is the time for stepping back to make the better leap."[10] And to show

---

7   To d'Alembert, 10 Oct. 1764, vol. 68, let. 145, p. 323.

8   To d'Alembert, 9 Oct. 1755, vol. 68, let. 4, p. 9.

9   From d'Alembert, 16 July, 1762, vol. 68, let. 102, p. 207.

10 From d'Alembert, 21 July, 1757, vol. 68, let. 30, p. 51.

that he never lost sight of this maxim, he answers Voltaire's animadversions on the article HELL: "Without doubt we have several wretched articles in our divinity and metaphysics, *but with divines for censors, and a privilege, I defy you to make them better. There are articles less exposed where all is set to rights again.*"[11]

Can there be a doubt left of the precise and determined intention of the Encyclopedists, when Voltaire exhorts d'Alembert to snatch the moment, whilst the attention of government is drawn off by other concerns: "During this war *with the parliament and the bishops*, the Philosophers will have fine play; *You have a fair opportunity of filling the Encyclopedia with those truths that we should not have dared utter twenty years ago,*"[12] or when he writes to Damilaville, "I can be interested by a good dramatic performance, but could be far more pleased with a good philosophical work that should for ever crush the wretch. *I place all my hopes in the Encyclopedia.*"[13] After such an avowal it would be useless to seek farther proof of this immense compilation being no other than the grand arsenal for all their sophisticated arms against religion.

Diderot, more open, even in his ambush reluctantly employed cunning. He does not hide how much he wished boldly to insert his principles; and

---

11   *Ibid.* Page 52.

12   To d'Alembert, 13 Nov. 1756, vol. 68, let. 11, p. 20.

13   To DamilaviUe, 23 May, 1764, vol. 58, let. 196, p. 360.

those principles are explained when he writes, "The age of Louis XIV only produced two men worthy of co-operating to the Encyclopedia," and these two men were Perrault and Boindin. The merits of the latter are more conspicuous than those of the former. Boindin, born in 1676, had lately died a reputed Atheist, and had been refused Christian burial. The notoriety of his principles had shut the French academy against him, and with such titles he could not have failed being a worthy co-operator.

Such then the object, such the intention of the conspiring authors. We see by their own confession, that they did not wish to compile for science, but for infidelity; that it was not the advancement of arts they sought, but to seize the moment, when the attention of the ruling authorities was drawn off, to propagate their impious calumnies against religion. They hypocritically utter some few religious truths, and *print the contrary of what they believed* on Christianity, but only the better to cover the Sophisms which they printed against it.

In spite of all their arts, however, men zealous for religion forcibly opposed the work. The Dauphin, in particular, obtained a temporary suspension of it; and various were the obstacles encountered by its authors. D'Alembert, wearied, had nearly forsaken it, when Voltaire, sensible of the importance of this first tool of the conspiracy, roused his drooping courage. He, far from abating, rather redoubled his efforts, asking for and incessantly sending fresh articles. He would extol per-

The object it meets and its success.

63

severance, he would show d'Alembert and Diderot the ignominy and shame redounding to their opponents.[14] He would urge them, conjure them by their friendship, or in the name of Philosophy, to overcome their disgust, and not to be foiled in so glorious an undertaking.[15]

At length the Encyclopedia was brought to a conclusion, and it made its appearance under the sanction of a public privilege. Triumphant in their first step, the conspirators saw in it but the forerunner of their future successes against religion.

Its co-operators.

That no doubt may exist as to the particular drift of this compilation, the reader must be made acquainted with the co-operators chosen by d'Alembert and Diderot, especially for the religious part. Their first divine was Raynal, a man just expelled from the Order of the Jesuits on account of his impiety, that very thing which constituted his chief and strongest recommendation to d'Alembert. Every one, unfortunately, knows how well he verified the judgement of his former brethren by his atrocious declamations against Christianity; but few are acquainted with the anecdote of his expulsion from among the co-operators; and that connects his story with that of another divine, who, without being impious himself, had been unfortunately drawn into the company of the Sophisters.

---

14   See his letters of the years 1755-6.

15   Letters of 5th Sept. 1752, 13th Nov. 1756, and particularly of 8th Jan. 1757, vol. 68.

This was the Abbé Yvon, an odd metaphysician, but an inoffensive and upright man; often in extreme indigence, and living by his pen when he thought he could do it with decency. In the simplicity of his heart he had written *The Defence of the Abbé de Prades*. I have heard him assert that not a single error could be found in that work, and on the first argument give up the point. With the same simplicity I have heard him relate, by what means he had co-operated in the Encyclopedia.

> I was in want of money (said he); Raynal met me and persuaded me to write a few articles, promising me a good reward. I acceded, and when my work was delivered at Raynal's study I received twenty-five Louis-d'ors. Thinking myself very well paid, I imparted my good fortune to one of the booksellers employed for the Encyclopedia, who seemed much surprised that the articles furnished by Raynal should not be his own. He was furious at the trick he suspected. A few days after this I was sent for to the office; and Raynal, who had received a thousand crowns for his pretended work, was obliged to refund me the hundred Louis-d'ors he had kept for himself.

This anecdote will not surprise those who are acquainted with Raynal's plagiary talents. His impiety was not indeed sufficient to prevent his dismission, but it preserved him within the pale of the fraternal embrace.

I must add, that the articles on God and on the Soul, furnished by the Abbé Yvon, are exactly those which grieved Voltaire to the heart, and for which d'Alembert and Diderot were obliged to have recourse to their art of references.

The third divine, or as d'Alembert styles him the second, for he never dared mention Yvon to Voltaire, was the Abbé de Prades, obliged to fly to Prussia for an attempt to impose on the Sorbonne by advancing his own impious propositions as those of religion. It was the cunning of this thesis which had misled the Abbé Yvon; but being soon discovered the parliament took it up. The author, nevertheless, was put under the protection of the King of Prussia by Voltaire and d'Alembert.[16]

We also owe it to the memory of the Abbé De Prades to relate (what his protectors would willingly conceal) that three years afterward he publicly retracted all his errors in a declaration signed the 6th of April 1754, bewailing his intimacy with the Sophisters, adding, *that one life could not suffice to bewail his past conduct.*[17] He died in 1782.

Another of their divines was the Abbé Morrelet, a man dear to Voltaire and to d'Alembert, who, playing on his name, called him the Abbé *Mordles* (*Bite 'em*), because, under pretence of attacking the Inquisition, he had fallen on (bitten) the church with all his might.[18]

Were we to enumerate the lay writers who co-operated in this work, we should find far worse than

---

16   To d'Alembert, 5 Sept. 1752, vol. 68, let. 3, p. 7.

17   Feller's *Hist. Dict.*

18   From d'Alembert, 16Juin, 1760, vol. 68, let. 65, p. 115—and to

these divines. But we will only mention the celebrated Dumarsais, a man so infamous, that the public authorities were obliged to interfere and destroy a school he had formed solely to imbue his pupils with the venom of his impiety. This unfortunate man also retracted his errors, but not till he lay on his death-bed. The choice of this man's pen shows the kind of co-operators which d'Alembert sought.

Far be it from me to confound in this class, such men as MM. de Formey or Jaucourt, particularly the latter, to whom, as we have already said, they were indebted for many articles. The only reproach that can attach to him is, that he should have continued his labours after he either saw or should have seen the drift of that vast compilation, wherein, intermixed with his toils, lay all the sophisms and calumnies impiety could invent.

Excepting these two men, we may comprehend nearly all the rest of the Encyclopedian writers in the following picture, drawn by Diderot himself. *It is judged by Diderot.*

> All that detestable crew, who, though perfectly ignorant, valued themselves on knowing every thing; who, seeking to distinguish themselves by that vexatious universality to which they pretended, fell upon every thing, jumbled and spoiled all, and converted this pretended digest of science *into a gulph, or rather a sort of rag-basket, where they promiscuously threw every thing half-examined, ill-digested, good, bad, and indifferent, but always incoherent.*

Thiriot, 26 Jan. 1762, vol. 57, let. 157, p. 320.

What a precious avowal as to the intrinsic merit of their work! especially after what he says as to their views, in describing the pains they had taken, the vexations it had caused them, and the art it had required to insinuate what they dared not openly write against prejudices (religion), in order to overthrow them without being perceived.[19]

But all these follies of the *rag-dealers* contributed to the bulk and accelerated the appearance of the volumes, the chiefs carefully inserting in each volume what could promote the grand object. Being at length terminated, all the trumpets sounded, and the journals of the party teemed with the praises of this literary achievement. The learned themselves were duped. Every one would have an Encyclopedia. Numerous were the editions, of all sizes and prices; but in every successive one, under the pretence of correction, greater boldness was assumed. About the time when the antichristian revolution was nearly accomplished, appeared *L'Encyclopedie par ordre des Matières*. When it was first undertaken, some deference was still paid to religion. A man of eminent merit, Mr. Bergier, a canon of Paris, thought it incumbent on him to yield to the pressing solicitations of his friends, lest the part treating of religion should fall into the hands of its greatest enemies. What was

A new one proposed.

---

19 The text in the original is far more extensive, where Diderot treats of the deficiencies of the Encyclopedia; but, not having it at hand, we quote from Feller's *Hist. Dic.*, art. Diderot.

easy to foresee came to pass. The name of a man who had combated the impious work of a Voltaire or a Rousseau naturally served as a cloak to this new digest, styled *The Encyclopedia methodised.*[20] This was on the eve of the French revolution, so that the petty infidels charged with the work, observed no farther bounds with regard to religion. This new work is more completely impious than the former, notwithstanding some excellent tracts of Mr. Bergier and of some others; and thus the Sophisters of the day perfected the first tool of the antichristian conspirators.

---

20 Nicolas-Sylvestre Bergier, *L'Encyclopédie méthodique*, 2 vols. (Paris: Panckoucke, 1788). —Ed.

Second means of the Conspirators.— The Extinction of the Jesuits.

he hypocrisy of Voltaire and d'Alembert had triumphed over every obstacle. They had so perfectly succeeded in their abuse of all who dared oppose the Encyclopedia, whom they represented as barbarians and enemies to literature; they had found such powerful support during the successive ministries of d'Argenson, Choiseul, and Malesherbes, that all the opposition of the grand Dauphin, of the clergy, and of the religious writers, could not avail, and this impious digest was in future to be looked upon as a necessary work. It was to be found in every library; whether at home or abroad, it was always to be referred to. Thence the simple mind in quest of science was to imbibe the poison of infidelity, and the Sophister was to be furnished with arms against Christianity. The conspirators, though proud of their first invention, could not dissemble that there existed a set of men whose zeal, whose learning, whose weight and authority, might one day counteract their undertaking. The church was defended by her bishops and all the lower clergy. There were, moreover, numerous orders of relgous always ready to join the seculars for her defence in the cause of Christianity. But before we treat of the means employed for the destruction of these defenders of the faith, we must show the plan formed by Frederick, whence they resolved on the destruction of the Jesuits, as the first step toward dismantling the church, and effecting the destruction of her bishops and of her different orders of priesthood.

General wish of the conspirators as to religious Orders.

In the year 1743 Voltaire had been sent on secret service to the Court of Prussia; and among his dispatches from Berlin we find the following written to the minister Amelot.

Frederick's first plan for the ruin of the church.

> In the last interview I had with his Prussian majesty, I spoke to him of a pamphlet that appeared in Holland about six weeks back, in which the secularization of ecclesiastical principalities in favour of the Emperor and Queen of Hungary was proposed as the means of pacification for the Empire. I told him that I could wish, with all my heart, to see it take place; that what was

Cæsar's was to be given to Cæsar; that the whole business of the church was to supplicate God and the princes; that by his institution, the Benedictine could have no claim to sovereignty, and that this decided opinion of mine had gained me many enemies among the clergy. He owned that the *pamphlet had been printed by his orders*. He hinted, that he should not dislike to be one of those kings to whom the clergy would conscientiously make restituion, and that he should not be sorry to embellish Berlin with the goods of the church. This is most certainly his grand object, and he means to make peace only when he sees the possibility of accomplishing it. It rests with your prudence to profit of this his secret plan, which he confided to me alone.[1]

At this time the court of Louis XV. began to be overrun with ministers who on religious matters thought like a Voltaire or a Frederick.—They had no ecclesiastical states, no ecclesiastical electors to pillage; but the possessions of the numerous religious orders dispersed through France could satiate their rapacity, and they conceived that the plan of Frederick might be equally lucrative to France. The Marquis d'Argenson, counsellor of state and minister of foreign affairs, was the great patron of Voltaire. It was he who, adopting all his ideas, formed the plan for the destruction of all religious orders in France. The progress of the plan was to be slow and successive, lest it should spread alarm. They were to begin with those orders that

Its effects on the court of Versailles.

D'Argenson's plans for the same object.

---

1   To Mr. Amelot, 8 Oct. 1743, vol. 53, let. 229, p. 474.

were least numerous; they were to render the entrance into the religious state more difficult; and the time of professions was to be delayed until that age when people are already engaged in some other state of life. The possessions of the suppressed were artfully to be adapted to some pious use, or united to the episcopal revenues. Time was to do away with all difficulties, and the day was not far off when, as lord paramount, the Sovereign was to put in his claim to all that belonged to the suppressed orders, even to what had been united, for the moment, to the sees of the bishops; the whole was to be added to his domains.

That the French ministry often changed, but that the plans of the cabinet never did, and that it always watched the favourable opportunity, was the remark of a shrewd and observing legate.—The plan for the destruction of religious orders had been made by d'Argenson, in the year 1745, though forty years after it still lay on the chimney-piece of Maurepas, then prime minister. I owe this anecdote to a person of the name of Bevis,[2] a learned Benedictine, and in such high repute with Maurepas, that he often pressed him to leave his hood, promising him preferment as a secular.—The Benedictine refused such offers; and it was not without surprise that he heard Maurepas tell him, when pressing him to accept his offer, *that secularization would one day be his lot*; he then gave him

---

2   He was in London at the time the first edition of this Volume
     was printing.

d'Argenson's plan, which had long been followed and would soon be accomplished.

Avarice alone could not have suggested this plan; as the mendicant orders, as well as the more wealthy, were to be destroyed.

It would have been folly to attempt its execution before the Encyclopedian Sophisters had prepared the way; it therefore lay dormant many years in the state offices at Versailles. In the mean time the Voltairean ministry, fostering infidelity, pretended to strike, while they secredy supported, the sophistical tribe. They forbade Voltaire to enter Paris, while *in amazement he receives a scroll of the king*, confirming his pension, *which had been suppressed twelve years before!*[3] He carries on his correspondence with the adepts, under the covers and under the very seals of the first secretaries and of the ministers themselves, who were perfectly conversant with all his impious plans.[4] It was this very part of the Antichristian Conspiracy that Condorcet meant to describe when he says: "Often a government would reward the Philosopher with one hand, whilst with the other it would pay his slanderer; would proscribe him, while it was proud of the soil that had given him birth; punished him for his opinions, but would have blushed not to have partaken of them."[5]

This perfidious understanding between the ministers of his most Christian Majesty and the An-

Choiseul's under-
standing with the Sophisters.

---

3   To Damilaville, 9 Jan. 1762, vol. 57, let. 152, p. 310.

4   To Marmontel, 13 Aug. 1760, vol. 56, let. 173, p. 353.

5   Condorcet's *Sketch on History*, 9th Epoch.

tichristian Conspirators hastened their progress, when the most impious and most despotic of ministers judged that the time was come for the decisive blow to be struck. This minisiter was the Duke of Choiseul; during the whole time of his power he was the faithful adept and admirer of Voltaire, who says, "Don't fear opposition from the Duke of Choiseul; I repeat it, I don't mislead you, he will be proud of serving you:"[6] or to Marmontel, "We have been a little alarmed by certain panics, but never was fright so unfounded. The Duke of Choiseul and Mad. de Pompadour know the opinions of the uncle and of the *niece*. You may send any thing without danger." In fine, he was so secure in the Duke's protection against the Sorbonne and the church, that he would exclaim, *"The ministry of France for ever; long live the Duke de Choiseul."*[7]

This confidence of the premier chief was well placed in Choiseul, who had adopted and acted upon all the plans of d'Argenson. The ministry prognosticated a great source of riches to the state in the destruction of the religious, though many of them did not seek in that the destruction of religion; they even thought some of them necessary, and the Jesuits were excepted. Unfortuntely, these were the very men with whom Choiseul wished to begin, and his intention was aleady known by the following anecdote:—Choiseul, one day, convers-

---

6 To d'Alembert, 9 July, 1760, vol. 68, let. 68, p. 121.

7 To Marmontel, 13 Aug. 1760, vol. 56, let. 173, p. 352, and 2 Dec. 1767, vol. 60, let. 200, p. 336.

ing with three ambassadors, one of them said, "If I ever chance to be in power, I will certainly destroy all religious orders excepting the Jesuits, for they are at least useful to education."—"As for my part (answered Choiseul), I will destroy none but the Jesuits; for, their education once destroyed, all the other religious orders will fall of themselves;" and his policy was deep! There can be no doubt but that destroying the Order in whose hands the majority of the colleges were at that time, would be striking at the very root of that Christian eduction which prepared so many for the religious state; in spite, therefore, of the exception, Choiseul still sought to sway the council by his opinion.

Why he begins with them.

The Jesuits were tampered with, but in vain; so far from acceding to the destruction of the other Orders, they were foremost in their defence; they pleaded the rights of the church; they supported them with all their weight, in their writings and their discourses. This gave occasion to Choiseul to remonstrate with the council, and to persuade them, that if they wished to procure to the state the immense resources of the religious possessions, it was necessary to begin with the *destruction of the Jesuits.*

This anecdote I only cite as having heard it among the Jesuits, but their subsequent expulsion strongly corroborates its veracity. Whether these religious deserved their fate or not is alien to my subject; I only wish to point out the hand that strikes, and the men who, as d'Alembert says, *gave the orders* for their destruction. Treating of the Antichristian Conspiracy, I have only to ascertain whether the destruction of the Jesuits was not conceived, urged, and premeditated, by the Sophistical Conspirators, as a means powerfully tending to the destruction of Christianity. Let us then examine what that body of men really was, and how necessarily odious they must have been to the conspirators from their general reputation. Let us, above all, hear the Sophisters themselves; let us see how much they interested themselves in their destruction.

What the Jesuits were.

The Jesuits were a body of twenty thousand men spread through all Catholic countries, and particurly charged with the eduction of youth. They did not, however, on that account, neglect the other duties of the ecclesiastic, but were bound by a particular vow to go as missionaries to any part of the globe, if sent, to preach the gospel. From their youth brought up to the study of literature, they had produced numberless authors, but more particularly divines, who immediately combated any error that might spring up in the church. Latterly they were chiefly engaged in France against the Jansenists and Sophisters, and it was their zeal in the defence of the church that made the King of Prussia style them *The Lifeguards of the Pope.*[8]

Opinion of the bishops on the Jesuits.

When fifty French prelates, cardinals, archbishops or bishops, assembled, were consulted by Lou-

---

8   From Frederick, 10 Feb. 1767, vol. 65, let. 154, p. 361.

is XV. on the propriety of destroying the Order, they expressly answered,

> The Jesuits are of infinite service to us in our dioceses, whether for preaching or the direction of the faithful, to revive, preserve, and propagate faith and piety, by their missions, congregations, and spiritual retreats, which they make with our approbation, and under our authority. For these reasons we think, Sire, that to prohibit them from instructing would essentially injure our dioceses, and that it would be difficult to replace them with equal advantage in the instruction of youth, and more particularly so in those provincial towns where there are no universities.[9]

Such in general was the idea entertained of them in all Catholic countries; it is necessary for the reader to be acquainted with it, that he may understand of how much importance their destruction was to the Sophisters. At the time, the Jansenists had the honor of it, and indeed they were very ardent in its promotion. But the Duke of Choiseul and the famous courtezan La Marquise de Pompadour, who then held the destiny of France, under the shadow and in the name of Louis XV., were not more partial to the Jansenists than to the Jesuits. Both confidants of Voltaire, they were consequently initiated in all the mysteries of the Sophisters,[10] and Voltaire, as he says himself, *would willingly*

---

9   Opinion of the Bishops, 1761.

10   To Marmontel, 13 Aug. 1760, vol. 56, let. 173, p. 352.

have seen all the Jesuits at the bottom of the sea, each with a Jansenist hung to his neck.[11]

The Jansenists were nothing more than the hounds employed in the general hunt by Choiseul, the Marquise de Pompadour, and the Sophisters; the minister spurred on by his impiety, the Marquise wishing to revenge an insult (as she called it) received from Père Sacy, a Jesuit. This Father had refused her the Sacraments, unless by quitting the Court she would in some sort atone for the public scandal she had given by her cohabitation with Louis XV. But, if we judge by Voltaire's letters, they neither of them needed much stimulation, as they both had always been great protectors of the Sophisters, and the minister had always favoured their intrigues as far as he could consistendy with circumstances and politics.[12] The following pages will show these intrigues; and we shall begin with d'Alembert, who writes in the most sanguine manner on their future victory over the Jesuits, and on the immense advantages to be derived to the Conspiracy by their downfall.

The avowals of d'Alembert.

> You are perpetuallky repeating *Crush the wretch*; for God's sake let it fall headlong of itself! Do you know what Astruc says? It is not the Jansenists that are killing the Jesuits, but the Encyclopedia; yes, the Encyclopedia: and that is not unlikely. This scoundrel Astruc is a second Pasquin, and sometimes says very good things.

11   To Chabanon, 21 Dec. 1767, vol. 60, let. 215, p. 362.

12   To Marmontel, 13 Aug. 1760.

I for my part see every thing in the brightest colours; I foresee the Jansenists naturally dying off
the next year, after having strangled the Jesuits
this; I foresee toleration established, the Protestants recalled, the priests married, confession
abolished, and *fanaticism* (religion) crushed;
and all this without its being perceived.[13]

The express words of the Conspirators show
what part they had in the destruction of the Jesuits.
They were indeed the true cause. We see what advantage they hoped to reap from it. They had kin-
dled the hatred, and procured the death warrant.
The Jansenists were to serve the Conspirators,
but were themselves to fall when no more wanted. The Calvinists were to be recalled, but only to
perish in their turn. To strike at the whole Christian Religion was their aim; and Impiety, with its
Sophisters, was to range uncontrolled throughout
an infidel world.

D'Alembert smiles at the poreblind parliaments
seconding with all their might the plans of the
Conspirators. It is in this idea that he writes thus
to Voltaire:

The laugh is no longer on the side of the Jesuits,
since they have fallen out with the Philosophers.
They are now at open war with the Parliament,
who find that the society of Jesus is contrary to
human society. This same society of Jesus on its
own part finds that the order of the Parliament
is not within the order of those who have com-

13   From d'Alembert, 4 May 1762, vol. 68. let. 100. p. 201.

mon sense, and Philosophy would decide that both the society of Jesus and the Parliament are in the right:[14]

and again, when he writes to Voltaire,

> This evacuation of the College of Louis le Grand (the Jesuits College at Paris) is of more importance to us than that of Martinico. Upon my word this affair is becoming serious, and the people of the Parliament don't mince the matter. They think they are serving religion, while *they are in reality forwarding reason without the least suspicion.* They are the public executioners, and *take their orders from Philosphy without knowing it.*[15]

Rapt in this idea, when he sees the Encyclopedian commands nearly executed, he openly avows the cause of his revenge, and even implores Heaven that his prey may not escape him. "Philosophy (says he) is on the eve of being revenged of the Jesuits, but who will avenge it of the other fanatics?— Pray God, dear Brother, that reason may triumph even in our days."[16]

And this day of triumph comes. He proclaims the long-concerted exploit: "At length," he cries, "on the sixth of next month, we shall be delivered from all that Jesuitical rabble; but will rea-

---

14 From d'Alembert, 9 July, 1761, vol. 68. let. 88, p. 168.

15 From d'Alemert, 4 May, 1762, vol. 68, let. 100, P., 201.

16 From d'Alembert, 8 Sept. 1761, vol. 68, let. 90, p. 173.

son by that have gained, or *the wretch* have lost ground?"[17]

Thus we see, that under this shocking formula the destruction of Christianity is linked with that of the Jesuits. D'Alembert was so thoroughly convinced of the importance of their triumph over that Order, that, hearing one day of Voltaire's pretended gratitude to his former masters, he immediately wrote to him,

> Do you know what I was told yesterday?—nothing less than that you began to pity the Jesuits, and that you were almost tempted to write in their favour; as if it were possible to interest any one in favour of people on whom you have cast so much ridicule. *Be advised by me; let us have no human weakness.* Let the Jansenitical rabble rid of us the Jesuitical, and do not prevent one spider from devouring another.[18]

Nothing could be more ill-grounded than this alarm. Voltaire was not the writer of the conclusions drawn by the Attorney-Generals of the Parliament (as d'Alembert had been informed, who himself had been the author of Mr. de La Chalotais, the most artful and virulent piece that appeared against the Jesuits).[19] Voltaire, however, was not

Of Voltaire.

---

17   From d'Alembert, 31 July, 1762, vol. 68, let. 102, p. 208.

18   From d'Alembert, 25 Sept. 1762, vol. 68, let. 105, p. 218.

19   For six decades the *procureur général* at the Parliament of Brittany, Louis-René de Caradeuc de La Chalotais (1701 – 1785) was a fierce opponent of the Jesuits, against who he

less active in composing and circulating memorials against them.[20]

If he suspected any great personage of protecting the Jesuits, he would write and use his utmost endeavours to dissuade them. It was for that purpose he wrote to the Mareschal de Richlieu, "I have been told, my Lord, that you have favoured the Jesuits at Bourdeaux:—try to destroy whatever influence they may have."[21] Again, he did not blush to upbraid Frederick himself with having offered an asylum to these unfortunate victims of their plots.[22] Full as rancorous as d'Alembert, he would express his joy at their misfortunes in the same gross abuse; and his letters show with what adepts he shared it.

> I rejoice with my brave chevalier (writing to the Marq. de Villevielle) on the expulsion of the Jesuits; Japan led the way in driving out those knaves of Loyola; China followed the example of Japan; and France and Spain have imitated the Chinese. Would to God that all the Monks were swept from the face of the earth; they are no better than those knaves of Loyola. If the Sorbonne

wrote two memoirs, *Comptes Rendus des Constitutions des Jesuites* (1761), which contributed greatly to the suppression of the order in France. In his 1763 *Essay on National Education (Essai d'Éducation Nationale* (1762), he gave Voltaire extravagant praise. —Ed.

20 To the M. d'Argence de Dirac, 26 Feb., 1762, vol. 57, let. 174, p. 352.

21 To the Due de Richelieu, 27 Nov. 1761, V. 57, let. 139, p. 281.

22 To Frederick, 8 Nov. 1773, vol. 66. let. 46. p. 112.

were suffered to act, it would be worse than the Jesuits. One is surrounded with monsters: I embrace my worthy chevalier, and exhort him to conceal his march from the enemy.[23]

What examples does the Philosophist of Ferney adduce! the cruelties of a Taikosama, who, while expelling and crucifying the missionary Jesuits, also murders thousands and tens of thousands of his subjects, in order to eradicate Christianity; and the Chinese, less violent indeed, but with whom every persecution against the missionaries has always been preceded or followed by a prohibition to preach the Gospel. Can a man build upon such authorities without forming the same wish?

It is to be remarked, that Voltaire dares not cite the example of Portugal, or of its tyrant Carvalho.[24] The truth is, that, with the rest of Europe, he is

---

23 To the M. de Villevielle, 27 April, 1767, V. 60, let. 102, p. 180.

24 I have seen well-informed persons, who thought that the persecution in Portugal was not entirely unconnected with the conspiracy of the Sophisters; that it was only a first essay of what might be afterwards attempted against the whole body. This might be. The politics and power of Choiseul, and the character of Carvalho, may add weight to this opinion. I candidly confess that I have no proof of their secret co-operations; and beside, the ferocious wickedness of Carvalho has been set in so strong a fight, (he was the jailor and murderer of so many victims declared innocent by the decree of the 8th of April 1771) that it would be useless to seek any other stimulator than his own heart in that shocking series of cruelties which distinguished his ministry. See the Memoirs and Anecdotes of the Marq. of Pombal; and The Discourse on History by the Comte d'Albon.

obliged to confess that the conduct of this minister in Portugal, with regard to the Father Malagrida and the pretended conspiracy of the Jesuits, *was the height of folly and the excess of horror*.[25]

It is always worthy of remark, that the conspiring Sophisters spared no pains to throw the odium of the assassination of Louis XV on the Jesuits; and more particularly Damilaville, whom Voltaire answers in the following manner:

> My Brethren may easily perceive that I have not spared the Jesuits. But posterity would revolt against me in their favour, were I to accuse them of a crime of which all Europe and Damien himself has cleared them. I should debase myself into the vile *echo of the Jansenists*, were I to speak otherwise.[26]

Notwithstanding the incoherency in their accusations against the Jesuits, d'Alembert, convinced of Voltaire's zeal in this warfare, sends him his *pretended history* of these Religious; a work, of the fallacy of which his own pen is the best guarantee, when he speaks of it as a means for the grand object:

> I recommend this work to your protection (he writes to Voltaire); I really believe it will be of service to the common cause, and that *superstition*, notwithstanding the many bows I pretend to make before it, will not fare the better for it. If

---

25   Voltaire's *Age of Louis XV*. chap. 33.
26   To Damilaville, 2 March, 1763, vol. 58, let. 35, p. 72.

I were, like you, far from Paris, I would certainly *give it a sound threshing* with all my heart,
with all my soul, and with all my strength; in
short, as they tell us we are to love God. But,
*situated as I am, I must content myself with
giving it a few fillips,* apologizing for the great
liberty I take; and I do think that I have hit it off
pretty well.[27]

Could the reader for a moment suppress his
indignation at the profligacy of the style, would
not the hypocrisy, the profound dissimulation,
of which these Sophisters speak so lightly, rouse
it anew? If the annals of history should ever be
searched, it would be in vain to seek a Conspiracy
the insidiousness of whose intrigues was of a deeper cast; and that from their own confession.

As to Frederick, his conduct during the whole
of this warfare is so singular, that his own words
alone can give a proper idea of it. He would call
the Jesuits, *The life-guards of the court of Rome,
the grenadiers of Religion*; and, as such, he hated
them, and triumphed with the rest of the Conspirators in their defeat. But he also beheld in them a
body of men highly useful and even necessary to
his state; as such, he supported them several years
after their destruction, and was deaf to the repeated solicitations of Voltaire and his motley crew.
One might be almost led to think that he liked
them; for he openly writes to Voltaire, "I have no

*Of
Frederick
and his
strange
conduct.*

---

27 From d'Alembert, 3 Jan. 1765, vol. 68, let. 151, p. 333.

reason to complain of Ganganelli;[28] he has left me my dear Jesuits, who are the objects of universal persecution. I will preserve a seed of so precious and so rare a plant, to furnish those who may wish to cultivate it hereafter."[29] He would even enter into a sort of justification with Voltaire on his conduct, so opposite to the views of the party.

"Although a heretic, and what is still more an infidel," says he,

> I have preserved that Order after a fashion, and for the following reasons:
> Not one Catholic man of letters is to be found in these regions, except among the Jesuits. We had nobody capable of keeping schools; we had no Oratorian Fathers, no Purists (Piaristes, or Fathers of Charity-schools) . . . . There was no other alternative, but the destruction of our schools, or the preservation of the Jesuits. It was necessary that the Order should subsist to furnish professors where they dropped off, and the foundation could suffice for such an expence; but it would have been inadequate to pay the salaries of laymen professors. It was moreover at the university of the Jesuits that the divines were taught, who were afterwards to fill the rectories. Had the Order been suppressed, there had been an end of the university; and our Silesian divines would have been obliged to go and finish their studies

---

28 Giovanni Vincenzo Antonio Ganganelli (1705 - 1774) Pope Clement XIV from 1769, suppressed the Society of Jesus in 1773 under pressure from the Bourbon monarchs. The reasons were political rather than theological. —Ed.

29 From Frederick, 7 July, 1770, vol. 65, let. 173, p. 408.

in Bohemia, which would have been contrary to the fundamental principles of our government.[30]

Such was the language of Frederick, speaking in his regal character, and such were the political reasons he so ably adduced in support of his opposition to the Sophisters. Alas! as I have already said, in Frederick there were two distinct men; one the great king, in which character he thinks the preservation of the Jesuits necessary; the other the impious Sophister, conspiring with Voltaire, and triumphant in the loss which religion had sustained in that of the Jesuits. In the latter character we find him freely exulting with the Conspirators, and felicitating d'Alembert, on this happy omen of the total destruction of Christianity. In his sarcastic style he writes,

> What an unfortunate age for the Court of Rome! she is openly attacked in Poland; her life-guards are driven out of France and Portugal, and it appears that they will share the same fate in Spain. The Philosophers openly sap the foundations of the apostolic throne; the hieroglyphics of the conjuror are laughed at, and the author of the Sect is pelted; toleration is preached, and so all is lost. A miracle alone could save the church. She is stricken with a dreadful apoplexy, and you (Voltaire) will have the pleasure of burying her, and of writing her epitaph, as you formerly did that of the Sorbonne.[31]

---

30   From Fred. 18 Nov. 1777, vol. 66, let. 127, p. 300.

31   From d'Alembert, 10 April, 1767, vol. 65, let. 154 p. 361.

When that which Frederick had foreseen really came to pass in Spain, he wrote again to Voltaire:

> Here is a new victory that you have gained in Spain. The Jesuits are driven out of the kingdom. Moreover, the courts of Versailles, of Vienna, and of Madrid, have applied to the Pope for the suppression of divers convents. It is said that the holy Father, though in a rage, will be obliged to consent. O cruel revolution! what are we not to expect in the next century? The axe is at the root of the tree. On one side, the Philosophers openly attack the abuses of a sainted superstition; on the other, *princes, by the abuses of dissipation*, are forced to lay violent hands on the goods of those recluse who are the props and trumpeters of fanaticism. This edifice, sapped in its foundations, is on the eve of falling; *and nations shall inscribe on their annals, that Voltaire was the promoter of the revolution effected during the nineteenth century in the human mind.*[32]

Farther avowals of d'Alembert and Voltaire

Long fluctuating between the feelings of the king and the Sophister, Frederick had not yet yielded to the solicitation of the conspirators. D'Alembert was particularly pressing in his. We see how earnestly he was bent on its success by the following letter which he wrote to Voltaire:

> My venerable Patriarch, do not accuse me of the want or zeal in the good cause; no one perhaps serves it more than myself. You would not

---

32   From Frederick, 5 May, 1767, vol. 65, let. 60, p. 378.

guess with what I am occupied at present? With nothing less, I assure you, than the expulsion of the Jesuitical rabble from Silesia; and your former disciple is but too willing on account of the numerous and perfidious treacheries which, as he says himself, he experienced through their means, during the last war. I do not send a single letter to Berlin without repeating, *That the Philosophers of France are amazed at the king of Philosophers, the declared protector of Philosophy*, being so *dilatory* in following the example of the kings of France and Portugal. These letters are read to the king, who is very sensible, as you know, to what the true believers may think of him; and this sense will, without doubt, produce a good effect by the help of God's grace, which, as the Scripture very properly remarks, turns the hearts of kings like a water-cock.[33]

It is loathsome to transcribe the base buffoonery with which d'Alembert was accustomed to season his dark plots; and to observe his clandestine persecution against a society of men whose only crime was their respect and reverence for Christianity. I pass over many more expressions of this stamp, or not less indecent. It will suffice for my purpose to show how little, how empty, how despicable, these proud and mighty men were, when seen in their true colors.

In spite of all these solicitations Frederick was invincible; and, fifteen years after, he still protect-

---

33   From d'Alembert, 29 Dec. 1763, vol. 68, let. 124, p. 269.

ed and preserved *his dear Jesuits.* This expression in his mouth, who at length sacrificed them to the conspiracy, may be looked upon as an answer to what d'Alembert had written of their treachery to the king. It might prove with what unconcern calumny, or supposed evidence of others, were adduced as proofs by him; for in another place he says, "Frederick is not a man to *confine within his royal breast* the subjects of complaint he may have had against them," as had been the case with the king of Spain, whose conduct in that respect had been so much blamed by the Sophisters.[34]

They fear the recall of the Jesuits.

These sophistical conspirators were not to be satisfied by the general expulsion of the Jesuits from the different states of the kings of the earth. By their reiterated war-hoop, Rome was at length to be *forced to declare the total extinction of the Order.* We may observe this by the manner in which Voltaire particularly interested himself for a work, whose sole object was to obtain that extinction. At length it was obtained. France too late perceiving the blow it had given to public education, without appearing to recoil, many of her leading men, sought to remedy the mistake, and formed the plan of a new society solely destined to the education of youth. Into this the former Jesuits, as the most habituated to education, were to be admitted. On the first news of this plan, d'Alembert spread the alarm. He sees the Jesuits returning

---

34   From d'Alembert, 4 May, 1767, vol. 68, let. 206, p. 434.

to life. He writes again and again to Voltaire. He sends the counter-plan. He lays great stress on the danger that *would result thence to the state, to the king, and to the Duke d'Aiguillon,* during whose administration the destruction had taken place. *He also insists on the impropriety of placing youth under the tuition of any community of priests whatever*: they were to be represented as ultramontanes by principle, and as anti-citizens. Our barking Philosophist then concluding in his cant to Voltaire, says, "*Raton* (cat), *this chestnut requires to be covered in the embers, and to be handled by a paw as dextrous as that of Raton; and so saying I tenderly kiss those dear paws.*" Seized with the same panic, Voltaire sets to work, and asks for fresh instructions. He considers what turn can be given to this affair, much too serious to be treated with ridicule alone. D'Alembert insists,[35] Voltaire at Ferney writes against the recall, and the conspirators fill Paris and Versailles with their intrigues. The ministers are prevailed upon; the plan is laid aside; youth left without instruction; and it is on this occasion that Voltaire writes, "My dear friend, I know not what is to become of me; in the mean time let us enjoy the pleasure of having seen the Jesuits expelled."[36]

This pleasure was but short; for d'Alembert, seized with a new panic, writes again to Voltaire:

---

35 From d'Alembert, 22 March, 1774, vol. 69, let. 128, p. 216.
36 To d'Alembert, 27 Apr. 1771, vol. 69, let. 64, p. 105.

I am told, for certain, that the Jesuitical rabble is about to be reinstated in Portugal in all but the dress. This new Queen appears to be a very *superstitious Majesty*. Should the King of Spain chance to die, I would not answer for that kingdom's not imitating Portugal. *Reason is undone should the enemy's army gain this battle.*[37]

When I first undertook to show that the destruction of the Jesuits was a favourite object of the conspirators, and that it was essentially comprised in their plan of overthrowing the Christian religion, I promised to confine myself to the records and confessions of the Sophisters themselves. I have omitted, for brevity's sake, several of great weight, even that written by Voltaire fifteen years after their expulsion, wherein he flatters himself *that by means of the court of Petersburg* he could succeed in getting them expelled from China, because "*those Jesuits, whom the Emperor of China had chosen to preserve at Pekin, were rather* CONVERTERS *than Mathematicians.*"[38]

Errors of the Sophisters.

Had the Sophisters been less sanguine or less active in the extinction of this order, I should not have insisted so much on that object. But the very warfare they waged was a libel on Christianity. What! they had persuaded themselves that the religion of the Christians was the work of man, and that the destruction of a few poor mortals was to shake it to its very foundations? Had they forgot-

---

37   From d'Alembert, 23 June, 1777, vol. 69, let. 182, p. 301.
38   To d'Alembert, 8 Dec. 1776, vol. 69, let. 173, p. 289.

ten that Christianity had flourished during four-teen centuries before a Jesuit was heard of? Hell might, indeed, open its gates wider after their de-struction, but it was written that they should not prevail. The power and intrigues of the ministers of France, of a Choiseul or a Pompadour, plot-ting with a Voltaire; of a de Aranda[39] in Spain, the public friend of d'Alembert, and the protector of infidelity; of a Carvalho in Portugal, the ferocious persecutor of the good; and the arts of many other ministers, dupes or agents of the sophistical con-spiracy, rather than politicians, may have extorted the bull of extinction from Ganganelli, by threats of schism: but did that pontiff, or any ther Chris-tian, believe that the power of the Gospel rested on the Jesuits?

No: the God of the Gospel reigns above, and he will one day judge the pontiff and the minister, the Jesuit and the Sophister.—It is not to be doubted that a body of twenty thousand religious dispersed throughout Christendom, and forming a succes-sion of men attending to the education of youth, and applying to the study of science both religious and prophane, must have been of the greatest utility both to church and state. The conspirators were not long before they perceived their error;

---

39 This name appears as 'D'Aranda' in the translation and as 'Daranda' in the French. The person referred to was Pedro Pablo Abarca de Bolea y Jiménez de Urrea, X conde de Aran-da (1719 - 1798). He was instrumental in getting Charles III to sign in 1767 the decree expelling the Society of Jesus from Spain. —Ed.

and though they had done the Jesuits the honour to look upon them as the base on which the church rested, they found that Christianity had other succours left, that new plots were yet necessary; and we shall see them with equal ardor attacking all other religious orders, as the third means of the Antichristian Conspiracy.

Third Means of the Conspirators.— Extinction of all Religious Orders.

The favorite measure of those who were inimical to religious orders, has been to endeavour to show their inutility both to church and state. But by what right shall Europe complain of a set of men, by whose labours she has been enabled to emerge from that savage state of the ancient Gauls or Germanni, by whom two-thirds of her lands have been cultivated, her villages built, her towns beautified and enlarged? Shall the State complain of those men who, sedulously attending to the cultivation of lands which their predecessors had first tilled, furnish sustenance to the inhabitants? Shall the inhabitant complain, when the vil-

Charges against religious Orders.

97

lage, the town, the country, from whence he comes would not have existed, or would have remained uncultivated, but for their care? Shall men of letters complain, when, should they even have been happy enough to have escaped the general ignorance and barbarity of Europe, they would perhaps, but for them, have been now vainly searching ruins in hopes of finding some fragment of ancient literature? Yes, complain; all Europe complain! It is from them that you learned your letters, and they have been abused without mercy. Alas! our forefathers learned to read, but we read perversely; they opened the temple of science, we half shut it again; and the dangerous man is not he who is ignorant, but the half wise who pretends to wisdom.

Had any one been at the trouble of comparing the knowledge of the least learned part of the religious orders, with that of the generality of the laity, I have no doubt but the former would greatly have excelled the latter, though they had received their ordinary education. It is true, the religious were not versed in the sophisticated science of the age; but often have I seen those very men who, upbraided with their ignorance, were happy in the sciences which their occupations required. Not only among the Benedictines, who have been more generally excepted from this badge of ignorance, but among all other orders, I have met with men, as distinguished by their knowledge, as by the purity of their morals. Alas! that I could extend this remark to the laity! This, indeed, is a language very different from that which the reader may have seen in the satiric declamations of the age; but will satire satisfy his judgement? In the annals of the conspiring Sophisters shall he find testimony borne of their services; and every scurrilous expression shall be a new laurel in their crown.

The Jesuits were destroyed; but the conspirators saw Christianity still subsisted, and they then said to each other, We must destroy the rest of the religious orders, or we shall not triumph. Their whole plan is to be seen in a letter from Frederick, to which Voltaire gave occasion by the following: "Hercules went to fight the robbers and Bellerophon chimeras; I should not be sorry to behold Herculeses and Belerophons delivering the earth both from Catholic robbers and Catholic chimeras."[1] Frederick answers on the 24th of the same month:

Frederick's plan.

> It is not the lot of arms *to destroy the wretch*; it shall perish by the arm of truth, and interested selfishness. If you wish me to explain this idea, my meaning is as follows:—I have remarked, as well as many others, that the places where convents are the most numerous, are those where the people are most blindly attached to superstition. No doubt, if these asylums of fanaticism were destroyed, the people would grow lukewarm, and see with indifference, the present objects of their veneration. The point would *be to destroy the cloisters*, at least to begin by

---

1   To Frederick, 3 March, 1767, vol. 65, let. 157, p. 369.

lessening their number. The time is come: the French and Austrian governments are involved in debts; they have exhausted the resources of industry to discharge them, and they have not succeeded; the lure of rich Abbeys and well-endowed convents is tempting. By representing to them the prejudice cloistered persons occasion to the population of their states, as well as the great abuse of the numbers of *Cucullati*, who are spread throughout the provinces; and also the facility of paying off part of their debts with the treasures of those communities, who are without heirs; they might, I think, be made to adopt this plan of reform; and it may be presumed, that after having enjoyed the secularization of some good livings, their rapacity would crave the rest.

Every government that shall adopt this plan *will be friendly to the Philosophers*, and promote the circulation of all those books which attack popular superstition, or the false zeal that would support it.

Here is a pretty little plan, which I submit to the examination of the patriarch of Ferney; it is his province, as father of the faithful, to rectify and put it in execution.

The patriarch may perhaps ask *what is to become of the bishops?* I answer, it is not yet time to touch them. To destroy those who stir up the fire of fanaticism in the hearts of the people, is the first step; and when the people are cooled, *the bishops will be but insignificant personages, whom sovereigns will, in process of time, dispose of as they please.*[2]

---

2   From Frederick, 24 March, 1767, vol. 65, let. 158, p. 370.

Voltaire relished such plans too much not to set a great value on them, and of course thus answered the King of Prussia:

> Your plan of attack against the *Christicole Superstition*, in that of the friar-hood, is worthy a great captain. The religious orders once abolished, *error* is exposed to universal contempt. Much is written in France on this subject; every one talks of it, but as yet it is not ripe enough. People are not sufficiently daring in France; bigots are yet in power.[3]

Having read these letters, it would be ridiculous to ask of what service religious orders could be to the church. Certain it is, that many had fallen off from the austerity of their first institutes; but even in this degenerate state we see Frederick making use of all his policy to over-turn them, because his antichristian plots are thwarted by the zeal and example of these religious, because he thinks the church cannot be stormed until the convents are carried as the outworks; and Voltaire traces the hand of the great captain, who had distinguished himself so eminently by his military science in Germany, in the plan of attack against the *Christicole Superstition*. These religious corps were useful then, though branded with sloth and ignorance; they were a true barrier to impiety. Frederick was so much convinced of it, that when the Sophisters had already occupied all the avenues of the throne,

---

3   To Frederick, 5 April, 1767, vol. 65, let. 159, p. 375.

he dared not direct his attacks against the Bishops, nor the body of the place, until the outworks were carried.

Voltaire writes to him thus on the 29th of July 1775:

> We hope that Philosophy, which in France *is near the throne*, will soon *be on it*. Yet that is but hope, which too often proves fallacious. There are so many people interested in the support of error and nonsense, so many dignities and such riches are annexed to the trade, that the hypocritres, it is to be feared, will get the better of the sages. Has not your Germany transformed your principal ecclesiastics into sovereigns? Where is there an elector or a bishop who will side with Reason, against a Sect that allows him two or three hundred thousand pounds a-year?[4]

Frederick continued to vote for the war being carried on against the religious. It was too early to attack the bishops. He writes to Voltaire, "All that you say of our German bishops it but too true; they are the hogs fattened on the tythes of Sion." (Such is their scurrilous language in their private correspondence).

> But you know likewise, that in the Holy Roman Empire, ancient custom, the golden bull, *and such antiquated fooleries as these*, have given weight to established abuses. One sees them, shrugs one's shoulders, and things jog on in the

---

4   Vol. 66, let. 93, p. 217.

old way. *If we wish to diminish fanaticism, we must not begin with the bishops.* But if we succeed in lessening the friarhood, especially the mendicant orders, the people will cool, and, being less superstitious, will allow the powers *to bring down the bishops* as best suits their states. *This is the only possible mode of proceeding.* Silently to undermine the edifice hostile to reason, is to force it to fall of itself.[5]

I began by saying, that the means of the conspirators would give new proofs of the reality of the conspiracy, and of its object. Can any other interpretation, than that of an Antichristian Conspiracy, be put on the language made use of in their correspondence? How can we otherwise understand, *such is the only possible mode of proceeding, to undermine* the edifice of that religion which they are pleased to denominate the *Christicole Superstition*, as fanatic or unreasonable; or in order to overthrow its pontiffs, to seduce the people from its worship? What then is conspiracy, if those secret machinations carried on between Ferney, Berlin, Paris, in spite of distance, be not so? What reader can be so infatuated as not to see, that by the establishment of Reason is only meant the overthrow of Christianity? It is indeed a matter of surprise, that the Sophisters should so openly have exposed their plans at so early a period.

In the mean time Voltaire was correct when he answered Frederick, that the plan of destruction

What plan was adopted in France.

---

5   From Frederick, 13 Aug. 1775, vol. 66, let. 95, p. 222.

had been ardently pursued in France ever since the expulsion of the Jesuits, and that by people who were in office. The first step taken was, to put off the period of religious professions until the age of twenty-one, though the adepts in ministry would fain have deferred it till the age of twenty-five. Of course, of a hundred young people who might have embraced that state, not two would have been able to follow their vocations; for what parent would let his child attain that age without being certain of the state of life he would embrace? The remonstrances made by many friends to religion caused the age fixed on by the edict to be that of eighteen for women, and twenty-one for men. This nevertheless was looked upon as an act of authority exercised on those who chose to consecrate themselves more particularly to the service of their God, and rescue themselves from the danger of the passions at that age when they are the most powerful. This subject had been very fully treated in the last Œcumenical Council, where the age for the profession of religious persons had been fixed at sixteen, with a term of five years to reclaim against their last vows in case they did not choose to continue the religious life they had undertaken. And it had always been looked upon as a right inherent to the church to decide on these matters, as may be seen in Chappelain's discourse on that subject. It would be ridiculous, after what has been said in this chapter, to repeat the favourite argument of their inutility to France. What! pious works, edification, and the instruction of the people, useless to a nation! Beside, France was a lively example that the number of convents had not hurt its population, as few states were peopled in so great a proportion. If celibacy was to be attacked, she might have turned her eyes to her armies, and to that numerous class of worldlings who lived in celibacy, and who perhaps ought to have been noticed by the laws. All further reclamations were useless. What had been foreseen came to pass according to the wishes of the ministerial Sophisters. In many colleges the Jesuits being very ill replaced, the youth, neglected in their education, left a prey to their passions, or looking on the number of years they had to wait for their reception into the religious state as so much time lost, laid aside all thoughts of that state, and took to other employments. Some few, from want, engaged; but rather seeking bread than the service of their God, or else prone to vice and to their passions, which they had never been taught to subdue, reluctantly submitted to the rules of the cloister. Already there existed many abuses, but these daily increased; and while the number of religious was diminishing, their fervour languished, and public scandals became more frequent. This was precisely what the ministers wanted, in order to have a plea for the suppression of the whole; while their masters, still more sanguine if possible, made the press teem with writings in which neither satire nor calumny were spared.

It is prosecuted by Briennes.

The person who seemed to second them with the greatest warmth was he who, after having persuaded even his companions that he had some talent for governing, at length added his name to those ministers whom ambition may be said to have blinded even to stupidity. This man was Briennes, Archbishop of Toulouse, since Archbishop of Sens, afterwards prime minister, then a public apostate, and at last died as universally hated and despised as Necker himself appears to be at this day. Briennes will be more despised when it shall be known that he was the friend and confidant of d'Alembert, and that in a commission for the reform of the religious orders he wore the mitre and exercised its powers as a d'Alembert would have done.

The clergy had thought it necessary to examine the means of reforming the religious, and of re-establishing their primitive fervor. The court seemed to enter into their views, named counsellors of state to join the bishops in their deliberations on this subject, and called it the *Commission of Regulars*. A mixture of prelates who are only to be influenced by the spirit of the church, and of statesmen solely acting from worldly views, could never agree; some few articles were supposed to have been settled; but all was in vain, and many, through disgust, abandoned the commission. Among the bishops were Mr. Dillon, Archbishop of Narbonne; Mr. de Boisgelin, Archbishop of Aix; Mr. de Cicé, Archbishop of Bourdeaux, and the famous Briennes, Archbishop of Toulouse.

man forms! These were far above the reach of calumny, or of a Briennes: a pretence could not even
be devised.

With a view to diminish the number of real nuns,
he thought that if he augmented those asylums for
canonesses who have a much greater communica-
tion with the world, and are therefore more easily perverted, novices would not be so numerous.
But by an inconceivable oversight (unless he had
some very deep and hidden scheme) these canonesses were in future to prove a certain number of
degrees of nobility to enter these asylums, which
before had been open to all ranks in the state. One
might have thought, that he meant to render the
real nuns odious to the nobility, and the latter to
all other classes, by applying foundations to particular ranks which had ever been common to all.

These were reflections to which Briennes little attended. He was laying his snares, while
d'Alembert smiled at the idea that ere long both
nuns and canonesses would add to the common
mass of ruin; but these sacred virgins baffled all
their cunning. Nothing less than the whole despotic power of the Constituent Assembly could
prevail against them. They were to be classed with
the martyrs of that bloody September; their fervor
was impassible.—Edicts worthy of Nero exulting in
the flames of burning Rome are necessary to drive
them from the Altar; cannons, and the satellites of
that Constituent Assembly, march against them to
enforce those edicts; and *thirty thousand women*

These
plans
consumat-
ed by the
National
Assembly.

are driven from their convents, in contradiction to a decree of that same assembly promising to let them die peaceably in their asylums. Thus was the destruction of religious orders completed in France. It was forty years since this plan had been dictated by the Sophisters to the ministers of his most Christian Majesty. But when accomplished, ministers are no more! . . . The sacred person of the king a prisoner in the towers of the Temple! . . . The object of the abolition of religious orders was fulfilled; and religion was savagely persecuted in the person of its ministers! But during the long period that preceded the triumph of the Sophisters they had resorted to many other means with which I have yet to acquaint my reader.

CHAPTER VII.

Fourth Means of the Conspirators.— Voltaire's Colony.

hilst the conspirators were so much occupied with the destruction of the Jesuits, and of all other religious orders, Voltaire was forming a plan which was to give to impiety itself both apostles and propagandists. This idea seems first to have struck him about the year 1760-61.— Always ruminating the destruction of Christianity, he writes to d'Alembert, "Could not five or six men of parts, who rightly understood each other, succeed, after the example of twelve scoundrels who have already succeeded."[1] The object of this un-

Object of this colony.

---

1 To d'Alembert, 24 July, 1760, vol. 68, let. 70, p. 127. To

derstanding has already been explained in a letter before quoted.

> Let the real Philosophers unite in a brotherhood, like the Freemasons; let them assemble and support each other; let them be faithful to the association. This secret academy will be far superior to that of Athens and to all those of Paris. But every one thinks only of himself, and forgets that his most sacred duty *is to annihilate the wretch.*[2]

The Conspirators never lost sight of this most sacred duty; but they met with various obstacles; religion was still zealously defended in France, and Paris was not yet a proper asylum for such an association. It appears also that Voltaire was obliged for some time to lay this plan aside; but taking it up again a few years afterwards, he applied to Frederick, as we are told by the editor of their correspondence, for leave "to establish at Cleves a little colony of French Philosophers, who might there freely and boldly speak the truth, *without fearing ministers, priests, or parliaments.*" Frederick answered with all the desired zeal, "I see you wish to establish the little colony you had mentioned to me.—I think the shortest way would be, for those men, or your associates, to send to Cleves, to see what would be most convenient for them, and what I can dispose of in their favor."[3]

It is seconded by Frederick.

---

d'Alembert, 24 July, 1760, vol. 68, let. 70, p. 127.

2   To d'Alembert, 20 April 1761, vol. 68, let. 85, p. 163.

3   From Frederick, 24 Oct. 1765, vol. 65, let. 142, p. 330.

It is to be lamented that many letters respecting this colony have been suppressed in their correspondence; but Frederick's answers are sufficient to convince us of the obstinacy of Voltaire in the undertaking, who, returning again to the charge, is answered,

> You speak of a colony of Philosophers who wish to establish themselves at Cleves. I have no objection to it. I can give them every thing, only excepting wood, the forests having been almost destroyed by your countrymen. But on this condition alone, that *they will respect those who ought to be respected,* and that they will keep within the *proper bounds of decency in their writings.*[4]

The meaning of this letter will be better understood when we come to treat of the Antimonarchial Conspiracy. Decency in their writings, one should think, would be of the first necessity even for their own views; as otherwise this new colony must have spread a general alarm, and governments would have been obliged to repress their barefaced impudence.

While on one side Voltaire was imploring the succour and protection of the King of Prussia for these apostles of impiety, on the other he was seeking Sophisters worthy of the apostleship. He writes to Damilaville, that he is ready to make a sacrifice of all the sweets of Ferney, and go and place himself at their head. "Your friend," says he,

---

4   From Frederick, 7 Aug. 1766, vol. 65, let. 146, p. 340.

persists in his idea. It is true, as you have observed, that he must tear himself from many objects that are at present his delight, and will then be of his regret. But is it not better to quit them through Philosophy than by death? What surprises him most is, that many people have not taken this resolution together. Why should not a certain philosophic baron labor at the establishment of this colony? Why should not so many others improve so fair an opportunity?

In the continuation of this letter we find that Frederick was not the only prince who countenanced the plan: "Two sovereign princes, *who think entirely as you do*, have lately visited your friend. One of them offered a town, provided that which relates to the grand work, should not suit."[5]

It was precisely at the time when this letter was written, that the Landgrave of Hesse-Cassel went to pay homage to the idol of Ferney. The date of his journey, and the similarity of his sentiments, can leave little doubt that he was the prince who offered a town to the colony should Cleves prove inconvenient.[6]

Meanwhile the apostles of this mock Messiah, however zealous as they were for the grand work, were not equally ready to sacrifice their ease. D'Alembert, idolized by the Sophisters at Paris, saw that he could be but a secondary divinity in the presence of Voltaire. That Damilaville, who

Not approved by the Conspirators.

_____

5   To Damilaville, 6 Aug. 1766, vol. 59, let. 234, p. 415.

6   To the Landgrave, 9 Sept. 1766, vol. 66. let. 64, p. 409.

was celebrated by the impious patriarch as personally hating God, was necessary for carrying on the secret correspondence in Paris. Diderot, the certain philosophic baron, and the remaining multitude of adepts, reluctantly cast their eyes on a German town where they could not with equal ease sacrifice in luxury and debauchery to their Pagan divinities. Such remissness disconcerted Voltaire. He endeavoured to stimulate their ardor by asking: "If six or seven hundred thousand Huguenots left their country for *the fooleries of Jean Chauvin*, shall not twelve sages be found who will make some little sacrifice to Reason, which is trampled on?"[7]

When he wishes to persuade them that their consent is all that is necessary to accomplish the grand object, he writes again, "All that I can tell you now by a sure hand is, that every thing is ready for the establishment of the manufacture. More than one Prince envies the honor of it; and from the borders of the Rhine unto the Oby, Tomplat (that is Plato Diderot) will be honored, encouraged, and live in security." He would then repeat the grand object of the conspiracy, in hopes of persuading the conspirators. He would try to inflame their hearts with that hatred for Christ which was consuming his own.—He would repeatedly cry out, *Cruch, crush the wretch! oh, crush the wretch—then crush the wretch.*[8]

---

7   To Damilaville, 18 Aug. 1766, vol. 59, let. 239, p. 423.

8   To Damilaville, 25 Aug. 1766, vol. 59. let. 243, p. 433.

It fails.

His prayers, his repeated solicitations, could not avail against the attractions of Paris. That same reason which made Voltaire willing to sacrifice all the pleasing scenes of Ferney, to bury himself in the heart of Germany, there to consecrate his days and writings to the extinction of Christianity; that reason, I say, taught the younger adepts that the sweets of Paris were not to be neglected. They were not the Apostles of the Gospel preaching temperance and mortification both by word and example; and in the end Voltaire, obliged to give up all hopes of expatriating his sophistical apostles. He indignantly expresses his vexation to Frederick a few years afterwards:

> I own to you, that I was so much vexed and so much ashamed of the little success I had in the transmigration to Cleves, that I have never since dared to disclose any of my ideas to your Majesty. When I reflect that a fool and an ideot like St. Ignatius should have found twelve followers, and that I could not find three Philosophers who would follow me, I am almost tempted to think that Reason is useless.[9]

"I shall never be reconciled to the non-execution of this plan; it was there that I should have ended my old age."[10]

Violent however as Voltaire was in his reproaches against the other Conspirators, the sequel of these Memoirs will show that he was unjustly so.

---

9   To Frederick, Nov. 1769, vol. 65, let. 162, p. 383.

10   To Frederick, 12 Oct. 1770, vol. 65, let. 179, p. 426.

D'Alembert in particular had far different plans to prosecute. He grasped at the empire of the academic honors; and, without exposing his dictatorship, or expatriating the adepts, by distributing these honors solely to the Sophisters he abundantly replaced Voltaire's so-much-regretted plan. This object, and the method by which it was promoted, shall be the subject of the ensuing Chapter.

CHAPTER VIII.

Fifth Means of the Conspirators.— The Academic Honors.

The protection which the sovereigns had given to men of letters had brought them into that repute which they so well deserved, until, abusing their talents, they turned them against religion and governments. In the French Academy glory seemed to be enthroned; and a seat within its walls was the grand pursuit of the orator and the poet; in short, of all writers, whether eminent in the historic or any other branch of literature. Corneille, Bossuet, Racine, Massillon, La Bruyère, La Fontaine, and all those authors who had adorned the reign of Louis XIV. were proud of their admission within this sanctuary of learning.

Real object of the Academies.

Morals and the laws seemed to guard its entrance, lest it should be prophaned by the impious. Any public sign of infidelity was a bar against admission even during the reign of Louis XV. Nor was the famous Montesquieu himself admitted, until he had given proper satisfaction as to certain articles contained in his *Persian Letters*. Voltaire pretends that he deceived the Cardinal de Fleury by sending him a new edition of his work, in which all the objectionable parts had been omitted. Such a mean trick was beneath Montesquieu; repentance was his only plea, and in his latter days little doubt can be left of his having repented sincerely. On his admission, however, impiety was openly renounced, and religion publicly avowed.

Boindin, whose infidelity was notorious, had been rejected, though a member of several other academies. Voltaire, for a long time unable to gain admission, at length succeeded merely through the influence of high protectors, and by the practice of that hypocrisy which we shall see him recommending to his disciples. D'Alembert, with great prudence, concealed his propensity to infidelity until he had gained his seat; and though the road to these literary honours had been much widened by the adepts who surrounded the court, he nevertheless thought that it would not be impossible, by dint of intrigue, to turn the scale; that if impiety had formerly been a ground of exclusion, it might in future be a title to admission, and that none should be seated near him but those whose writings had

Plan laid by d'Alembert.

rendered them worthy abettors of the Conspiracy and supporters of its sophisticated arts. His *forte* was petty intrigue, and so successfully did he practice it, that in latter times the titles of Academician and Sophister were nearly synonimous. It is true that he sometimes met with obstacles; but the plot formed between him and Voltaire for the admission of Diderot will be sufficient to evince what great advantages they expected would accrue to their conspiracy by this new means of promoting irreligion. D'Alembert first proposes it. Voltaire receives the proposal with all the attention due to its importance, and answers, "You wish Diderot to be of the academy, it must then be brought about." The king was to approve of the nomination, and D'Alembert feared ministerial opposition. It is to this fear that we owe the account Voltaire has given of Choiseul. He therein mentions his partiality to the Sophisters, and declares that so far from obstructing their plots, he would forward them with all his power. "In a word," he continues,

Intrigues for the admission of Diderot.

> Diderot must be of the academy; it will be the most noble revenge that can be taken for the play against the Philosophers. The Academy is incensed at Le Franc de Pompignan; and it would willingly give him a most swingeing slap.[1]—I will make a bonfire on Diderot's admis-

---

1   Marriage to a wealthy widow had enabled the vain and arrogant Jean-Jacques Le Franc, Marquis de Pompignan (1709 - 1784), to dedicate himself fully to literature. Marmontel tells in his memoirs that having grown accustomed to applause at

sion. Ah! what a happiness it would be, if Helvétius and Diderot could be received together.[2]

D'Alembert would have been equally happy in
such a triumph; but he was on the spot and saw the
opposition made by the Dauphin, the Queen, and
the Clergy. He answers, "I should be more desirous
than yourself to see Diderot of the academy. *I am
perfectly sensible how much the common cause
would be benefited by it*; but the impossibility of
doing it is beyond what you can conceive."[3]

Voltaire, knowing that Choiseul and La Pompadour had often prevailed against the Dauphin,
ordered d'Alembert not to despond. He takes the
direction of the intrigue on himself, and places

---

his academies of Montauban and Toulouse, Pompignan went
to Paris in search of glory, where he was largely unknown but
enjoyed enough esteem to be heard. His application to join the
Academie française was not immediately successful, however,
which injured his vanity. When he was finally admitted in 1760,
fury at the years of repeated rejections combined with a desire
to please the Dauphin, whom he knew disapproved of Voltaire
and the Encyclopædists; accordingly, he used his speech at his
formal introduction to attack the aforementioned, a number
of whom were seated in the audience. They responded with
such a barrage of satire—Voltaire even feeling rejuvenated by
the joy of ridiculing Pompignan—that in time it became impossible for the marquis to leave his quarters without being
subjected to mockery; Paris having thus become uncomfort-
able, he left, buried himself in his townhouse in Montauban,
and dedicated himself to gardening, poetry, and translations
from the classics, never again to appear at the Academie. —Ed.

2   To d'Alembert, 9 July 1760, vol. 68, let. 68, p. 121.

3   From d'Alembert, 18 July 1760, vol. 68. let. 69, p. 123.

his chief hopes on the Courtesan. "Still further, (says he), she may look upon it as an honor, and make a merit of supporting Diderot. Let her undeceive the king, and delight in quashing a cabal which she despises."[4] What d'Alembert could not personally undertake, Voltaire recommends to the courtiers, and particularly to the Count d'Argental: "My divine Angel! (would he write) do but get Diderot to be of the Academy; it will be the boldest stroke imaginable in the game that reason is playing against fanaticism and folly (*that is, religion and piety*) . . . . Impose for penance on the Duke de Choiseul, to introduce Diderot into the Academy."[5]

The secretary of the academy, Duclos, is also called in as an auxiliary by Voltaire, who gives him instructions to insure the success of the recipiendary adept.

> Could not you represent, or cause to be represented, how very essential such a man is to you for the completion of some necessary work? Could not you, *after having slyly played off that battery, assemble seven or eight of the Elect*, and form a deputation to the King, to ask for Diderot as the most capable of forwarding your enterprize? Would not the Duke of Nivernois help you in that project, would not he be the speaker on the occasion?[6] The bigots will

---

4 To d'Alembert, 24 July, 1760, vol. 68, let. 70, p. 126.

5 To the Count d'Argental, 11 July 1760, vol. 56, let. 153, p. 315.

6 The Duke (1716 - 1798) occupied seat number 4 of the Acade-

say, that Diderot has written a metaphysical work which they do not understand: *Let him say that he did not write it, and that he is a good Catholic—it is so easy to be a Catholic.*[7]

It may be an object of surprise to the reader and to the historian, to see Voltaire straining every nerve, calling on dukes and courtiers, not blushing at the vilest hypocrisy, advising base dissimulation, and that merely to gain the admission of one of his fellow Conspirators into the Academy; but this surprise will cease when they see d'Alembert's own words: *I am perfectly sensible how much the common cause would be benefited by it*; or in other words, the war we are waging against Christianity. These words will explain all his anxiety. And to get admitted within the sanctuary of letters the man the most notorious for infidelity, would it not be confirming the error which the government had committed, in letting itself be led away by the hypocritical demonstrations of a Voltaire or a d'Alembert? Would it not have been crowning the most scandalous impiety with the laurels of literature, and declaring that Atheism, so far from being a stain, would be a new title to its honors? The most prejudiced must own it would have been an open contempt for religion; and Choiseul and La Pompadour were conscious that it was not yet time to allow the Conspirators such a triumph. D'Alembert even shrunk back when he beheld the clamours it

---

mie. —Ed.

7   To Duclos, 11 Aug. 1760, vol. 56, let. 171, p. 349.

would excite, and for the present desisted. But the critical moment was now come, when the ministers secretly abetted what they publicly professed a desire to crush. D'Alembert persisted in his hopes, that with some contrivance he might soon be able to exclude from literary honours all writers who had not offered some sacrifice at least to the Antichristian Sophistry; and he at length succeeded.

Having shown how highly d'Alembert had conceived of the importance that the French Academy, converted into a club of irreligious Sophisters, would be to the Conspiracy, let us examine the merits of some of those who were admitted among its members. And, first, we find Marmontel, perfectly coinciding in opinion with Voltaire, d'Alembert, and Diderot. Then, in succession, La Harpe the favorite adept of Voltaire; Champfort, the adept and hebdomadary co-adjutor of Marmontel and La Harpe; one Le Mierre, distinguished by Voltaire as *a staunch enemy to the wretch,* or Christ;[8] an Abbé Millot, whose sole merit with d'Alembert was his total oblivion of his priesthood,[9] and with the public his having transformed the history of France into an antipapal one; a Briennes, long since known to d'Alembert as an enemy to the church, though living in its bosom; a Suard, a Gaillard, and lastly a Condorcet, whose reception enthroned the fiend of Atheism within the walls of the academy.

Success of the Conspirators, and list of the first Academicians.

8   To Damilaville, 15 June, 1761, vol. 57, let. 70, p. 143.

9   From d'Alembert, 27 Dec. 1777, vol. 69, let. 190, p. 312.

It does not appear why Mr. de Turgot did not succeed in his election, though aided by all the intrigues of d'Alembert and Voltaire.[10] The reader who casts an eye on their correspondence will be surprised to see of what concern it was to them to fill this philosophical Sanhedrim with their favorite adepts. There are above thirty letters on the admission of them, and on the exclusion of those persons who were friendly to religion. Their intrigues, whether through protection or any other means, were at length so successful, that in a few years, the name of Academician and Atheist or Deist were synonimous. If there were yet to be found among them some few men, especially bishops, of a different stamp from Briennes, it was a remains of deference shown them, which some might have mistaken for an honour; but they should have looked upon it as an insult, to be seated next to a d'Alembert, a Marmontel or a Condorcet.

There was however among the forty a layman much to be respected for his piety. This was Mr. Beauzée. I one day asked him, how it had been possible, that a man of his morality could ever have been associated with men so notoriously unbelievers?

> The very same question (he answered), have I put to d'Alembert. At one of the sittings, seeing that I was nearly the only person who believed in God, I asked him, how he could ever have

---

10   To d'Alembert, 8 Feb. 1776, vol. 69, let. 151, p. 256.

thought of me for a member, when he knew that my sentiments and opinions differed so widely from those of his brethren? D'Alembert, (added Mr. Beauzée) without hesitation answered, I do not wonder at your question; but we were in want of a skilful grammarian, and among our party not one had made himself a reputation in that line. We knew that you believed in God; but we cast our eyes on you, being a good sort of man, for want of a Philosopher to supply your place.

Thus was the sceptre wrested from the hands of science and virtue, by the hand of impiety. Voltaire had wished to place his conspirators under the protection of the Royal Sophister; d'Alembert stopped their flight, and made them triumph in the very states of that monarch who gloried in the title of Most Christian. His plot, better laid, conferred the laurels of literature solely on the impious writer, whilst he who dared defend religion was to be covered with reproach and infamy. The French academy, thus converted into a club of infidels, was a far better support to the Sophisters conspiring against Christianity, than any colony which Voltaire could have conceived. The academy infected the men of letters, and these perverted the public opinion by that torrent of impious productions which deluged all Europe. These were to be instrumental in bringing over the people to universal apostasy, and will be considered by us, as the sixth means for the Antichristian revolution.

CHAPTER IX.

Sixth Means of the Conspirators.— Inundation of Antichristian Writings.

hat for these forty years past, and particularly for the last twenty of Voltaire's life, all Europe has been overrun with most impious writings, under the forms either of pamphlets, systems, romances, or feigned histories, is one of those self-evident truths which needs no proof. Though I shall in this place confine myself only to a part of what I have to say on the subject, I will show how the chiefs of the conspiracy acted in concert, in the production, the multiplication and distribution of them, in order to disseminate their poisons throughout Europe.

Concert of the chiefs in their writings.

The method to be observed in their own works was particularly concerted between Voltaire, d'Alembert, and Frederick. We see them, in their letters, imparting to each other the different works they are writing against Christianity, their hopes of success, and their methods of insuring it. We see them smile at the snares which they have laid against religion; and that particularly in those works and systems which they affected most to consider as indifferent to, or as rather promoting than attacking religion. In that style d'Alembert was inimitable. The following example will convince the historian, or the reader, of the consummate art of this crafty Sophister.

D'Alembert's devices with regards to *systems.*

It is well known with what immense pains the Philosophers of our day have been forming their pretended physical systems on the formation of the globe, their numerous theories and genealogies of the earth. We have seen them diving into mines, splitting mountains, or digging up their surface in search of shells, to trace old ocean's travels, and found their epochs. These numerous researches (according to them) had no other end but the advancement of science and of natural Philosophy. Their new epochs were not to affect religion; and we have reason to believe, that many of our naturalists had no other object in view, as many of them, real men of learning, of candour in research, and capable of observation, have rather furnished arms against, than forwarded those vain systems by their studies, labours, and peregrinations: not such was the case with d'Alembert and his adepts. They soon perceived that these new epochs and systems drew the attention of divines, who had to maintain the authenticity of, and the truth of the facts contained in the books of Moses, the rudiments of Revelation. To baffle the Sorbonne and all the defenders of holy writ, d'Alembert writes a work under the title of *The Abuse of Criticism*, a palpable defense of all those systems. The main drift of the work was, while showing a great respect for religion, to prove that neither revelation, nor the credibility of Moses, could be in the least affected by these theories or epochs, and that the alarms of the divines were ungrounded. Many pages were occupied in proving that these systems could only serve to raise our ideas to the grand and sublime. That, so far from *counteracting the power of God, or his divine wisdom*, they only *displayed it more clearly*; that considering the object of their researches, *it less became the divine, than the natural Philosopher to judge them.* Divines are represented *as narrow-minded, pusillanimous, and enemies to reason*, and terrified at an object which did not in the least concern them. He is very pointed in his writings against those feigned panics; and among other things, says, "They have sought to connect Christianity with systems purely philosophical. In vain did religion, so simple and precise in its tenets, constantly throw off the alloy that disfigured it; it is from that alloy that the notion has arisen of its being attacked in works where in fact nothing was farther from the minds of the writers."[1] These are precisely the works in which *a much longer space of time is required* for the formation of the universe, than the history of the creation, as delineated by Moses, leaves us at liberty to suppose.

Who would not have thought d'Alembert convinced, that all those physical systems, those theories, *and that longer space of time*, so far from overturning Christianity, would only serve to raise the grandeur and sublimity of our ideas of the God of Moses and of the Christians? But that same d'Alembert, while seeking this *longer space of time*, anticipated his applause to the He which his travelling adepts were about to give to Moses and to revelation. Those adepts, rambling in the mountains of the Alps or the Appenines, are the men whom he points out to Voltaire *as precious to Philosophy*. It is he who, after having been so tender for the honor of Moses and revelation, writes to Voltaire,

> This letter, my dear companion, will be delivered to you by Desmarets, a man of merit and of sound Philosophy, who wishes to pay his respects to you on his journey to Italy, where he purposes *making such observations on natural history, as may very well give the lie to Moses.* He will not say a word of this to the master of the sacred palace; but if, perchance, *he should discover that the world is more ancient than even the septuagint pretends, he will not keep it a secret from you.*[2]

---

1   *The Abuse of Criticism*, Nos. 4, 15, 16, 17.

2   From d'Alembert, 30 June, 1764, vol. 68, let. 137, p. 302.

It would have been difficult to use more art, He directs
though it were to point the hand of an assassin; Voltaire.
d'Alembert would sometimes direct Voltaire, when
shafts were to be sent from Ferney which could
not yet be shot from Paris. On these occasions the
theme was already made, and only needed the last
gloss of Voltaire's pen.

When, in 1763, the Sorbonne published that famous thesis which foretold what the French revolution has since taught the sovereigns of Europe
on the evil tendency of this modern Philosophism
to their very thrones, d'Alembert, in haste, informs
Voltaire of the necessity for counteracting an impression so detrimental to the conspiracy. He shews
Voltaire how to impose on the kings themselves,
and how to involve the church in all their doubts
and suspicions. In tracing this master-piece of art
and cunning, he reminds him of the contests long
since extinct between the priesthood and the empire, and instructs him in the art of throwing odium and suspicion on the clergy.[3] Many other plans
are proposed to the patriarch according to circumstances.[4] Those were (in his style) the chestnuts that
Bertrand (d'Alembert) *pointed out under the ashes,
and which Raton* (Voltaire) was to help him draw
out of the fire with *his delicate paw.*

---

3   From d'Alembert, 18 Jan. 1773, vol. 69, let. 90, p. 150, and 9
    Feb. let. 96, p. 160.

4   From d'Alembert, 26 Feb. 1774, vol. 69, let. 125, p. 210, and 22
    March, let. 128, p. 216.

Voltaire
acts in
perfect
concert,

Voltaire did not fail, on his part, to inform d'Alembert and the other adepts of what he himself wrote, or of the steps he took with ministry. Thus, as a prelude to the plundering decrees of the revolution, he gave Count d'Argental notice of the memorial he had sent to the Duke de Praslin, to prevail on that minister to deprive the clergy of part of its maintenance by abolishing tythes.[5]

These secret memorials, the anecdotes, whether true or slanderous, against the religious writers, were all concerted among the conspirators and their chiefs.[6] Even the smiles, the witticisms, insipid epigrams of the adepts, were under the direction of Voltaire, and used by him as forwarding the conspiracy. He, better than any man, knew the powers of ridicule, and would often recommend its use to the adepts in their writings and their conversation. "Do your best (he writes to d'Alembert) to preserve your cheerfulness; always endeavour *to crush the wretch*. I only ask five or six witticisms a day; they would suffice. *It* would not get the better of them. Laugh, Democritus; make me laugh, and the sages shall carry the day."[7]

Voltaire was not always of the same opinion with regard to this attack on Christianity. This method was not sufficiently elevated for a Philosopher! and

---

5   To the Count d'Argental, 20 June, 1764, vol. 58, let. 130, p. 243.

6   To d'Alembert, 16 Jan. 1757, vol. 68, let. 18, p. 31, and 23 Jan. let. 20, p. 35.

7   To d'Alembert, 30 Jan. 1764, vol. 68, let. 128, p. 279.

he soon after adds, in his quality of chief, "*To the flood of jests and sarcasms, there should succeed, some serious work, which however should be worth reading, for the justification of the Philosophers, and the confusion of the wretch.*"[8] This work, notwithstanding the exhortations of the chief, and his union with the adepts, never was executed. But, on the other side, the press teemed with deistical and atheistical works fraught with calumny and impiety. Monthly or weekly some new production of the most daring impiety was printed in Holland. Such were the *Philosophic Soldier, The Doubts, Priestcraft, Blackguardism Unveiled,*[9] which are among the most profligate that the Sect has produced. One might have thought (such was his zeal in promoting the sale of them) that Voltaire alone had monopolized this traffic of impiety. He received notice of the publications, which he communicated to his brethren at Paris. He recommended their procuring and circulating them; upbraided them with their little ardor in spreading them abroad, while he himself dispersed them all around him.[10] To stimulate them, he would write that it was out of these works *that all the German youth learned to read; that they were the universal catechisms from Baden to Moscow.*[11]

and urges the circulation of these works.

8   To d'Alembert, 23 June, 1760, vol. 68, let. 67, p. 119.

9   *Le Militaire philosophe, Les Doutes, L'Imposture sacerdotale, Le Polissonisme devoilé.*

10   See his letters to Count d'Argental, to Mad. du Dessant, and particularly to d'Alembert, 13 Jan. 1769, vol. 69, let. 2, p. 5.

11   To Ct. d'Argental, 26 Sept. 1766, vol. 59, let. 270, p. 480.

When he thought that Holland could not sufficiently infect France with these profligate writings,
he would select those which d'Alembert was to get
privately printed at Paris, and then distribute them
by thousands. Such, for example, was the pretended *Survey of Religion* by Dumarsais.

> They have sent me, (these are Voltaire's own
> words) *a work of Dumarsais,* ASCRIBED *to
> Saint-Évremond.* It is an excellent work (that
> is to say, precisely one of the most impious). I
> exhort you, my dear brother, to prevail on some
> one of our faithful and beloved to reprint this
> little work, which may do a great deal of good.[12]

We find the like exhortations, or rather more pressing, with regard to the *Last Will of Jean Meslier*,
of that famous Curate of Etrepigni, whose apostacy and blasphemies could make a still stronger
impression on the minds of the populace. Voltaire
would complain that there were not so many copies of that impious work in all of Paris, as he himself had dispersed throughout the mountains of
Switzerland.[13]

D'Alembert was himself obliged to apologize as
if he had been indifferent and deficient in point of
zeal; but particularly for not having dared, at the
entreaties of Voltaire, to print in Paris *and distrib-*

---

12 To d'Alembert, 13 Dec. 1763, vol. 68, let. 122, p. 263.
13 From d'Alembert, 31 July, 1762, vol. 68, let. 102, p. 207, and to
    d'Alembert, 15 Sept. let. 104, p. 214.

ute four or five thousand copies of John Meslier's last will. His excuse manifests the consummate conspirator, who knows how to wait the proper moment, and take precautions to ensure that success which too great precipitancy might have ruined.[14] By what he writes to Voltaire on a master-piece of impiety entitled *Good Sense*, we see that he was perfectly aware of the effect which these impious works had on the minds of the people; that he knew when they were to be multiplied, or cast into the hands of the vulgar; he says, "This production (*Good Sense*) is a work much more to be dreaded than the *System of Nature*." It really was so, because, with greater art and unconcern, it leads to the most unqualified Atheism; and for that reason we see d'Alembert setting forth the advantages to be derived from it to the conspiracy, if it were abridged, though already but small, so *as to cost no more than five-pence, and thus to be fitted for the pocket and the reading of every cook-maid.*[15]

D'Alembert excuses himself.

These low intrigues, however, were not the only means to which the Sophisters resorted to evade the law, and overrun all Europe with these Antichristian productions. They were supported at court by powerful men, or ministerial adepts, who knew how to silence the law itself; or, if it ever was to speak, it was only to favour the better this impious traffic, at another time, in spite of the magistracy. The duke de Choiseul and Malesherbes

Ministers promote their circulation.

14   From d'Alembert, 31 July, 1762, *Ibid.*

15   From d'Alembert, 15 Aug. 1775, vol. 69, let. 146, p. 249.

were again the promoters of this grand plan for robbing the people of their religion, and insinuating the errors of Philosophism. The former, with the assurance of ministerial despotism, threatened the Sorbonne with all the weight of his indignation, when by their public censures they sought to guard the people against those ephemerous productions. It was this strange exertion of authority which made Voltaire exclaim, *Long live the ministry of France; above all, "long live the Duke of Choiseul!"* [16]

Malesherbes, who, having the superintendency over the whole trade of printing and bookselling, was hence enabled to evade the law both in the introduction and circulation of these impious writings, was on that point in perfect unison with d'Alembert. Both would willingly have hindered the champions of religion from printing their replies to that legion of infidels then rising in France; but the time was not yet come. With his pretended toleration, Voltaire was indignant, that under a philosophic minister the apologists of the Gospel should still have access to the press; and d'Alembert is obliged to plead in his defence, that Malesherbes, so far from favoring the antiphilosophic works, had reluctantly been obliged *to submit to superior orders* which he could not resist.[17] Not content with a simple connivance, such excuses were unsatisfactory to Voltaire; nothing

---

16　To Marmontel, 2 Dec. 1767, vol. 60, let. 200, p. 336.

17　From d'Alembert, 28 Jan 1757, vol. 68, let. 21, p. 37.

less than the authority of kings could satisfy his zeal, and he has again recourse to Frederick. This inundation of impious books[18] was to have been

_____

18 Were I not pretty well acquainted with a certain numerous class of readers, I might consider as superfluous the observations I am about to make on the doctrine of those works which Their the chiefs of the conspiracy, independently of their own, sought doctrine. to circulate through all classes of society. I have not only to satisfy men hard to convince, but to persuade men who will resist evidence itself, unless it overwhelms them. In spite of all the proofs we have already adduced of the Conspiracy formed and carried on by Voltaire, d'Alembert, Frederick, Diderot, and their adepts, against the vitals of Christianity, will nobody again assert, that the Sophisters only levelled their writings at the abuses, or at least that Catholicism was their only aim; and that they never meant to attack the divers other religions that are within the pale of Christianity, whether at Geneva or London, in Germany or Sweden. The extreme falsity of such an argument renders it absurd. If we do but reflect for a moment on the nature of those works which the Sophisters circulated with so much zeal, can we suppose that they wished to disseminate That the other principles than those preached up in these works? Let us conspir- appeal to them, and see if the destruction of abuses, or even of acy was Catholicism alone, could have been their sole object. general,

We have seen that the works so highly recommended by proved Voltaire and d'Alembert are particularly those of Fréret, Bou- by these langer, Helvétius, John Meslier, Dumarsais, and Maillet; or works. at least they bear the names of those Sophisters. They are, as we have before said, the *Philosophic Soldier*; the *Doubts* or the *Sage's Scepticism*; and *Good Sense*; whose authors remain unknown. I will lay before the reader the divers opinions broached by the writers so much commended by the Sophisters, concerning those points which cannot be invalidated without overthrowing the very foundation of Christianity; and then let any one conclude that the Conspiracy only impugned abuses, or some particular branch of Christianity.

The belief of the existence of a God belongs to every religion that is Christian; let us then examine their doctrine as to a God.

Doctrine
of these
works On
God.

FRÉRET tells us expressly, "*The universal cause, that* GOD *of the Philosophers, of the Jews, and of the Christians, is but a chimera and a phantom.*" The same author continues: "*Imagination daily creates fresh chimeras, which raise in them that impulse of fear; and such is the phantom of the Deity.*" (Letter from Thrasybulus to Lucippus, p. 164 to 254.)

The author of GOOD SENSE, that work which d'Alembert wishes to see abridged, in order to sell it for five-pence to the poor and ignorant, is not so emphatical; but what is his doctrine? "*That the phenomena of nature only prove the existence of God to a few prepossessed men,*" that is to say, full of false prejudices; "*that the wonders of nature, so far from bespeaking a God, are but the necesssary effects of matter prodigiously diversified.*" (No. 36 and *passim.*)

THE PHILOSOPHIC SOLDIER does not deny the existence of God; but he starts, in his first chapter, with a monstrous comparison *between Jupiter* and *the* GOD *of the Christians*; and the pagan god carries all the advantage of the discussion.

According to CHRISTIANITY UNVEILED, which appeared under the name of Boulanger, it is more reasonable to admit with Manes of a *twofold God*, than of the God of Christianity. (Page 101.)

The author of THE DOUBTS, or of Scepticism, informs the world, "That they cannot know whether a GOD really exists, or whether there is the smallest difference *between good and evil, or vice and virtue.*" Such is the drift of the whole of that work. (Particularly 100 & 101.)

On the
Soul.

We find the same opposition to Christianity in their doctrines on the spirituality of the SOUL. With FRÉRET, "every thing that is called Spirit, or Soul, *has no more reality than the phantoms, the chimeras, or the sphinxes.*" (Letter from Thrasybulus.)

The Sophister of the pretended GOOD SENSE heaps up arguments anew to prove, that it is the body that feels, thinks, and judges; and that the SOUL *is but a chimera.* (No. 20 and 100.)

HELVÉTIUS pronounces, "That we are in an error when we *make of the* SOUL *a spiritual being; that nothing* can be more

absurd; and that the SOUL *is not a distinct being from the body.*"
(*Of the Spirit,* and *Of Man and His Education,* no. 4 and 5.)

BOULANGER tells us decidedly, "That the immortality of the
Soul, so far from stimulating man to the practice of virtue, is
nothing but a *barbarous, desperate, fatal tenet*, and contrary
to all legislation." (Antiquity Unveiled, p. 15.)

If from these fundamental tenets, essential to every religion
as well as to Catholicism, we pass on to MORALITY, we shall
find FRÉRET teaching the people that "all ideas of *justice and
injustice, of virtue and vice, of glory and infamy,* are purely
arbitrary and dependent on custom." (Letter of Thrasybulus.) On Moral-
ity.

HELVÉTIUS will at one time tell us, that the only rule by
which *virtuous actions* are distinguished from *vicious ones,*
is the law of princes, and public utility. Elsewhere he will say,
"that *virtue,* or *honesty,* with regard to individuals, is no more
than the *habit of actions personally advantageous,* and that
self-interest is the sole scale by which the actions of man can
be measured;" In fine, "that if the virtuous man is not happy
in this world, we are justified in exclaiming, *O Virtue! thou
art but an idle dream.*" (*On the Mind,* discourse 2nd and 4th.)

The same sophister also says, that "*sublime virtue and enlightened wisdom* are only the fruits of those passions *called
folly*; or, that stupidity is the necessary consequence of the ces-
sation of passion. That to moderate the passions is to ruin the
state. (*Idem.,* discourse 2d and 3d, Chap. 6, 7, 8, and 10.) That
conscience and remorse are nothing but the *foresight* of those
physical penalties to which crimes expose us. That the man who
is above the law can commit, without remorse, the dishonest act
that may serve his purpose." (*Idem, Of Man,* vol. 1st, sect. 2d,
chap. 7.) That it *little imports* whether men are vicious, if they
be but enlightened. (*Idem.,* no. 9, chap. 6.)

The fair sex too will be taught by this author, that "MODESTY
*is only an invention of refined voluptuousness:—*that MORAL-
ITY has nothing to apprehend from *love,* for it is the passion
that *creates genius,* and *renders man virtuous.*" (*Idem,* Disc.
2d, chap. 4 and 15, &c.) He will inform children, that "the
commandment of loving their father and mother is more the
work of education than of nature." (*Of Man,* chap. 8.) He will

Frederick acts in concert with Voltaire.

the prime object of his colony. As yet unconsoled for the failure of that plan, he writes to the king of the Sophisters,

tell the married couple, that "the law which condemns them to live together becomes *barbarous and cruel* on the day they cease to love each other." (*Of Man*, sect. 8, &c.)

In vain should we seek among the other works that the chiefs of the conspirators wished to circulate a more Christian MORALITY. DUMARSAIS, as well as Helvétius, knows no other virtue but what *is useful*, nor vice but that which *is hurtful* to man upon earth. (*Essay on Prejudices*, chap. 8.) The PHILOSOPHIC SOLDIER thinks that so far from being able to offend God, *men are obliged to execute his laws.* (Sect. 20.) The author of Good Sense so much praised by the leaders, tells them that to think we can offend God, *is to think ourselves stronger than God.* (Sect. 67.) He would even teach them to answer us, "If your God leaves to men the *liberty of damning* themselves, *why should you meddle with it?* Are you wiser than that God whose rights you wish to avenge?" (Sect. 135.)

Boulanger, in the work so much admired by Frederick and Voltaire, asserts that the *fear of God*, so far from being the beginning of wisdom, *would rather be the beginning of folly.* (*Christianity Univelied*, in a note to p. 163.)

It would be useless to the reader, and irksome to ourselves, were we to carry these quotations any farther. Those who wish to see these texts, and numberless others of the same kind, may peruse the HELVIAN LETTERS. But certainly here is enough to demonstrate, that conspirators who wished to circulate such works, were not levelling solely at the Catholic religion, much less at a few abuses. No; it is evident, that every Altar where Christ was adored was to be overthrown, whether Anglican, Calvinist, or Protestant.

The base project of throwing into circulation four or five thousand copies of John Meslier's Last Will would fully prove the design of annihilating every vestige of Christianity, since this Last Will or Testament is nothing but a gross declamation against the doctrines of the Gospel.

144

*Were I younger and had I health, I would will-
ingly quit the house I have built and the trees
I have planted, to go and dedicate with two or
three Philosophers the remainder of my life,
under your protection, to the printing of a few
useful books. But, Sire, cannot you, without exposing yourself, have some of the Berlin booksellers encouraged to reprint them, and to distribute them throughout Europe at a price low
enough to ensure their sale.*[19]

This proposal, which transformed the King of
Prussia into the hawker-general of Antichristian
pamphlets, did not displease his protecting majesty. "You may (answers Frederick) *make use of our
printers as you please*; they enjoy perfect liberty,
and as they are connected with those of Holland,
France, and Germany, I have no doubt but that
they have means of conveying books whithersoever they may think proper."[20]

Even at Petersburg Voltaire had found hawkers
of these impious productions. Under the protection and by the influence of Count Schouvallow,
Russia was to petition Diderot *for leave to be honoured with* the impression of the Encyclopedia,
and Voltaire is commissioned to announce that
triumph to Diderot.[21] The most impious and most
seditious work that Helvétius had written was then
reprinting at the Hague, and the Prince Gallitzin

---

19   To Frederick, 5 April, 1767, vol. 65, let. 159, p. 374.
20   To Frederick, 5 May, 1767, vol. 65, let. 160, p. 378.
21   To Diderot, 25 Sept. 1762, vol. 57, let. 242, p. 475.

dared to *dedicate it to* THE EMPRESS OF ALL THE RUSSIAS. Here Voltaire's zeal was out-run by his success. He could not help remarking, with what amazement the world would see such a work inscribed to the most despotic sovereign on earth; but while he smiled at the imprudence and folly of the Prince adept, he exultingly beheld *the flock of sages silently increasing,* for princes themselves were no less eager than himself in the circulation of these antichristian writings. We find this account repeated three different times in his letters to d'Alembert; so great was his joy, and so confident was he of annihilating all idea of Christianity in the minds of the people by these means.

In this chapter we have treated only of the solicitude with which the chiefs sought to infuse the poison of their writings into the minds of the people; hereafter we shall see the means employed by the Sect to extend it to the hovel or the cottage, and to imbue the rabble with its impious principles, though we have seen Voltaire despising such a conquest.

CHAPTER X.

Of the Spoliations and Violences Projected by the Conspirators, and Concealed under the Name of Toleration.

f all the arts put in practice by the conspirators, none, perhaps, has succeeded better with them, than the perpetual appeal in all their writings to *toleration, reason, and humanity*, which Condorcet tells us they had made their *war-hoop*.[1] In fact, it was natural enough, that men who appeared so deeply impressed with these sentiments should gain the attention of the public: But were they real? Did the conspiring Sophisters mean to content themselves with a true toleration? As they acquired strength, did they mean to grant

What their toleration really was.

---

1   *Sketch on History.* Epoch 9.

to others what they asked for themselves? These questions are easily solved; and it would be useless for the reader to seek the definition of each of these high-sounding words imposed upon the public, when their private and real sentiments are to be seen in their continued cry of *Crush Religion*. To cast an eye on their correspondence, is sufficient to identify the plans of these conspiring Sophisters with those of the Jacobins their successors. Do not the Pétions, the Condorcets, and the Robespierres, adopt their wishes and execute their plans under the same mask of toleration?

Spoliations premeditated by Voltaire.

Plunder, violence, and death have marked the toleration of the revolutionists. Nor were any of these means foreign to the first conspirators, whose language the latter had adopted. As to spoliations, I have already said that Voltaire, as early as the year 1743, was plotting with the King of Prussia to plunder the Ecclesiastical Princes and the Religious Orders of their possessions. In 1764, we have seen him sending a memorial to the Duke of Praslin on the abolition of tythes, in hopes of depriving the clergy of their sustenance.[2] In 1770, he had not abandoned his plan when he writes to Frederick, "I wish to God that Ganganelli had some good domain in your neighbourhood, and that you were not so far from Loretto . . . . It is noble to scoff at these Harlequin *Bull-givers*; I like to cover them with ridicule, but *I had rather* PLUNDER *them*."[3]

---

2   To the Count d'Argental, 20 June, 1764, ut supra.

3   To Frederick, 8 June, 1770, vol. 65, let. 172, p. 405.

These various letters prove to the reader, that the chief of the Conspirators only anticipated the plundering decrees of the Jacobins, and the revolutionary incursion their armies have made to Loretto.

Frederick, assuming the kingly tone, seems for an instant so shocked at these spoliations, as to have forgotten that he had been the first to propose them. He answers,

Rejected and approved by Frederick.

> Were Loretto adjoining to my villa, I would not touch it. Its treasures might tempt a Mandrin, a Conflans, a Turpin, a Rich . . . . or their fellows. It is not that / reverence donations consecrated by sottish stupidity; but what the *public* venerates should be spared. When one looks upon one's self as gifted with superior lights, compassion for others, and commiseration for their weakness, should make us unwilling to shock their prejudices. It is to be lamented, that the pretended Philosophers of our days are not ot the same way of thinking.[4]

But the Sophister soon prevails over the monarch; and Frederick is no longer of opinion that spoils of the church are to be left to a Mandrin: the very next year, coinciding with Voltaire, he writes to him, "If the new minister of France is a man of sense, he will neither be weak nor foolish enough to restore Avignon to the Pope."[5]—He recurs to his means of *silently undermining the edifice*, by first

---

4   From Frederick, 7 July, 1770, vol. 65, let. 173, p. 409.

5   From Frederick, 29 June, 1771, vol. 66, let. 10, p. 25.

plundering the Religious Orders, that they might then strip the bishops.[6]

D'Alembert's advice.

D'Alembert, on his side advised, that the clergy should be first deprived of that consequence they enjoyed in the state, before they were plundered of their possessions. Sending to Voltaire his task, almost ready made, that he might speak out what d'Alembert dared not utter himself, he tells him, "that he must not forget (if it could be done delicately) to add to the first part a little appendix, or an attractive postscript, on the danger both to states and kings, in suffering the clergy to form a separate and distinct body, with the privilege of holding regular assemblies."[7]

As yet this doctrine was new both to kings and states; they had never perceived this pretended danger of letting the clergy form a distinct body in the nation, as did the nobility and the third order; but these conspiring chiefs were anticipating the horrors of the revolution, the plunders and murders of their Jacobin successors and disciples.

Violent measures wished for by Voltaire.

Violent and sanguinary edicts, decrees of deportation and of death, were not foreign to the wishes of the conspiring chiefs. How frequent soever the words of toleration, humanity, and reason, may be in Voltaire's mouth, it would be a great error in judgment to think that those were the only arms he wished to employ against the Christian Religion. When he writes to Count Argental, "Had I but a

---

6   From Frederick, 13 Aug. 1775, vol. 66, let. 95, p. 222.

7   From d'Alembert, 9 Feb. 1773, vol. 69, let. 96, p. 161.

hundred thousand men, I well know what I would do with them,"[8] and to Frederick, "Hercules went to fight the robbers and Bellerophon chimeras; I should not be sorry to behold Herculeses and Bellerophons delivering the earth both from Catholic robbers and Catholic chimeras;"[9] it was not toleration that dictated those wishes; and one is tempted to conclude, that he would not have been sorry to behold the massacre of the Clergy by the Herculeses and Bellerophons of the sanguinary September. Have we not observed him wishing to behold *every Jesuit at the bottom of the ocean, each with a Jansenist hung to his neck?* When, with the view of avenging Helvétius and Philosophism, he does not blush to ask. *Could not the moderate and discreet proposal of strangling the last Jesuit with the guts of the last Jansenist,* bring matters to some compromise? In reading this, can we reasonably infer, that the humanity and toleration of Voltaire would have been greatly shocked at the sight of ships stowed with the Catholic Clergy by a Le Bon, as a preparatory step to submerging them in the ocean!!!

Frederick seemed to be nearer to simple toleration when he thus answered Voltaire: "It is not the lot of arms to destroy *the wretch.*—It will perish by those of truth."[10] At length he begins to think that force must strike the last blow at Religion. He is

By Frederick.

---

8   To the Count d'Argental, 16 Feb. vol. 57, let. 28, p. 60.

9   To Frederick, 3 March, 1767, vol. 65, let. 157, p. 369.

10   From Frederick, 25 March, 1767, vol. 65, let. 158, Page 370.

not averse to this force, and we see him willing to employ it had the occasion offered when he writes to Voltaire,

> To Bayle, your forerunner, and to yourself, no doubt, is due the honor of that Revolution working in the minds of men. But, truly to speak, it is not yet complete; bigots have their party, and *it will never be perfected but by a superior force: from government must the sentence issue that shall crush the wretch.* Enlightened Ministers may forward it, *but the will of the sovereign must accede.* Without doubt this will be effectuated in time; but neither of us can be spectators of that long-wished for moment.[11]

There can be no doubt but that the long-sought for moment was that, when impiety, enthroned, should cast aside the mask of toleration, with which it had necessarily disguised itself: Julian-like, would not Frederick also have resorted to superior force at that desired period? Would he not have seconded the Sophisms of the Conspirators with that sentence which was to issue from the Sovereign? He would have spoken as a master; and under Frederick might not the reigns of a Domitian or a Julian have been renewed, when apostacy, exile, or death, were the only alternatives left to a Christian's choice.—But to reconcile this superior force, this sentence of the government that is *to crush*, with what d'Alembert says of that Prince in

---

11   From Frederick, 8 Sept. 1775, vol. 66, let. 97, p. 230.

a letter to Voltaire, is difficult: "I believe him at his last shift, and it is a great pity. Philosophy will not easily find a Prince like him, tolerant through indifference, (which is the true style) and an enemy to superstition and fanaticism."[12]

But with d'Alembert even that mode of tolerating, through indifference did not exclude underhand persecutions; nor would it have been incompatible with this man's rage and phrenzy, so openly expressed in his letters to Voltaire, to see a whole nation destroyed solely for having shewn its attachment to Christianity. Could toleration through indifference dictate the following fines?

D'Alembert.

> A-propos of the King of Prussia, he has at length got a-head again. And I, as a Frenchman and a thinking being, am quite of your opinion, that it is a great happiness both for France and for Philosophy. Those Austrians are a set of insolent capuchins who hate and despise us, *and whom I could wish to see annihilated with the superstition they protect.*[13]

It would be useless to remark in this place, that these very Austrians whom d'Alembert wishes to see annihilated, were then the allies of France, at war with that very King of Prussia whose victories he celebrates. These circumstances might serve to show, how much more philosophism swayed the heart of the Sophister, than the love of his country;

---

12   From d'Alembert, 27 Jan. 1762, vol. 68, let. 95, p. 187.

13   From d'Alembert, 12 Jan. 1763, vol. 68, let. 113, p. 237.

and that toleration would not have hindered the Conspirators from betraying their king or country, could they by that event have made a new attack on Christianity.

We plainly see, that all these inhuman wishes were rather expressed by inadvertency, than the avowed object of their correspondence. They were preparing the road for those seditious and ferocious minds, that were to perpetrate what the Sophisters could at that time only devise.—The day of rebellion and murder was not yet come; with the same wishes circumstances had not distributed to them the same parts to act. Let us then examine what characters the first chiefs performed, and by what services each one in particular, signalizing his zeal in the Antichristian Conspiracy, prepared the reign of his Revolutionary adepts.

CHAPTER XI.

Part, Mission and Private Means of Each of the Chiefs of the Antichristian Conspiracy.

n order to attain the grand object of the conspiracy, in short to crush the Christ whom they pursued with unrelenting hatred, all the general plans and means they had concerted were judged insufficient. Each individual was to concur with his own means, with those which his faculties, his situation, or peculiar mission, enabled him to exert.

Voltaire was endowed with all those talents which adorn the eminent writer; and no sooner was the confederacy formed than he turned them all against his God. During the last five and twenty years of his life, he declares himself, *that he had*

Voltaire's services,

no other object in view than to vilify the wretch.[1]
Before that period he had shared his time between
poetry and impiety; but henceforward he is solely
impious. One might have thought that he wished
to vomit forth himself more blasphemies and calumnies against the God of Christianity, than had
the whole class of Celsi, or Porphyrii during all
ages. In the large collection of his works (more
than forty volumes in 8vo.) Romances, Diction-
aries, Histories, Memoirs, Letters and Commen-
taries, flowed from his pen, embittered with rage
and breathing the wish of crushing Christ. "I finish all my letters," would he write, "by saying,
crush the wretch, as Cato was used to finish his
harangues. Such is my opinion and let *Carthage
be destroyed.*"[2]

In this immense collection it would be in vain
to seek any particular system of Deism, of Materialism, or Scepticism. They all form one common
mass. We have seen him conjuring d'Alembert to
unite all these diverging Sects in the common attack against Christ; and his own heart may be said
to have been their focus. He cared not whence the
storm arose, or whose the hand that struck; the
subversion of the Altar was his only aim. The religious authors, and we ourselves, have shown
him fickle in his systems, and daily adopting new
opinions, and that from his own works;[3] we be-

ardor,

contradic-
tions,

---

1   Letter to Damilaville, May, 1761, vol. 57, let. 58, p. 117.

2   To Damilaville, 26 July, 1762, vol. 57, let. 225, p. 446.

3   See Helvian Letters, and particularly letter 34 and 42.

hold twenty different men in him alone, but each of them equally hateful. Rage accounts for his contradictions; even his hypocrisy flows from the same source. This latter phenomenon is not sufficiently known; it must have its page in history; but let Voltaire himself speak as to the extent and original cause of so base a conduct.

During that inundation of Antichristian books in France, government would sometimes, though remissly, take cognizance of their authors. Voltaire himself had been prosecuted on account of his first impious writings. When declared premier chief, he thought that more caution became his pre-eminence, lest any legal proof should be acquired of his impiety. The better to attack, and the more securely to *crush Christ*, he conceals himself under his very banners; he frequents his temples, is present at his mysteries, receives into his mouth the God he blasphemed; and if annually at Easter he received, it was but more audaciously to blaspheme his God. To so monstrous an accusation incontestable proofs shall be brought.

On the 14th of Jan. 1761, Voltaire sends a performance, (I know not what, but which the editor of his works supposes to be an epistle to Mademoiselle Clairon, a famous actress in those days,) to one of his female adepts, the Countess of Argental, whom he styles his angel. Beyond a doubt, it was a most scandalous production; since only the chosen of the elect are favored with it, or rather since to them alone Voltaire *dared* send it. In short, what-

hypocrisy and communions.

ever was the subject, it was accompanied with the following letter.

Will you amuse yourself with the perusal of this scrap: will you read it to Mademoiselle Clairon? None but yourself and the Duke de Choiseul are in possession of it; you will tell me presently that I grow very daring, and rather wicked in my old age. Wicked! No; I turn Minos, and judge the wicked. But take care of yourself. There are people, I know, who do not forgive; and I am like them. I am now sixty-seven years old. I go to the parochial mass. I edify my people. I am building a church. *I receive communion there*; and, zounds, I will be buried there, in spite of all the hypocrites. I believe in Jesus Christ consubstantial with God, and in the Virgin Mary mother of God.—Ye base persecutors, what have you to say to me? Why, you have written *La Pucelle*. No, I never did. You are the author of it; it was you that gave ears to Joan's palfrey. I am a good Christian, a faithful servant of the king, a good lord of the parish, and a proper tutor for a daughter. I make curates and Jesuits tremble. I do what I please with my little province about as big as the palm of my hand (his estate extended about six miles); I am the man to dispose of the Pope whenever I please. Now, ye raggamuffins, what have you to say to me?—These, my dear angels, are the answers I would make to the Fantins, Grisels, Guyons; or to the little black monkey, &c.&c.[4]

---

4   vol. 57, let. 8, p. 15.

CHAPTER XI

The female adepts might indeed laugh at the tone and style of such a letter; but will the judicious reader see it in any other light, than as the production of an insolent old man, who, proud of his protections, is nevertheless determined impudently to lie, and to set forth the most orthodox profession of faith, should religious writers accuse him of impiety, and to combat the laws with denials or make a merit of his sacrilegious communions; and the infidel talks of hypocrites and base cowards!

Such odious artifice seems to have shocked the Count d'Argental himself; for on the 16th of February following, Voltaire writes to him,

> Had I a hundred thousand men, I would know what use I would make of them; but as I have them not, *I will receive at Easter*, and you may call *me hypocrite as much as you please*; Yes, by God! I will receive the sacrament, and that in company with Mad. Denis and Mademoiselle Corneille; and if you say much, I will put the *Tantum ergo* into verse, and that in cross rhimes.[5]

It appears that many more of the adepts were ashamed of this meanness in their chief. He himself at length thinks it necessrary to write to d'Alembert on the subject; to whom he says, "I know there are people who speak ill of my Easter devotions. It is a penance I must resign myself to, in expiation of my sins. - - - - *Yes, I have received my Easter com-*

5   vol. 57, let. 28, p. 60.

*munion, and what is more, I presented in person
the hallowed bread*; - - - - after this, I could boldly
defy both Molinists and Jansenists."[6]

If these last words do not sufficiently declare
the motives of his hypocrisy, the following letter,
also to d'Alembert, will do away all doubt; it is only
three days posterior to the last:

> What, in your opinion, should the sages do
> when surrounded by senseless barbarians?
> There are times when *one must imitate their
> distortions, and speak their language. Mute-
> mus clypeos* (let us change our bucklers). In
> fact, what I have done this year, *I have already
> done several times before*; and please God I will
> do it again.[7]

This is the same letter too in which he particularly recomends that *the mysteries of Myrtra
should not be divulged,* and which he concludes
with this terrible sentence against Christianity.
*The monster must fall pierced by a hundred in-
vincible hands; yes, let it fall beneath a thousand
repeated blows.*

With this profound dissimulation,[8] Voltaire combined all that dark-dealing activity, which the oath

---

6   To d'Alembert, 27 April 1768, vol. 68, let. 228, p. 476.

7   To d'Alembert, 1 May 1768, vol. 68, let. 229, p. 477.

8   If I may credit men who knew Voltaire in the earlier part of
     his literary triumphs, he was then no stranger to this profound
     hypocrisy. The following anecdote I learned from men who
     knew him well. It was singular enough, that Voltaire had a
     brother, an arrant Jansenist, who professed all the austerity

of crushing the God of Christianity could suggest to the premier chief of the Antichristian Sophisters. Not content with his partial attacks, he had recourse to whole legions of adepts from the east to the west; he encouraged, pressed, and stimulated them in this warfare. Present every where by his correspondents, he would write to one, "Prevail on all the brethren, to pursue *the wretch in their discourses and in their writings, without allowing him one moment's respite*."—To another he would say, "*make the most earnest, though the most prudent efforts to crush the wretch.*" Should he observe any of the adepts less ardent than himself, he would extend his Philippics to all: "*They forget* (says he) *that their principal occupation ought to be to crush the monster.*"[9] [The reader has not forgotten that

Pressing exhortations to the adepts,

---

of manners which that Sect affected. The Abbé Arouet, heir to a considerable fortune, would not see his impious brother, and openly declared that he would not leave him a halfpenny. But as his health was weak, and his life could be of no long duration, Voltaire did not give up all hopes of the inheritance; he turned Jansenist and acted the devotee. On a sudden he appears in the Jansenistical garb; with a large slouched hat, he runs from church to church, taking care to choose the same hours as the Abbé Arouet; and there, with a deportment as contrite and humble as Deacon Paris himself, kneeling in the middle of the church, or standing with his arms crossed on his breast, his eyes cast on the ground, on the Altar, or on the Christian orator, he would hearken or pray with all the compunction of the penitent sinner reclaimed from his errors. The Abbé believed in his brother's conversion, exhorted him to persevere, and died leaving him all his fortune. The Jansenist's cash was, however, all that Voltaire retained of his conversion.

9　See Letters to Thiriot, Saurin, and Damilaville.

monster, wretch, and *Christ* or *Religion,* are synonimous in his mouth.] Satan could not have been more ardent, when, in the war of hell against heaven, he fought to stir up his legions against the Word. He could not more urgently exclaim, We must triumph over the Word, or meanly serve: shame in defeat could not be expressed more forcibly by Satan than by Voltaire, when he cries out to his adepts, *"Such is our state, that we shall be the execration of mankind, if* (in this war against Christ) *we have not the better sort of people on our side*; we must therefore gain them cost what it will; labour then in the vineyard; *oh, crush the wretch,*[10] - - - - *I tell you, crush the wretch."*

corre-
spond-
ence.

So much zeal had made him the idol of the party. The adepts flocked from all parts to see him, and went away fired with his rage. Those who could not approach, consulted him by letter, and laid their doubts before him; they would crave to know whether there really was a God, if they really had a soul, &c. Voltaire, who knew nothing of the matter, smiled at his own power; but always answered, that the God of the Christians was to be crushed. Such were the letters he received every week.[11] He himself wrote a prodigious number in the same blasphemous style. The reader must have seen the collection in order to believe that the heart or hatred of one single man could dictate, or that one hand could pen them, and that without considering his many

10   To d'Alembert, 13 Feb. 1764, vol. 68, let. 129, p. 282.

11   To Mad. du Dessant, 22 July, 1761, vol. 57, let. 87, p. 181.

other blasphemous works. In his den at Ferney, he would be informed of, and see all; he would personally direct every thing that related to the conspiracy. Kings, princes, dukes, marquisses, petty authors or citizens, might write to him, provided they were but impious. He would answer them, strengthen them, and encourage them all in their impiety. In short, to extreme old age, his life was that of a legion of devils, whose sole and continued object was to crush Christ and overthrow his Altar.

Frederick the Sophister, though on a throne, was not less active, nor less astonishing in his activity. This man, who alone did for his kingdom all that a king could do, and even more than both king and ministers in most other countries do, out-stripped the Sophisters also in their Antichristian deeds. As a chief of the conspiracy, his part, or rather his folly, was to protect the inferior adepts, if any of them chanced to fall under prosecution by what was called fanaticism. When the Abbé Desprades[12] was obliged to fly the censures of the Sorbonne and the decrees of Parliament, the sophistical monarch presented him with a canonicate at Breslaw.[13] Etallonde de Morival, a hair-brained youth, flies the vengeance of the laws, after having broken the public monuments of religion; he is received, and the colours of a

Frederick's services.

---

12 Jean-Martin de Prades (1720 - 1782). He supplied the article on Certitude to the Encyclopedia. —Ed.

13 To d'Alembert, 5 Sept. 1752, vol. 68, let. 3, p. 7. [The canonries were of Oppel and Guglau. Of Breslau was the Bishop, Philip

regiment are entrusted to his hands.[14] If his armies require money, his treasures are exhausted; but not so to the adepts. In the very height of war, their pensions, and particularly d'Alembert's, are regularly paid.

He was sometimes, it is true, seen to lay aside the Sophister, and think it beneath a monarch to be connected with a set of *blackguards, coxcombs, and visionary fools*.[15] But those were little sallies which the Sophisters easily overlooked; his philosophism would return; he was one of their's again; and his hatred to Christianity would once more engage his whole attention. He would then spur on Voltaire himself; he would urge and solicit him impatiently for new writings, and the more impious the work, the more he approved of it.—Then with Voltaire and d'Alembert he would demean himself even to their artifices; he would, above all, admire the hand that struck unseen, or, as he expresses himself, that method of filliping the *wretch*, while loading him with civilities.[16]

---

von Schaffgotsch, with whom the Abbé entered negotiations with a view to a recantation of the doctoral thesis that had led to him being censured. Frederick induced him to 'return to the bossom of the Church' and Pope Benedict XIV and Cardinal Tercin wrote the formula of recantation that was to be signed by the Abbé. This done, the Faculty of Paris re-inscribed him in their record of bachelors. He later became archdeacon of Guglau. —Ed.]

14   To d'Alembert, 8 Dec. 1772, vol. 69, let. 82, p. 134.

15   His Dialogues of the 1 lead.

16   From Frederick, 16 March, 1771, vol. 66, let. 6, p. 16.

Then, assuming the tone of disgusting flattery, he would stile Voltaire the God of Philosphy. "He would fancy him ascending Olympus, loaded and satiated with glory, *the conqueror of the wretch,* supported by the genii of Lucretius and Sophocles, of Virgil and Locke, seated on a car beaming with light, and placed between Newton and Epicurus." [17] He paid homage to him for the Antichristian Revolution which he saw preparing.[18] Unable to triumph by so many titles himself, he would acquire that of being laborious; and even those impious works, whether in rhyme or in prose, published under his name, are not the only productions of the royal Sophister. Many he privately ushered into circulation, and which never could have been thought to be those of a man who had the duties of a throne to fulfil. Such, for example, was his extract of Bayle. More impious than Bayle himself, he only rejects the useless articles, in order to condense the poison of the rest. His *Akakia* too, and that *Discourse on the History of the Church* so much extolled, as well as its preface, by the abettors of impiety. In short, his productions were numberless, in which Voltaire finds no other fault but the eternal repetitions (like his own) of the same arguments against religion.[19]

---

17 From Frederick, 25 Nov. 1766, vol. 65, let. 151, p. 353.

18 To Frederick, 10 Feb. 1767, vol. 65, let. 154, p. 361.

19 Correspondence of Voltaire and the King of Prussia, let. 133, 151, 159, &c. &c. vol. 65.

Hence we see, that it was not enough for Frederick to forward the conspiracy by his counsels, and to give refuge to its agents; but he would also, by his constancy and application to infect Europe with his impieties, aspire to the rank of chief. If he was inferior to Voltaire, it was in his talents, and not in his hatred; but had Voltaire been destitute of the support of a Frederick, he could not have risen to the height he aimed at. Possessed of the secret, he would willingly have initiated all kings to the mysteries of the conspiracy; and of all, he was the king who gave it the chief support. His example was still more powerful than his writings; and it may be justly said, that his reign was that of a sceptered infidel.

Diderot's services.

Placed in an humbler sphere, Diderot and d'Alembert began their several missions with a game that well characterized their apostleship. Both were actuated by its spirit; but neither had yet acquired that reputation which they afterwards gained more by their impiety, than by their abilities. The coffee-houses at Paris were their first stage. There unknown, first in one then in another, they would begin an argument on religious matters, Diderot the assailant and d'Alembert the defendant. The objection was forcible and pointed, the energy and tone of Diderot was invincinble. The reply was weak, but made with all the apparent candour of a Christian, who wished to maintain the honor and truth of his religion. The idle Parisians, who generally resorted to these places, would hearken and admire, and sometimes take a part in the dispute. Diderot then insisted, resumed, and pressed the argument. D'Alembert, in return, owned that the difficulty appeared unanswerable, and then withdrew as if ashamed, and regretting, that neither his divinity, nor his love for religion, could furnish him with arguments for its defense. Our two disputant friends would soon meet to felicitate each other on the good success of their sham conflict, and on the impression they had made upon the crowd of ignorant hearers, who had been completely duped. They then make a fresh appointment; the dispute was taken up again; the hypocritical advocate for religion makes a new display of his zeal, but submits to the superior arguments of Atheism. At length the police, informed of their game, attempted to put a stop to it: but it was too late; these sophisms had spread through the different societes, never to be eradicated. Hence arose, in great part, that fury which soon became fashionable with all the youth of Paris, of disputing on matters of faith; and that still greater folly, of looking on objections as insuperable which immediately disappear when, in search of truth, we seek to know it, and follow it, in spite of those passions which militate against it. It was on occasion of the coffee-house disputations, that the lieutenant of the police upbraiding Diderot with propagating Atheism, that madman proudly answered, *It is true, I am art Atheist, and I glory in it.* "Why Sir," replied the minister, "you would know, were you in my place, that even had no God existed, it would be necessary to have invented one."

However much the brain of this Atheist might have been heated, the fear of the Bastille put a period to his apostleship. The minister would have been more correct in his office, had he threatened him with Bedlam. We refer the reader to the Helvian Letters, where are recorded his numberless titles to a place there.[20] He was in fact the boasting madman of the conspiracy. They wanted a man of this cast, who would utter all the absurd and contradictory impieties which his brain could invent. Such are the ideas with which he filled his different writings his pretended *Philosophic Thoughts*; his *Letter on the Blind*; his *Code*, and his *System of Nature*.

This last work gave great offense to Frederick, who even refuted it, for reasons we shall explain in the Antimonarchial Conspiracy. And indeed d'Alembert always kept the author's name a profound secret. He would not even own it to Voltaire, though he was as well acquainted with it as myself. But Diderot was not the sole author of this famous system. To build this chaos of nature, which, destitute of *intelligence*, had made man intelligent, he had associated with two other Sophisters, whose names I will not mention for fear of error, not having paid sufficient attention to them to be certain; but as to Diderot I am certain, being previously ac-

---

20   Letters LVII. and LVIII.

quainted with him. It was he who sold the manuscript, to be printed out of France, for the sum of one thousand livres. I had the fact from the man who paid them, and who owned it when he came to know better those impious Sophisters.

Notwithstanding all these follies, Diderot, was nevertheless, in Voltaire's eyes, the *illustrious philosopher, the brave Diderot,* and one of the most useful knights of the conspiracy. The conspirators proclaimed him the *Great Man;* they sent him to foreign courts as the *Admirable Man;* yet whenever he had been guilty of some notable piece of folly, they were silent, or even disowned him. This was the case in particular when at the court of Empress of Russia.

Formerly, at all courts a fool was kept for amusement; fashion had substituted a French Philosopher, and little had been gained in point of common sense. But the Empress Catherine soon perceived, that much might be lost with respect to public tranquillity. She had sent for Diderot, judging *his imagination to be inexhaustible.* She classed him *among the most extraordinary men that ever existed;*[21] and she was correct in her judgement, for Diderot behaved himself in such an extraordinary manner, that her majesty thought it necessary to send him back to the place he came from. He consoled himself, in his disgrace, with the idea that the Russians were not yet ripe for the sublimity of his philosophy. He set off for Paris in a bannian, with a velvet cap on

---

21 From Catherine, 7 Jan. 1774, vol. 67, let. 134, p. 286.

his head. His footman, like a king at arms, preceded; and when they were to pass through any town or village, he would cry out to the gazing multitude, "it is Diderot the *Great Man* that is passing."[22] Such was his equipage from Petersburg to Paris. There he was to support the character of the extraordinary man, whether writing in his study, or dealing out in divers companies his philosophic absurdities; always the bosom friend of d'Alembert, and the admiration of the other Sophisters. He finished his apostleship by his *Life of Seneca*, in which he sees no other difference between him and his dog, but that of their dress; and by his *New Philosophical Thoughts*, where God is supposed to be the *Animal Prototype*, and mortals so many little particles flowing from this great animal, and successively metamorphosed into all sorts of animals until the end of time, when they are all to return to the divine substance whence they had originally emanated.[23]

Diderot would madly utter in public all those absurdities which Voltaire would impiously assert. It is true, that none of them gained credit; but religious truths were enfeebled by these assertions wrapped in frothy discourse and philosophic pomp. Men cease to believe the religion of Christ, thus perpetually reviled in these writings; and that was all the Sophisters aimed at. The part which Diderot acted was thereby rendered so essential to the conspiracy.

---

22 Feller's *Historical Dictionary.*

23 *New Philosophical Thoughts*, Page 17 and 18. The whole is exposed in the Helvian Letters, XLIX.

Who can reconcile this antichristian zeal, ever emphatic, and in a state of ebullition when his imagination is heated, with that real admiration which he often expressed for the Gospel? The following is an anecdote I had from Mr. Beauzée, a member of the academy. Going one day to see Diderot, he found him explaining a chapter of the Gospel to his daughter, as seriously and with as much concern as the most Christian parent could have done. Mr. Beauzée expressed his surprize. "I understand you," said Diderot, "but in truth where could I find better lessons to give her?"

D'Alembert would never have made such an avowal as this. Though the constant friend of Diderot, we find throughout their lives, and their philosophic course, that same difference which marked their first essays in the apostle-ship. Diderot spoke out whatever he thought at the moment, d'Alembert never said a word but what he wished to say. I will defy any one to find his real opinion on *God*, or on the *soul*, except in his private correspondence with the conspirators. His works have all the obscurity and cunning of iniquity, but he is the fox that infects and then burrows himself. Easier would it be to follow the meanderings of the eel, or trace the windings of the serpent gliding through the grass, than to discover the tortuous course he follows in those writings which he owns.[24]

D'Alembert's services.

---

24 From the criticism made of his works in our Helvian Letters the result is this: d'Alembert will never declare himself a sceptic, or whether he knows of the existence of a God or not. He

No body was ever more true to Voltaire's maxim of strike, but hide your hand. The avowal he makes of his bows to religion, while he is striving to pull it to pieces,[25] might save the historian the trouble of seeking those numerous proofs with which the works of this Sophister abound. To make himselt amends for this perpetual restraint under which, from his dissimulation, he was himself forced to write, by means of his pupils, or in their produc-

---

will even let you think that he believes in God; and then begin by attacking certain proofs of a Deity; he will tell you that, from zeal for the Deity, man must know how to choose among those proofs. He will end by attacking them all, with a *yes* on one object, and a *no* a little while on the same; he will entangle the minds of his readers, he will raise doubts in them, and smile to see them fallen without perceiving it, into the very snare he had prepared for them. He never tells you to attack religion, but he will tempt you with a stand of arms, or place them in your hands ready for combat. (*See his Elements of Philosophy and our Helvian Letters*, let. xxxvii). He will never declaim against the morality of the church or the commandments of God; but he will tell you that *there does not exist a single catechism on morality fitted to the capacities of youth*; and that it is to be hoped there will at length appear a Philosopher who will supply that *desideratum* (See *Elem. of Phil.* No. 12). He will not pretend to deny the sweets of virtue; but he will tell you, "that philosophers would have better known our nature, had they been satisfied with simply confining the happiness of this life to the exemption from pain." (*Preface of the Encyclopedia*). He will not offend his reader by obscene descriptions, but he will tell him. Art. HAPPINESS, "Men all agree as to the nature of happiness; they declare it to be the same as pleasure, or at least they are indebted to pleasure for all that is most delicious in it." And thus his young pupil is transformed into an Epicurean without knowing it.

25 From d'Alembert, 3 Jan. 1765, vol. 68, let. 151. p. 333.

tions, he would speak more boldly. When he returned them their works, he would artfully insinuate an article, or plan a preface; but so much the worse for the pupil, if he underwent the punishment incurred by the master. Morellet, still a youth, though already a graduate among the divines of the Encyclopedia, had just published his first essay in philosophism. This was a manual with which Voltaire was enchanted; above all he valued the Preface; *it was one of the finest lashes ever given by Protagoras.* The youth was taken up and sent to the Bastille. The real Protagoras, or d'Alembert, who had so well taught him the art of *lashing*, never owned the whip, as may be supposed.[26]

On the whole, d'Alembert would have been but of little use to the Conspirators, had he confined himself to his pen. In spite of his quibbling style, and of his epigrams, his talent of wearying his readers left them an antidote. Voltaire, by giving him another mission, better suited his genius. He had reserved to himself the ministers, dukes, princes, and kings, and all those sufficiently initiated to forward the Conspiracy; but charged d'Alembert with the care of training the young adepts: *"Endeavour,"* he writes expressly, *"endeavour on your part to enlighten youth as much as you are able."*[27]

He is charged with training youth.

Never was a mission more actively, more zealously, nor more ably fulfilled. It is to be remarked, that however secret d'Alembert may have been in

---

26   To Thiriot, 26 Jan. 1762, vol. 57, let. 157, p. 320.
27   To d'Alembert, 15 Sept. 1762, vol. 68, let. 104, p. 214.

all the ther parts he acted in the conspiracy, he was not unwilling that his zeal in this particular should be observed. He was the general protector of all young men who came to Paris possessed of any talents. Had they any fortune of their own, he dazzled them with crowns, premiums, and even with the academic seats, of which he absolutely disposed, either as perpetual secretary, or as being irresistible in all those petty intrigues wherein he so much excelled. The reader has already seen what a master-stroke it was for the Conspirators to have filled with their adepts this tribunal of European Mandarines presiding over the empire of letters. But his power in this point extended far beyond Paris. He writes to Voltaire, "I have just got Helvétius and the Chevalier de Jaucourt admitted into the academy at Berlin."

D'Alembert was particularly attentive to such of the adepts as were intended to train others, or to fulfil the functions of private or public professors, or of tutors in private families; but particularly in the latter, when the pupil, by his rank or wealth, might hereafter be a protector of the Conspirators, or more amply remunerate his teacher. This was the true method of imbuing youth with the real principles of the conspiracy. D'Alembert was perfectly aware of its importance, and took his measures so well that he succeeded in spreading such tutors and preceptors throughout all the countries of Europe, and deserved the title of the most fortunate propagator of philosophism.

The proofs he cites of their progress will suffice to show the choice he had made. "Here is, my dear Philosopher," he exultingly writes to Voltaire, "here is what was pronounced at Cassel on the 8th of April, in presence of his highness the Landgrave of Hesse-Cassel, of six princes of the empire, and of a most numerous assembly, by a *Professor of History which I gave to his Highness the Landgrave.*" This was a discourse full of the grossest invectives against the Church and the Clergy, as *obscure fanatics, praters crosiered or unmitred, with or without a cowl.* Such was the style of the professor and such the proofs adduced by d'Alembert of the victories daily gained by his adepts over religious ideas, and of the sentiments they instilled into their pupils.[28]

It was, above all, of importance to the conspirators to place such tutors about young princes and children hereafter destined to govern nations. The correspondence of Voltaire and d'Alembert lays open their intrigues on this point, and the powerful support which they expected from it.

The court of Parma was seeking men worthy of presiding over the education of the young infant; and when they placed the Abbé de Condilhac and De Leire[29] at the head of his Instructors, they flattered themselves with having succeeded; as they little thought that these two men were to inspire the young prince with the irreligious ideas of the

---

28   From d'Alembert, 1 July, 1772, vol. 69, let. 77, p. 124.

29   Abbé Michel Deleyre. —Ed.

Sophisters. The Abbé de Condilhac, in particular, had by no means the reputation of an Encyclopedian Philosopher; and it was long ere they became sensible of their error, which could only be remedied by the total subversion of all that these two tutors had done. The whole would have been foreseen, had they known that Condilhac was the particular friend of d'Alembert, who always looked up to him as a man precious to the self-created Philosophers; or had they known that the choice of these two men was only the effect of an intrigue in which Voltaire glories, when he writes to d'Alembert, "It appears to me that the Parmesan child will be well surrounded; he will have a Condilhac and a De Leire. If, with all that, he is a bigot, *grace must be powerful indeed.*"[30]

These wishes and artifices of the Sect were so well propagated, that in spite of Louis the XVI.'s attachment to religion, they sought to place new Condilhacs about the heir to the crown; and as they succeeded in discarding the bishops from the education of the young Dauphin, they would willingly have excluded all ecclesiastics; but, despairing of so complete a success, they sought to make the choice fall on some clergyman, who, like Condilhac, would inspire the illustrious pupil with the principles of the Sophisters. I am acquainted with one of those men with whom they dared to tamper. They offered him the place of tutor to the

---

30 To d'Alembert, 17 Nov. 1760, vol. 68, let. 77, p. 174 and from
    d'Alembert, 3 Jan. 1765, let. 151, p. 335.

Dauphin, being, as they said, sure of getting it for him, and of thereby making his fortune; *but on condition* that when he taught the young prince his Catechism, he would take care to insinuate, that all religious doctrine, as well as all the mysteries of Christianity, were only prejudices and popular errors, of which a prince should indeed be informed, but which he should never believe; and that in his private lessons he would instil, as true doctrine, all the errors of Philosophism.—Fortunately, this priest answered, that he knew not how to sacrifice his duty to his fortune; more fortunately still, Louis XVI. was not a man to encourage such intrigues. The Duke d'Harcourt, named to preside at the education of the Dauphin, took the advice of some bishops, and chose (to read lectures on religion to his pupil) a clergyman perfectly competent to the task, as he was then superior of the College of La Fleche. Alas! why must we felicitate this tender youth on his premature death? While yet the Sophisters of infidelity could not flatter themselves with the subversion of the throne of his ancestors, were they not infusing their poisons to transform him at least into an impious king? And when the throne was overturned, would he, more than his young brother, have escaped the hands of the Sophisters of rebellion?

Many other adepts, with the same zeal to enthrone Philosophism and to prepare the way for the Antichristian Revolution in divers other courts, showed the same activity. At Petersburg they had beset the Empress; they had persuaded her, that some Sophister, and that of the first class, ought to be entrusted with the education of her son. d'Alembert was named, and the Count Schouvallow was ordered by his sovereign to make the proposal in her name.—D'Alembert simply received the offer as proof *that Voltaire had no reason to be displeased with his mission, and that philosophy was sensibly reaching the throne.*[31] Whatever advantages he might have expected to reap from such a commission, he prudently declined; he preferred the petty empire he swayed in Paris as chief of the adepts, to the precarious favor of courts, and of that in particular whose distance from the center of the conspiracy could not have permitted him to act the same part in it.

King of the young adepts, he did not confine his protection to those of Paris alone, but to the remotest parts of Russia would he extend his paternal care; he would follow their progress, share their destiny, or protect them in adversity.—When he found his power insufficient, he would have recourse to Voltaire's credit; he would write, for instance:

> The poor Bertrand is not lucky. He has petitioned fair Kate (the Empress of Russia) to restore to liberty five or six giddy-headed Velches.

---

31 To d'Alembert, 25 Sept. 1762, vol. 68, let. 106, p. 219, and the 2 Oct. following.

He had conjured her, in the name of Philosophy; he had drawn up, under that sacred name,
the most eloquent pleading that from memory
of monkey was ever made, and Kate pretends
not to understand it.[32]

This was as much as to say to Voltaire, try in your
turn whether you can succeed better, and do for
them what you have so often done for other adepts
whose misfortunes I have made known to you.

This understanding equally subsisted in all that A spy to
regarded the conspiracy; little satisfied with point- Voltaire.
ing out works that were to be refuted, or with giving the sketch of some new impious brochure, he
would also be the spy over every religious author.
It has often been an object of surprise, to see Voltaire, so familiar with the anecdotes of the private
lives of those whose works he pretended to refute,
though generally they are slanderous, sometimes
ridiculous, but always foreign to the question.
He was indebted to d'Alembert for them. Whether true or false, the latter always chose such as
could attach ridicule to the person of the authors,
knowing how well Voltaire could substitute ridicule for proof, or wit for sound argument. Those
who doubt this fact may consult d'Alembert's
letters on the Père Berber, or the Abbé Guenée,
whom Voltaire himself could not but admire; or
those concerning Messrs. Le Franc, Caveirac[33] or

---

32 From d'Alembert, 18 Jan. 1773, vol. 69, let. 90, Page 151.

33 Jean Novi de Caveirac (1713 - 1782), prior of Cubiérettes and a

Sabbatier[34], and on many others whom Voltaire hardly ever combats, but with the weapons that d'Alembert had furnished.

His petty societies and clubs.

Voltaire on his part spared nothing that could raise the importance of d'Alembert. He would recommend him to all his friends; he would introduce him into every little society, or petty philosophic club; for these were already forming in Paris, to be one day absorbed by the great club of the Jacobins. Some indeed would have been styled aristocratical, as they were the weekly meetings of *Counts*, *Marquisses*, or *Chevaliers*, personages already too consequential to bend their knee before the Altar of their God. Here would they debate on prejudices, superstition, or fanaticism. They would scoff at J. C. and his priests, or smile at the simplicity of the adoring populace. They also thought of shaking off the yoke of religion, leaving indeed just what was necessary to keep the rabble in awe. The female adept, the Countess du Deffant, held the chair, and continued her philosophic education under the particular direction of Voltaire, by whose orders she studied Rabelais, Polymbrock, Hume, the *Tale of the Tub*, and other such romances.[35]

---

defender of the Jesuits. —Ed.

34 Antoine Sabatier de Castres (1742 - 1817) came to Paris in 1766, where he was protected by Helvétius and where he joined the Philosophes; however, he later joined the defenders of religion. —Ed.

735 Letters of Voltaire to Mad. Dessant, particularly 13 Oct. 1759, vol. 56, let. 90, p. 182.

D'Alembert was far from being at his ease in these aristocratical clubs; he even disliked this female adept. Voltaire on the contrary, knowing what advantages were to be drawn from them, wished him to belong to them all, and would introduce him by his letters. His introduction was less difficult into some other clubs, and particularly into that where Mad. Necker presided, when she had snatched the sceptre of Philosophy from the hands of all the other adepts of her sex.[36]

Our two chiefs mutually assisted each other by imparting their plans for drawing off the people from their religion. One, in particular, cannot certainly be omitted in these memoirs; it denotes too clearly the intentions of the conspirators, and it shows how far their views extended. It was not indeed the invention of d'Alembert; but he was aware of the advantages Philosophism would derive from it, and, strange as was the plan, he flattered himself with the execution of it.

His plan for rebuilding the temple of Jerusalem.

It is well known what strength the Christian religion draws from the fulfilling of the prophecies, and particularly from those of Daniel, and of Christ himself, on the fate of the Jews and of their temple. Julian the apostate, in order to give the lie to Christ and to the prophet Daniel, had sought to rebuild the temple. It is also known, that flames bursting forth from the earth at divers times, and

---

36 To d'Alembert, 21 June, 1770, vol. 69, let. 31, p. 59, and to Mad. Fontaine, 8 Feb. 1762, vol. 57, let. 167, p. 336.

devouring the workmen, had obliged him to desist from the undertaking. D'Alembert was not ignorant of this act of the divine vengeance having been ascertained by a multitude of eye-witnesses. He had undoubtedly seen it recorded in Ammianus Marcellinus, an author of unquestionable authority, for he was a friend of Julian, and like him a Pagan. But this did not hinder him from writing to Voltaire,

> You probably know, that at this present time, there is in Berlin one of the circumcised, who, expecting Mahomet's paradise, is in the mean time gone to wait on your former disciple in the name of the Sultan Mustapha. Writing to that country the other day, I mentioned, that if the king would but say a word, it would be a fine opportunity to have the temple of Jerusalem re-built.[37]

That word was not said by the former disciple, and d'Alembert gives the following reason to Voltaire: "I have no doubt but that we should have succeeded in our negotiation for the re-building of the temple of the Jews, if your former disciple had not been afraid of losing some circumcised worthies, who would have carried away thirty or forty millions with them."[38] Thus, in spite of all their inclination to give the lie to the God of the Christians, even the sordid interest of the Conspirators was to add a new proof to his doctrines.

37 Front d'Alembert, 8 Dec. 1763, vol. 68, let. 121, p. 261.
38 From d'Alembert, 29 Dec. 1763, vol. 68, let. 124, p. 269. i

Voltaire had not, eighteen years after, given up the plan, nor lost all hopes of accomplishing it. Seeing that d'Alembert had not succeeded with Frederick, he endeavoured to prevail with the Empress of Russia. He writes to her, "If your Majesty is in a regular correspondence with Ali Bey, I implore your protection with him; I have a little favor to ask of him; it is to re-build the temple of Jerusalem, and to recal the Jews, who will pay him a large tribute, and thereby make a mighty lord of him."[39]

Voltaire when nearly eighty still persisted in this plan, by which he was to prove to the people, that Christ and his prophets were impostors. Frederick and d'Alembert were also far advanced in their career; and the time was not far distant, when they were to appear before that very God whom they had daringly styled a wretch, and against whom they had never ceased to direct their malice.

I have now laid before my readers the means and the industry with which they sought to overturn the altars, to annihilate the dominion of the faith, to destroy the priests of God, and to substitute the hatred and ignominy of him whom the Christians adore, to his religion. I had promised not so much the history, as the real demonstration of the Conspiracy; and in exposing its object, its extent, or its means, I have not resorted to hearsay or vague report, for proof.—My proofs are their own words; the comparison of their letters and of their mutual communications carries conviction.

39   To Catherine, 6 July, 1771, vol. 6>7, let. 82, p. 172.

My readers may henceforth reconcile this conspiracy, and its means, with that revolution operated by the Jacobins. They may already perceive, that the latter, in destroying the altars of Christ, only execute the plots of the Sophisters their fore-runners and masters.

Was there a temple to be overthrown, a depredatory decree against the church to be passed by the Jacobins, of which we have not already seen the plan? Are not the Marats and the Robespierres figured by Voltaire in his Hercules and Bellerophon? And if whole nations are to be crushed in hatred to Christianity, have we not seen that wish formally expressed by d'Alembert? Every thing teaches us (the hatred of the father gaining strength in the breast of the son, and the plots propagating), that when force shall coalesce with impiety, they can only generate a race brutal and ferocious.

But this force to be acquired by the Conspirators supposes a successive progress. Before it could throw off the mask, it was requisite that the number of adepts should be augmented, and that the arms of the multitude should be secured to them. I am about to show their successes under the reign of corruption in the divers orders of society during the lives of the chiefs.—Hence history will hereafter more easily conceive and explain what they were during the reign of terror and devastation.

CHAPTER XII.

Progress of the Conspiracy.— First Class of Protectors.— Crowned Adepts.

oltaire's grand object, as we have seen, was to hurry away that whole class of men, styled by the conspirators the better sort, and infuse into them his hatred for Christ and his religion; to have left his gospel to none but the rabble, and to them only in case they could not efface it from their minds. Under this denomination of *the better sort*, they comprehended all who were distinguished either by power, rank, or riches; and, after them, all people of education or instruction, and honest citizens ranking above what Voltaire calls rabble, footmen, cooks, &c. It is an observation worthy the historian, that the Antichristian

Conspiracy first makes its progress in the most illustrious part of this class; among princes, kings, emperors, ministers and courts; among those, in short, who may be styled the great.

If a writer dares not utter these truths, let him throw aside his pen; he is too base and unworthy of treating such important subjects of history. He who has not the courage to tell kings, that they were the first to league in the conspiracy against Christ and his religion, and that it is the same God who has permitted the conspirators first to threaten, shake, and silently undermine their thrones, then openly to scoff at their authority; the man, I say, who dares not hold such language is only abandoning the powers of the earth to their fatal blindness. They would continue to hearken to the impious, to protect impiety, and support its dominion, to let it circulate and spread from the palace to the city, from the towns to the country, from the master to the servant, from the lords to the people. And would not such crimes call down vengeance from heaven? Will not heaven have crimes too numerous to avenge upon nations not to curse them with luxury and discord, with ambition and conspiracies, or with all those scourges which portend the downfall of nations? Had the monarch alone throughout his empire raised his head against his God, who has told us that the crimes of the chief shall not be avenged upon his people? Once more, I say, let the historian be silent, if he dares not utter the truth. Should he seek the causes of a revolution in its agents, he would meet a Necker, a Brienne, a Philippe d'Orléans, Mirabeaux, and Robespierres; a confusion in the finances, factions among the great, insubordination in the armies, the people agitated and disquieted, and at last seduced. Will he, by that, know whence these Neckers, Mirabeaux, or Robespierres, have arisen; whence this confusion in finance, this spirit of faction, this insubordination of the armies, or the seduction of the divers classes of the state? He will have seized but the last thread of the conspiracy. He will have seen empires in their agony, but he will have overlooked that slow fever which consumed them, while the violence of the fit is reserved to that last crisis which precedes dissolution. He will describe the calamities which every one has seen, but will he be the nearer to the remedy? Let the historian reveal the secrets of the masters of the earth, to ward from them the conspiracy which shall fall back upon them; and what secrets do we reveal? secrets publicly printed for these ten years past in their own correspondence with the chief of the conspiracy. It is too late to attack us on that point. Those letters were printed, to the great scandal of the public, to discover the favor of the impious man with the sovereigns of the earth; and when we show this protection avenged upon the sovereigns, it is not their shame we are seeking to divulge, it is their misfortunes and those of their people that we make known; the remedy then spontaneously manifesting itself, may avert or prevent much greater evils. Such a motive is more than an equivalent to all that could induce us to be silent.

In the correspondence of the conspirators there is more than one letter which deposes against the Emperor Joseph II. with all the possible evidence of such testimony, that he was initiated and had been admitted into all the mysteries of the Antichristian Conspiracy by Frederick.

In the first of these letters Voltaire announces his victory in these terms: "You have afforded me great pleasure by reducing the infinite to its real value. But here is a thing far more interesting: *Grimm assures us, that the Emperor is one of ours. That is lucky*; for the Duchess of Parma, his sister, is against us."[1]

In another letter, Voltaire, exulting in so important a conquest, writes to Frederick: "A Bohemian of great wit and Philosophy, called Grimm, has informed me that you have initiated the Emperor into our holy mysteries."[2] In a third, Voltaire, after enumerating the princes and princesses whom he reckoned among the adepts, adds these words: "You have also flattered me with the Emperor's being in the way of perdition; *that would he a good recruit for Philosophy*."[3] This alludes to a letter written by Frederick to Voltaire a few months before, in which he says,

---

1   To d'Alembert, 28 Oct. 1769, vol. 69, let. 13, p. 27.

2   To Frederick, Nov. 1769, vol. 65, let. 162. p. 383.

3   To Frederick, 21 Nov. 1770, vol. 65, let. 181. p. 432.

> I am setting off for Silesia, and shall meet the
> Emperor, who has invited me to his camp in
> Moravia; not to fight, as formerly, but to live as
> good neighbors. He is an amiable prince, and
> full of merit. *He likes your works and reads*
> *them as often as he can. He is the very reverse*
> *of superstitious.* In fine, he is an Emperor such
> as Germany has not for a long time seen. We
> neither of us like the ignorant and barbarous,
> but that is not a reason for exterminating them.[4]

Now that we are acquainted with Frederick's
idea of a prince, *The very reverse of superstitious,*
and who reads Voltaire's works as often as he
can, his encomiums are easily understood. They
truly point out an Emperor such as Germany had
not *for a long time seen,* that is, an Emperor as
irreligious as Frederick himself. Both the date and
the last words, *but that is not a reason for exter-*
minating them, recalls to our mind a time when
Frederick, thinking the Sophisters too daring and
hasty, sought himself to repress their imprudence,
lest it might overthrow the whole political system
of governments. It was not yet time to employ *su-*
perior force, or to pass the *last sentence.* The war
against Christ then resolved on between Frederick
and Joseph was not to be a war of Neros and Di-
ocletians; it was silently to undermine. Such was
that which Joseph waged, as soon as the death of
Maria Teresa left him at liberty to act. He carried
it on with hypocrisy; for Joseph, as unbelieving

---

4   From Frederick, 18 Aug. 1770, vol. 65, let. 175, p. 416.

as Frederick, wished to be looked upon as a very religious prince, and would often protest that the slightest attack on Christianity was the most distant from his ideas. During his travels through Europe he continued to take the sacraments, and perform his Easter devotions at Vienna and Naples, with that exterior piety, which could not seem to coincide with the hypocrisy of those of Voltaire at Ferney. He carried his dissimulation so far, that in passing through France he refused to call at Ferney, though very near and fully expected there by Voltaire. It is even said, that in turning away he affectedly observed, *That he could not bear to see a man, who, by calumniating religion, had given the severest blow to humanity.* What credit is to be given to this affirmation I will not pretend to decide; but certain it is, that the philosophers did nevertheless look upon Joseph as one of theirs. The flight of Voltaire was soon pardoned. It was everywhere asserted, that the Emperor's admiration had not diminished for the premier in impiety; that he would have willingly visited him, but that he had refrained through regard to his mother, *who at the solicitations of the priests had made him promise that he would not see him during his journey.*[5]

Notwithstanding his reserve and his dissimulation, the war which Joseph waged soon became one of authority and oppression, of rapine and vi-

---

5   See note to the letter of the Count de Touraille, 6 Aug. 1777, vol. 63, p. 387.

olence; and was very nigh ending in the extermination of his own subjects. He began by the suppression of a large number of monasteries; this, we have seen, was a leading feature in Frederick's plan: he seized on a great part of the ecclesiastical property; so would Voltaire have done, for he exclaims. *But I had rather plunder them*: Joseph II tore from their cells and cloisters even to those Carmelite nuns whose extreme poverty could afford no bate to avarice, and whose angelic fervor left no room for reform. He was the first who gave to the world the public spectacle of holy virgins driven to wander into distant countries, even as far as Portugal, to seek an asylum for their piety. Innovating at pleasure in the church, he only anticipated that famous constitution of the clergy called civil by the Jacobin legislators, and which prepared the way to the butchery at the Carmes. The sovereign pontiff thought it incumbent on him to leave Rome and pass into Austria, and, in the capacity of common father of the faithful, personally to represent to the emperor the laws and rights of the church. Joseph II. received him with respect, and permitted all that homage and public veneration to be shown to Pius VI., which his virtues and his dignity equally demanded. He did not, however, discontinue his war of oppression. He did not expel the bishops, it is true, but he gave them much trouble; for, constituting himself as it were the superior of a seminary, he would permit no lectures to be read, but by those professors whom he had chosen, and whose doctrine, like that of *Camus*, tended only to forward the grand apostacy. At length these secret persecutions and depredations gave rise to murmurs. The wearied Brabanters revolted. Since that, we have seen them call in those very Jacobins who, promising them the free exercise of their religion, and more artful than Joseph, are now consummating his work. Had they been less tormented in matters of faith by Frederick's adept, the Brabanters would have been less impatient under the yoke of Austria; had they been fraught with greater zeal and affection for the Emperor Joseph, they would have better seconded, and had more confidence in the virtues of Francis II. They would with greater force have opposed that invasion which we have seen extend to the very banks of the Danube. Should history lay the blame on Joseph, let it look back to that day when he was, by Frederick, initiated into the mysteries of Voltaire. It is the emperor *adept* that shall be found guilty of this war of extermination, which has threatened even the throne of his successors.

In the sequel of this work we shall see Joseph repenting of the war he had waged against Christ, when he beheld philosophism attacking both himself and his throne. He will then attempt, but too late, to repair his fault. He will fall a melancholy victim.

Many other sovereigns are mentioned in the correspondence of the conspirators, as having imprudently engaged in these plots. D'Alembert complaining to Voltaire of the obstacles he sometimes encountered from the public authorities, and which he terms *persecutions,* at length consoles himself by adding, "But we have on our side the Empress Catherine, the King of Prussia, the King of Denmark, the Queen of Sweden and her son, many Princes of the Empire, and all England."[6] Much about the same time Voltaire writes to the King of Prussia, "I know not what Mustapha thinks (on the immortality of the soul); my opinion is, that he does not think at all . . . . As for the *Empress of Russia, the Queen of Sweden your sister, the King of Poland, and Prince Gustavus* son of the Queen of Sweden, I believe that I know what they think."[7]

Voltaire effectually knew it. The letters of these sovereigns could not leave him in the dark; but had we not those letters to adduce in proof, we now see an Emperor, an Empress, a Queen, and four Kings, already enlisted under the banners of the conspirators.

In bringing to light this horrid Conspiracy, let not the historian abandon himself to false declamation, nor draw inferences still more deceptive. Let him not pretend to say to the people, Your kings have shaken off the yoke of Christ; it is but just that you should throw off that of their dominion. Such reasoning would be to blaspheme Christ, his doctrines, and his examples. The arm of vengeance is

False inferences to be avoided in speaking of the royal adepts.

---

6   To d'Alembert, 23 Nov. 1770, vol. 69, let. 47, p. 83.

7   To Frederick, 21 Nov. 1770, vol. 65. let. 181, P, 432.

reserved to God alone. For the happiness of subjects, to preserve them from revolutions and all the
horrors of rebellion, he alone can smite the apostate
on the throne. Let not the Christian apostatize, but
let him be subject to his lawful prince. To join revolt to impiety is not averting the scourge ot heav-
en; it is only adding anarchy, the most terrible of all
political scourges; it would not be a bar against the
Sophister of impiety, but the consummation of the
Conspiracy of the Sophisters of sedition against the
throne and all the laws of civil society. Such was the
fate of the unfortunate Brabanters when in rebellion
against the Emperor Joseph. They pretended to the
right of rejecting their lawful sovereign, and they
are become the prey of Jacobins; they called insurrection to the aid of religion, and that religion pro-
scribes insurrection against all lawful authority. At
the time that I am now writing, the fulminating reports made to the Convention forbode those dreadful decrees which, levelling the religious worship,
the privileges, and the churches of the Brabanters
to the standard of the French revolution, shall pun-
ish them for their error. When therefore the historian shall report the names of those sovereigns who
unfortunately were initiated, and conspired against
their God, let his intention be to recal them to their
religion; let him not be led away by false inferences
so adverse to the peace of nations. No; let him insist
on the duties which religion imposes on the people;
let him teach them what they owe to Cæsar and to
every public authority.

Of the royal protectors all are not to be classed with Voltaire, Frederick, or Joseph. All had tasted of the impious cup of infidelity, but all did not equally wish to imbue their people with its poison.

Immense was the distance between Frederick and this Empress, in whom the conspirators placed so much confidence. Seduced by the talents and homage of their premier chief, Catherine may have owed to him her first taste for literature; she almost devoured those works which she had mistaken for masterpieces, whether in history or philosophy, totally ignorant of their being disguised solely to forward the ends of impiety. On the fallacious encomiums of the Sophisters she boldly pronounced, *That all the miracles in the world could never wipe out the alleged disgrace of having hindered the printing of the Encyclopedia.*[8] But we never see her, like Frederick (to obtain the fulsome flattery of the Sophisters) pay to impiety a degrading court. Catherine would read their works;—Frederick would circulate them, compose himself, and wish to see them devoured by the people. Frederick would propose plans for the destruction of the Christian religion, Catherine rejected all those proposed to her by Voltaire. She was tolerant by nature, Frederick only from necessity. He would have been no longer so, had his policy permitted him, in following the dictates of his hatred, to call in *a superior force* to effect the overthrow of Christianity.[9]

Catherine II. Empress of Russia.

---

8   From Catherine, 22 Aug. 1765, vol. 67, let. 3, p. 8.

9   Those who, as men of literature, shall criticize the correspond-

Nevertheless, Catherine was a royal adept; she had the secret of Voltaire, and applauded the most famous of our infidels.[10] She was even willing to entrust the heir of her crown in the hands of d'Alembert; her name constantly appears among the protecting adepts in the writings of the Sophisters, nor can the historian suppress the fact.

Christiern VII. King of Denmark. The claims of Christiern VII., King of Denmark, to the title of adept are also founded on his correspondence with Voltaire. Among the numerous services rendered by d'Alembert, I should not have omitted the pains he had taken to prevail on different powers and great personages to subscribe to

---

ence of this Empress, will find an amazing difference between her manner and that of the King of Prussia. The former is that of a woman of wit, who often plays upon Voltaire in the most agreeable manner. With her light style and full of taste, she never forgets her dignity; she at least will not be seen to degrade herself to the gross dialect of scurrility and blasphemy; while Frederick in his, truly the pedantic Sophister, will be as void of shame in his impiety, as he is of dignity in his encomiums. When Voltaire wrote to Catherine, "We are three, Diderot, d'Alembert, and myself, who raise altars to you;" (22 Dec. 1766, vol. 67, let. 8, p. 17) she answers, "Pray leave me, if you please, on earth; there I shall be more near at hand to receive your letters and those of your friends." (9 Jan. 1767, let. 9. p. 18.)—Nothing so perfectly French can be found in Frederick's; we only have to regret, that it was addressed to a set of infidels. Catherine wrote Voltaire's own language in perfect purity, while Frederick could have had little pretensions to the hero, had he not handled his sword better than his pen.

10 From Catherine, 26 Sept. 1773, vol. 67, let. 129, p. 280, and 7 Jan. 1774, let. 134, p. 285.

the erection of a statue in honor of Voltaire. I could have shown the Sophister of Ferney modestly pressing d'Alembert to collect these subscriptions, and in particular that from the King of Prussia, who hardly waited their solicitations. This triumph of their chief was too desirable for the Conspirators, and Christiern VII. eagerly contributed.

A first letter, with a few compliments, might not be thought sufficient to constitute an adept, but we have Voltaire's own authority for naming the King of Denmark; and beside, among those compliments we find one exactly in the style of Frederick, "You are now occupied in delivering a considerable number of men from *the yoke of the clergy, the hardest of all others*; for the duties of society are only imprinted in their heads, *and never felt in their hearts. It is well worth while to be revenged of the barbarians.*"[11] Unfortunate Monarchs! Such was the language held to Marie Antoinette, in the days of her prosperity, by those corruptors. But in her misfortunes, when she witnessed the loyalty and the sensibility of those barbarians at the Thuileries, she exclaimed, "Alas! how we have been deceived! We now plainly see how much the clergy distinguish themselves among the faithful subjects of the king."[12] May the king that is led away by Philosophism never be reduced to the same experiment; may he learn at least from one revolution, that there is a yoke more *hard* and terrible than

---

11   From Christiem, 15 Dec. 1770, vol. 67, let. 44, p. 371.

12   I heard this anecdote in the midst of the revolution; and such

that of the clergy, which Voltaire his master had taught him to calumniate.

It is our duty to add, that with regard to this prince, as well as to many others who were seduced by the Sophisters, the conspirators had taken advantage of their youth. At that period of life, the writings of Voltaire could easily make impression on men who were not, because they were kings, better versed than other people in what they had not learned; nor were they able to discriminate truth from error, in objects where the want of knowledge is more to be dreaded than inclination or the passions.

At the time of his journey into France Christiern was but seventeen years of age; but even then, young as he was, he had, to use d'Alembert's expression, *the courage to say at Fontainebleau* that Voltaire *had taught him to think.*[13] Men about the court of Louis XV., of a different way of thinking, wished to hinder his young majesty from learning to think still more like Voltaire, and from seeing in Paris the adepts or most celebrated of his disciples. These however obtained admission; and to judge how well they understood improving their opportunity, we need only observe d'Alembert writing to Voltaire, "I had

expressions were necesssary to shew that she was recovered from those prejudices she had imbibed against the clergy, and which appeared to have redoubled after the second journey which her brother made to Versailles.

13   From d'Alembert, 12 Nov. 1768, vol. 68, let. 239, p. 494.

seen that prince at his own apartments, together with several of your friends. He spoke much about you, *of the services that your works had rendered, of the prejudices you had rooted out,* and of the enemies that your *liberty in thinking* had made you. You easily guess what my answers were."[14] D'Alembert has a second interview, and again writes, "The King of Denmark scarce spoke to me but of you. I can assure you, he had rather have seen you at Paris, than all the entertainments with which they have surfeited him."[15] This conversation had been but of short duration; but d'Alembert made amends in a discourse on Philosophy which he pronounced at the academy, in presence of the young monarch. Numerous were the adepts who were present, and they loudly applauded; the youthful monarch joined in the applause. Such, in short, is the opinion he carries away with him of that pretended Philosophy, (thanks to d'Alembert's new lectures!) that no sooner is he informed of a statue to be erected to the premier chief of the conspirators, than he sends a very *handsome subscription,* for which Voltaire acknowledges himself to be indebted to the lessons of the academical adept.[16] How much these lessons have since been forgotten by Christiern VII., I cannot pretend to say. Events have taken place since his Danish Majesty had learned

---

14   From d'Alembert, 6 Dec. 1768, vol. 68, let. 240, p. 496.

15   From d'Alembert, 17 Dec. 1768, let. 242, p. 496.

16   To d'Alembert, 5 Nov. 1770, vol. 69, let. 46. p. 81.

to think from Voltaire, sufficient to have given him a very different opinion of the *services* that the works of his master have rendered to empires.

Similar artifices were made use of with regard to Gustavus, King of Sweden. That prince also came to Paris, to receive the homage and lessons of the self-created philosophy. He was as yet but Prince Royal, when, already extolling him as one whose protection was insured to the Sect, d'Alembert writes to Voltaire,

> YOU LOVE REASON AND LIBERTY, my dear brother; and one can hardly love one without the other. Well then, I here present to you a *worthy republican philosopher*, who will talk PHILOSOPHY and LIBERTY with you. It is Mr. Jennings, chamberlain to the King of Sweden.—He has compliments to pay you from the *Queen of Sweden and the Prince Royal, who in the North* PROTECT *that philosophy* so ill received by the princes in the South. Mr. Jennings will inform you of the *progress that* REASON *is making in Sweden* under those happy auspices.[17]

At the time that d'Alembert was writing this letter, Gustavus, who was soon to restore royalty to the rights it had lost long since in Sweden, was no doubt ignorant that those great men, which he so much protected, were *Philosophers* superlatively *republican*. He was equally blind to the ultimate (and to him fatal) fruit of this conspiring Philoso-

---

17   From d'Alembert, 19 Jan. 1769, vol. 69, let. 3, p. 7.

phy, when on his accession to the throne he wrote to their premier chief, "I daily pray the Being of beings, that he may prolong your days, so precious to humanity, and so necessary to the progress of REASON and TRUE PHILOSOPHY."[18]

The prayer of Gustavus was heard; the days of Voltaire were prolonged; but he who was suddenly to shorten the days of Gustavus was born; he, grasping the dagger, was soon to sally forth from the occult school of Voltaire. For the instruction of kings, let the historian compare the gradual steps of this unfortunate prince, and those of the adept and assassin.

Ulrica of Brandenbourg had been initiated into the mysteries of the Sophisters by Voltaire himself. So far from rejecting his principles, she did not even feel herself offended at the declaration of a passion which he was daring enough to express.[19] When Queen of Sweden, she more than once pressed the Sophister to come and end his days near her person.[20] She knew no means of giving a stronger proof of her staunchness in the principles she had received, than, during Voltaire's first residence at Berlin, to make the infant king imbibe them with his milk. She initiated Gustavus, and wished to be the mother of the Sophister as well as of the king; and indeed we constantly see both the mother

18 From Gustavus, 10 Jan. 1772, vol. 67, let. 51, p. 379.
19 It was for this princess that Voltaire composed the Madrigal *Souvent un peu de Verité*.
20 Her letters to Voltaire, anno 1743 and 1751, vol. 67.

and the son ranking together among the adepts of whom the Sophisters thought themselves the most secure. Such then was the gradation of the unfortunate Gustavus. Voltaire initiated Ulrica, and Ulrica initiated her son.

On the other hand, Voltaire initiated Condorcet, and Condorcet, seated in the club of the Jacobins, initiated Ankestron. A pupil of Voltaire, Ulrica, teaches her son to ridicule the mysteries and scoff at the altars of Christ. Condorcet also, a disciple of Voltaire, teaches Ankestron to scoff at the throne and sport with the lives of kings.

When public report announced that Gustavus III. was to command in chief the confederate armies against the French revolution, Condorcet and Ankestron were members of the great club; and the great club resounded with the cry of, Deliver the earth from kings! Gustavus was doomed for the first victim, and Ankestron offers himself for the first executioner. He leaves Paris and Gustavus falls under his hand.[21]

The Jacobins had just celebrated the apotheosis of Voltaire, they also celebrate that of Ankestron.

Voltaire had taught the Jacobins that *the first of kings was a successful soldier*: they teach Ankestron, that the first hero was the assassin of kings; and they placed his bust beside that of Brutus.

Kings had subscribed to the erection of a statue to Voltaire; the Jacobins erect one to Ankestron.

---

21   Journal of Fontenai.

Lastly, Voltaire's correspondence shows Ponia-towski, King of Poland, to have been of the number of the protecting adepts. That king had known our hilosophers in Paris, and was one day to fall a victim to Philosophism! He had done homage to their chief, and written to him, "M. de Voltaire, every contemporary of a man like you, who knows how to read, who has travelled, and has not been acquainted with you, must feel himself unhappy; you might be allowed to say, *Nations shall pray, that kings may read me.*"[22] Now, when the king has seen men, who, like himself, had read and cried up the works of Voltaire, attempting in Poland the revolution they had wrought in France; when, a victim of that revolution, he has seen his sceptre vanish from his hand, how different must be his prayer? Does he not regret that nations have known Voltaire, or that kings have ever read his works? Those days which d'Alembert had foretold, and which he longed to see, are at length come, and that without being foreseen by the royal adepts. When the misfortunes of religion shall fall back upon them, let them read what d'Alembert says to Voltaire, "Your former illustrious protector (the King of Prussia) began the dance; the King of Sweden led it on; Catherine imitates them, and bids fair to outdo them both. How I should enjoy seeing the string run off in my time."[23] And indeed

Ponia-towski, King of Poland.

---

22 From Stanislaus, 21 Feb. 1767, vol. 67, let. 41, p. 367.

23 From d'Alembert, 2 Oct. 1762, vol. 68, let. 107, p. 221.

the string has begun to run with a vengeance. Gustavus, King of Sweden, dies by the dagger: Louis XVI., King of France, on the scaffold: Louis the XVII. by poison: Poniatowski is dethroned:[24] the Stadtholder is driven from his country; and the adepts, disciples of d'Alembert and his school, laugh as he would have done himself at those sovereigns who, protecting the impious in their conspiracy against the Altar, had not been able to foresee that the disciples of those same conspirators would conspire against their thrones.

These reflections anticipate, contrary to my intention, what I have to unfold in the second conspiracy; but such is the union of the Sophister of Impiety with the Sophister of Rebellion, that it is hard to separate the progress of the one from the ravages of the other. It is the intimacy of this union, which has forced us to lay before the eyes of the protecting monarchs one of the most important lessons that history could produce.

I cannot conclude this chapter without remarking, that among the kings of the North, in whose protection the Sophisters so often exult, the name of his Britannic Majesty is not so much as mentioned. This silence of the conspirators is above all the encomiums they could have bestowed. Had they sought a king beloved by his subjects, and deservedly so; had they sought, I say, a king good, just, compassionate, beneficent, zealous to main-

---

24   And since the publication of the first edition of this volume is
     dead. He died at Petersburg, Feb. 11, 1798.

tain the liberty of the laws and the happiness of his empire, then George III. might have been extolled as the Solomon of the North, he might have been their Marcus Aurelius, or Antoninus. They found him too wise to coalesce with vile conspirators who knew no merit but impiety, and hence the true cause of their silence. It is an honour for a prince to be omitted in their records, who in this terrible revolution has been so conspicuous by his activity in stopping its progress, and by his noble generosity in relieving its victims.

It is also a justice which the historian owes to the kings of the South, to say, that the conspirators, so far from ranking them among their adepts, complained that they had not yet attained to the height of their sophisticated Philosophy.

CHAPTER XIII.

Second Class of Protectors.— Princes and Princesses

I n the second class of protecting adepts, I shall comprehend those persons who, without being on the throne, enjoy a power over the people nearly equal to that of kings, and whose authority and example, adding to the means of the conspirators, gave them reason to hope that they had not sworn in vain the destruction of the Christian religion.

In this class of protectors Voltaire particularly mentions the *Landgrave of Hesse-Cassel*. The care with which d'Alembert had chosen the professor of history whom we have already mentioned, shows how much the Sophister abused his confidence. He

Frederick, Landgrave of Hes- se-Cassel.

was much imposed upon when he confided in the philosophy of Voltaire; he permitted him in some sort to direct his studies, and he could hardly have fallen into the hands of a more perfidious tutor. A letter, dated the 25th Aug. 1766, will suffice to show in what sources the august pupil was directed to seek lessons of wisdom. "Your Serene Highnesss has shown," the corruptor writes,

> a desire of seeing some new productions worthy your attention. There is one that has just made its appearance, entitled *The Necessary Collection*. You will find there, in particular, a work of Lord Bolingbroke's, which appears to me one of the most forcible things ever written against superstition. I believe it is to be found at Frankfurt; but I have a copy of it sewed, which I will send to your Highness, if agreeable.[1]

For a prince who really was desirous of instruction, what lessons were to be found in this collection! The name of Bolingbroke does not sufficiently denote how far they tended to pervert his religion; but we know that Voltaire often published, under that name, works far more impious than those of the English philosopher; and that he was the author of several of those which he particularly recommended in that collection.

Left to himself for the solution of doubts occasioned by such readings, and unfortunately prejudiced against those who might have solved them,

---

1   Vol. 66, let. 63, p. 408.

he threw himself headlong into studies which he had mistaken for those of truth, and of the most transcendent philosophy. When he could receive these lessons from Voltaire himself, the illusion was so great, that his Highness would flatter himself, and really believe that he had found a means of soaring far above the vulgar. He would lament the absence which deprived him of the lessons of his master, and, thinking himself under real obligations, would say to him,

> I left Ferney with the greatest regret. . . . I am delighted to find that you approve of my way of thinking. I try as much as possible to divest myself of all prejudices; and if in that I differ in opinion from the vulgar, it is to my conversation with you, and to the perusal of your works, that I am solely indebted for it.[2]

That he might give some proof of his proficiency in the school of Philosophism, the illustrious adept was wont to impart to his master the new discoveries he had made, and which he looked upon as unanswerable objections against the sacred writ. "I have been making," he would write to his hero,

> for some time past reflections on Moses, and on some of the historians of the New Testament, to me apparently just. Might not Moses be a natural child of Pharaoh's daughter, whom that

---

2   To the Landgrave of Hesse-Cassel, 9 Sept. 1766, vol. 66, let. 64, p. 109.

> princess caused to be brought up? It is not cred-
> ible that the daughter of a king should have tak-
> en such care of a Hebrew child, whose nation
> was so much abhorred by the Egyptians.[3]

Voltaire could easily have solved such a doubt, by
making his pupil observe that he was gratuitous-
ly slandering the fair sex, whose benevolence and
tenderness would readily lead them to take compassion on a child exposed to such danger. Many
would naturally do what Pharoah's daughter did,
and would show it still greater care and attention,
as the child was exposed to national enmities. Had
Voltaire wished to give his illustrious pupil the
rules of sound criticism, he would have hinted,
that to destroy a fact both simple and natural, his
Highness supposed one truly incredible: a princess
who wishes to give her child a brilliant education,
and begins by exposing it to be drowned, for the
pleasure of going to seek it on the banks of the Nile
at a given time; an Egyptian princess, who, loving
her child, and knowing how much the Egyptians
hated the Israelites, causes this child to be suckled
by an Israelite, leaves it to believe that it was born
of that nation, which its mother detests; and afterwards, to render this child odious to the Egyptians,
persuades them of the same; a mystery still more
singular is, that the birth of an infant who became
the man the most tremendous to the Egyptians has
always remained a secret; that the whole court of

---

3   *Ibid.* 1 Nov. 1766, let. 65, Page 411.

Pharoah obstinately believe him to be an Israelite, and that at a time when, to have declared Moses an Egyptian, would have sufficed to destroy his power with the Israelites and to have saved Egypt. Such arguments might have been used by Voltaire to make his Highness sensible of the impropriety, in sound criticism, of combating a fact both simple and natural by suppositions the most distant from probability. But such suppositions were consonant with that hatred which Voltaire bore to Moses and the sacred writ; he was better pleased to see his disciples ignorantly launching into infidelity, than to teach them the rules of sound cnticism.

Voltaire again applauds his adept when his Highness pretends that the *brazen serpent*, isolated on the mountain, *did not a little resemble the god Esculapius* in the temple of Epidaurus, holding a stick in one hand and a serpent in the other, with a dog at his feet; that the cherubim, displaying their wings over the ark, *were not unlike the sphinx* with the woman's head, the tour claws, body, and tail of a lion; that *the twelve oxen standing under the brazen sea*, and bearing that enormous vessel, twelve cubits in breadth and five in height, filled with water for the ablutions of the Israelites, bore a strong resemblance to the god Apis, or to the ox elevated on the Altar and beholding all Egypt at its feet.[4]

His Highness concludes, that Moses appeared to have introduced among the Jews many ceremo-

---

4   *Ibid.* 1 Nov. 1766.

nies which he had taken from the Egyptians.[5] The historian will at least remark, that it would have been easy for the conspirators to have undeceived an adept who sought only to be instructed. While we lament his Highness having been the dupe to such masters, we are in justice obliged to show how frankly he sought the truth, when he continues writing to Voltaire:

> As to what regards the New Testament, there are stories in it, of which *I should wish to be better informed.* I cannot understand the massacre of the innocents. How could King Herod have ordered all those infants to be slain, not having the power of life and death, as we see in the history of the Passion, where we find it was Pontius Pilate, governor of the Romans, who condemned Jesus Christ to death.[6]

Had he referred to the proper sources of history, had he consulted any other but that professor of history which d'Alembert had given him, or any other masters than those vain Sophisters, this prince, who wished for and deserved better information, would have seen this slight difficulty vanish from before his eyes. He would have learned, that Herod of *Ascalon*, surnamed the *Great*, and who might have been more properly called the ferocious, he who ordered the massacre of the innocents, was king of all Judea and of Jerusalem,

---

5   *Ibid.*

6   *Ibid.*

and is not the person mentioned in the Passion. He would have further learned, that the latter was Herod *Antipas*, who had only been able to obtain of the Romans one-third part of his father's dominions, and being simply Tetrarch of Galilee, had not the same power over the other provinces. Hence there can be little room for surprise at his not exercising the power of life and death in Jerusalem, though we see Pilate inviting him to exercise that right by sending Jesus Christ before him, as he had before tried and sentenced St. John the Baptist.

As to the ferocious Herod of *Ascalon*, his Highness would have learned, that this prototype of Nero had caused the infants at Bethlehem to be slain by the same power with which he had murdered Aristobulus and Hircanus, the one the brother, the other an octagenarian, and grand-father to the queen; by the same power also did he put to death Mariamne his queen and her two children; Sohemus his confidant, and numbers of his friends and nobles of his court, who had the misfortune to displease him. Reading of these numerous murders, of such unheard-of tyranny, and particularly that this Herod of *Ascalon*, on the point of death, and fearing lest the day of his decease should prove a day of public rejoicing, had caused all the chiefs of the Jews to be shut up in the Circus, commanding they should be massacred at the moment he himself expired; such lectures, I say, could have left little doubt in the mind of the illustrious adept, whether this Herod exercised the right of life and death. He would not then have suspected the Evangelists of forging a fact like that of the massacre of the innocents; a fact so recent, that many Jews then living had been witnesses to it. He would have reflected, that impostors would discovered, or in so public a manner shamed; and all his objections against this massacre of the innocents would not have availed against his faith in the Gospel.

But he was nurtured in the same objections with his master; he studied the sacred writ through the same medium; and Voltaire, who had fallen into thousands of the grossest errors on those sacred writings, carefully avoided referring his disciples to those answers which he had received from the religious writers.[7]

Though we blend these slight discussions with our memoirs, we will not add to the bitterness with which so many princes, who have been seduced by these impious chiefs of the Sophisters, now reproach themselves. We will not say to them,

> With what strange blindness were you smitten? It was your duty to study the sacred writings, to learn how to become better, and to render your subjects more happy; and you have debased yourselves by entering the lists with the conspirators, that like them you may dispute against Christ and his prophets. If doubts arise on religion, why appeal to those who have sworn its ruin. The day will come when the God of the

---

7   See the errors of Voltaire in the Letters of some Portuguese Jews.

> Christians shall raise doubts on your rights, and
> will refer your subjects to the Jacobins for their
> solution. They are in your dominions, seated in
> your palaces ready to applaud, as Voltaire did,
> your objections against Christ and his prophets.
> Answer to their sword the objections they make
> to your laws.

Let us forbear these reflections; let us simply remark, as history must, how very unfortunate these
princes must have been, who, seeking instruction,
had applied to men whose sole object was to make
them efficient to the destruction of the Altar, as the
first step towards the overthrow of their thrones.

In the number of the protecting adepts history will find itself necessitated to insert the names
of many princes whose states at this present moment feel the sweets of this new Philosophy. In the
account given by d'Alembert to Voltaire of those
foreign princes who would not travel through
France without doing homage to the conspiring
Sophisters, we see him extol the *Prince of Brunswick* as deserving *the kindest welcome*, and particularly so, when put in competition with the
Prince of Deux Ponts, who only protects *Fréron
and such like rabble*, that is to say religious authors.[8] The Jacobin army at this day proves which
of those two princes was most mistaken in his protection. It will be still better seen when in these
memoirs we come to treat of the last and deepest
conspiracy of the Jacobins.

The Prince of Brunswick.

---

8   From d'Alembert, 25 June, 1766, vol. 68, let. 185, p. 396.

Louis Eugene, Duke, and Louis, Prince of Wirtemberg.

Charles Theodore, Elector Palatine.

The Princess Anhalt-Zerbst.

To this prince we must add *Louis Eugene, Duke of Wirtemberg*,[9] and *Louis, Prince of Wirtemberg*, who both equally gloried in the lessons they received from Voltaire. The former writes to him, "When at Ferney I think myself a greater philosopher than Socrates himself."[10] The latter, not content with encomiums on the premier chief, petitions for the most licentious and the most impious work Voltaire had ever penned, I mean the poem of Joan d'Arc, or *The Maid of Orléans.*

Charles Theodore, Elector Palatine, would at one time solicit the impious Sophister for the same master-piece of obscenity, or for philosophic lectures; at another, he would press and conjure him to repair to Manheim, that he might there receive his lectures anew.[11]

Even those adepts who, through modesty, should have shrunk back at the very name of such a production, even the *Princess Anhalt-Zerbst*, sends thanks to the author, who had been impudent enough to send her a present more worthy of Aretino.[12]

The historian cannot but remark the eagerness of these mighty adepts for so profligate a work, as

---

9   An old spelling of Wüttemberg. —Ed.

10 From Duke of Wirtemberg, 1 Feb. 1763, vol. 66, let. 43, p. 380.

11 The 20 Oct. and 29 Dec. 1754, vol. 67, let. 15 and 16, p. 336-7.

12 From the Princess Anhalt-Zerbst, 25 May 1751, vol. 67, let. 9, p. 329, and April 1762, let. 35, p. 360. [The English translation has 'Aretine' here, but the French has 'l'Aretin', meaning, Pierre l'Arétin, which is what Pietro Aretino is known as in France. Besides a playwright and poet, Aretino was an infamous satirist and blackmailer. Nashe described him as '. . .

an awful testimony what charms depravity of morals gave to the productions of the Sophisters. The empire of the conspirators will cause less surprise when we reflect how prevalent their Sophisms became over the mind when they had once tainted and perverted the heart. This is a reflection we reluctantly make; but it is too apposite to the history of Philosophism, and to the cause and progress of the Antichristian Conspiracy, to be suppressed. We know the reverence due to great names, but we cannot on that consideration conceal the truth. Let those look to it whose shame is brought to the light; while longer to conceal it would be to betray at once their own interests, that of their people, the safety of their thrones, and that of the Altar.

Her Highness Wilhelmina, *Margravine of Bareith*, ranking among the protecting adepts, affords to the historian the opportunity of laying open a new cause of the progress of the Antichristian Sophisters, of the weight they acquired from the vanity of their school, and from their pretensions to a superiority of light above the vulgar. Wilhelmina, Margravine of Bareith.

It is far from being the lot of all men to argue with equal success on religious or philosophical topics. Without being wanting in the respect due to that precious half of mankind, we may observe in general, I think, that women are not born with minds congenial with philosophy, metaphysics,

___

one of the wittiest knaves that ever God made'. Milton referred to him as 'that notorious ribald of Arezzo'. —Ed.]

or divinity. Nature has compensated this want of research and meditation by the art of embellishing virtue by that sweetness and vivacity of sentiment which often proves a surer guide than all our reasonings. They do the good peculiarly allotted to them better than we do.—Their homes, their children, are their real empires, that of their lessons lie in the charm of example, more efficacious than all our syllogisms. But the female Sophister, philosophizing like a man, is either a prodigy or a monster; and prodigies are not common. The daughter of Necker, the wife of Roland, as well as Mesdames du Deffant, d'Espinasse,[13] Geoffrin, and such like Parisian adepts, in spite of all their pretensions to wit, can lay no claim to the exception. If the reader is indignant when he finds the name of the Margravine of Bareith on the same line, let his indignation fall upon the man who inspired her with such pretensions. Let an opinion be formed of the masters, by the tone she assumed with them to insure their approbation. The following is a specimen of the style of this illlustrious adept, aping the principles and the jests of Voltaire, in order to captivate his approbation at the expence of St. Paul.

> Sister Guillemetta to Brother Voltaire, greetings.—I received your consoling epistle. I swear

---

13   Barruel seems to be referring to Jeanne Julie Éléonore de Lespinasse (1732 - 1773) who, after living in Madame Deffant's apartments, where the latter held a fashionable salon, set up her own rival salon in Paris after her older hostess grew jealous of her increasing influence. —Ed.

by my favorite oath, that it has edified me infinitely more than that of St. Paul to Dame Elect. The latter threw me into a certain drowsiness that had the effect of opium, and hindered me from perceiving the beauties of it. Yours had a contrary effect; it drew me from my lethargy, and put all my vital spirits in motion again.[14]

We have no knowledge of any Epistle of St. Paul to Dame Elect; but Sister Guillemetta, like Voltaire, burlesquing what she had, as well as what she had not read, means no doubt to speak of St. John's Epistle to Electa. This contains no other compliment but that of an apostle applauding the piety of a mother, who rears her children in the way of life, exhorting her charity, and guarding her against the discourse and schools of seducers. It is rather unfortunate, that such lessons should have been opium for the illustrious adept. It is probable that Voltaire would have found a dose in the following letter, had it come from any other hand but that of Sister Guillemetta. We will however copy it, as making an epoch in the annals of Philosophism. We shall see in it the female adept attempting to give lessons to Voltaire himself, anticipating Helvétius by mere dint of genius, and without perceiving it copying Epicurus. Before she commences, Sister Guillemetta assures Voltaire of the friendship of the Margrave, and had carefully invoked the *Genius of Bayle*.[15] One day she thought

---

14   25 Dec. 1751, vol. 66, let. 7, p. 322.
15   12 Juin, 1752, vol. 66, let. 12, p. 330.

herself inspired with the whole of it, and immediately writes to *Brother Voltaire*,

> God, you say (in the Poem of the Law of Nature), has bestowed on all men justice and conscience to warn them, as he has given them all what is needful. As God has bestowed on man justice and conscience, these two virtues must be innate in man, and become an attribute of his existence. Hence it necessarily follows, that man must act in consequence, and that he cannot be just or unjust, or without remorse, being unable to combat an instinct annexed to his essence. Experience proves the contrary. If justice was an attribute of our being, chicane would be banished. Your counsellors in Parliament would not lose their time as they do, in disturbing all France about a morsel of bread given or not. The Jesuits and the Jansenists would equally confess their ignorance in point of doctrine . . . Virtue is barely accidental . . . Aversion to pain and love of pleasure have induced men to become just—Disorder can beget nothing but pain. Quiet is the parent of pleasure, I have made the human heart my particular study, and I draw my conclusions on what has been, from what I see.[16]

There is extant a play intitled, *Divinity dwindled into a Distaff*. This letter of her Highness the Margravine of Bareith, dwindled into Sister Guillemetta, may perhaps furnish the same idea for Philosophy. But, consigning over the female

---

16   1 Nov. 1752, vol. 66, let. 13, p. 331.

Socrates to the Molières of the day, the historian will draw from the errors of this female adept a more serious lesson on the progress of the Antichristian Conspiracy. He will behold a new cause in the mortifying limits of the human intellect, and the vanity of its pretensions, which in certain adepts seem precisely to expand itself, in as much as nature had, from the weakness of their understanding, seemed naturally to insinuate modesty and humility.

Sister Guillemetta fears for liberty, if it be true that God has given to man a conscience, the necessary sense of right and wrong. She was ignorant then, that man, with the eyes that God has given him to see and know his road, is nevertheless free to go where he pleases. She has made a particular study of the human heart, and she has not learned, that man often sees what is best, but will do the worst! She thinks herself in the School of Socrates; and, with Epicurus, she only *sees the aversion of pain and the love of pleasure*, as the principle of justice and virtue. She tells us, in short, probably without even perceiving it, that if chicane is not banished, it is because our attorneys have not a sufficient aversion to indigence; that if our vestals are not all chaste, it is because they do not sufficiently love pleasure; and after that, in presence of *her Highness*, Parliaments, Jesuits, Jansenists, and undoubtedly the whole Sorbonne, with the whole faculty of divinity, must confess their ignorance *in point of doctrine.*

Frederick William, Prince of Prussia.

With more genius, but less confidence in his own lights, Frederick William, Prince Royal of Prussia, presents us with quite another species of adept. Indefatigable in the field of victory, he dares not answer for himself: he knows what he could wish to believe, but not what he ought to believe; he fears to lose himself in reasoning. His soul repeats that he must be immortal; he fears her voice misleads him, and Voltaire is to decide for him. When in the field of Mars, he has the confidence and activity of a hero; but when he is to reflect on futurity, he has all the modesty and the humility of a disciple, almost the unconcern of a sceptic. The authority of his master is to save him the trouble of research, and that master is Voltaire.

> Since I have taken the liberty of conversing with you, he respectuously writes, suffer me to ask, for my own instruction only, whether as you advance in years you find no alteration necessary in your ideas on the nature of the soul—I don't like to bewilder myself in metaphysical reasonings; but I could wish not to die entirely, and that such a genius as yours were not to be annihilated.[17]

Like a man who can assume every tone, Voltaire answered,

> The King of Prussia's family is much in the right, not to consent to the annihilation of his

17   12 Nov. 1770, vol. 66, let. 69, p. 416.

soul. - - - It is tue, that it is not well known what a soul is, as nobody has ever seen one. All that we know is, that the eternal Master of nature has endowed us with the faculty of feeling and knowing virtue. That this faculty survives us after our death, is not demonstrated; but then the contrary is not better proved. - - - There are none but quacks who pretend to be certain; we know nothing of the first principles. Doubt is not an agreeable state, but certainty is a ridiculous one.[18]

I know not what effect this letter had on the serene and respectful disciple; but we see the premier chief varying his means of power over his princely adepts, as much as he did over the citizens of Haarlem. When the King, Frederick, wrote to him in so resolute a tone, *man once dead, there is nothing left*; he takes care not to reply, that certainty is a *ridiculous state*, that *quacks only are certain*. No; Frederick, King of Prussia, is always the first of philosophic kings.[19] And a week after, Frederick, Prince Royal, only wishes to be confirmed on the immortality of his soul; then it is, that, notwithstanding all the troubles and disquietudes of Scepticism, the dubitation of the sceptic is the only rational state for the tme Philosopher. Such a state will suffice, as he then beholds his adepts no longer belonging to the religion of Christ, and that

18   28 Nov. 1770, vol. 66, let. 70, p. 417.
19   From Frederick, 30 Oct. 1770, vol. 65, let. 180, p. 429, and to Fred. 21 Nov. 1770, p. 433.

is sufficient for his plans. He will leave the king materialist, and resolute in his opinions, notwithstanding his own irresolution and uncertainty, by encomiums and admiration. He leaves Eugene of Wirtemberg in astonishment at the master he coincides with in opinion. Wilhelmina of Bareith, more daring than her master, is permitted to argue. He cuts short, and threatens with ridicule and quackery, the humble adept who seeks to reclaim and allay the ire of his master. To one he dictates his principles; to another he peremptorily declares that man is condemned to the total ignorace of the *first principles*; and he is not the less the idol of the astonished Princes. He does not the less transform them into the protectors of his school and of the conspirators; and such is the success with which he flatters himself, that, writing to his dear Count d'Argental, he says, "AT PRESENT THERE IS NOT A GERMAN PRINCE WHO IS NOT A PHILOSOPHER;"[20] that is to say, the Philosophist of impiety! There certainly are exceptions to be made from such an assertion; but it will prove at least how much these abettors of impiety flattered themselves with the progress they were making among sovereigns and princes,—and to whom impiety was one day to prove so fatal!

---

20 To the Count d'Argental, 26 Sept. 1766, vol. 59, let. 270, p. 480; and this is written as a proof of the great success the distribution of bad books had had in that unfortunate country.— See above, Page 69.

Third Class of Protectors.— Ministers, Noblemen and Magistrates.

I t was in France that Philosophism had taken all the forms of a true Conspiracy; and it was in France also, that it had made its greatest ravages among the rich and powerful. It had not gained the throne of Bourbon as it had many of the northern thrones; but it would be in vain for history to dissimulate, that Louis XV., without being of the Conspiracy, powerfully helped the Antichristian Conspirators. He never had the misfortune of losing his faith; he even loved religion; but during the last thirty-five years of his life, he so little practised it, the dissoluteness of his morals and the public triumph of his courtezans answered so little to the title of His Most Christian Majesty, that he might almost as well have been a disciple of Mahomet.

Sovereigns are not sufficiently aware of the evils they draw on themselves by swerving from morality. Some have supported religion only as a curb on their subjects; but woe be to them who only view it in that light. In vain shall they preserve its tenets in their hearts; it is their example that must uphold it. Next to the example of the clergy, that of kings is the most necessary to restrain the people. When religion is used only as a policy, the vilest of the populace will soon perceive it; they will look upon it as a weapon used against them, and sooner or later they will break it, and your power vanishes. If without morals you pretend to religion, the people will also think themselves religious in their profligacy; and how often has it been repeated, that laws without morals are a mere phantom? But the day will come when the people, thinking themselves more consequent, will throw aside both morals and tenets, and then where shall be your curb?

Such were the discourses often held by the Christian orators in presence of Louis XV. He without morals was soon surrounded by ministers destitute of faith, who could have seldomer deceived him, had his love for religion been stimulated by practice. After the death of the Cardinal de Fleury some are to be found, the Marechal de Belle-Isle and Mr. de Bertin for example, who are not to be confounded in that class of adepts;

but then we successively find near his person Mr. Amelot in the foreign department, Mr. d'Argenson in the same; the Duke de Choiseul, de Praslin and Mr. de Malesherbes, also the Marquise de Pompadour as long as she lived, and all these were intimately connected with Voltaire, and initiated in his Conspiracy. We have seen him make application to *Mr. Amelot* on the destruction of the clergy. This minister had sufficient confidence in Voltaire to intrust him with a secret and important mission to the King of Prussia; and Voltaire, in return, does not conceal from him the use he had made of his mission against the church. He confided no less in that *Duke de Praslin,* to whom he had sent his memorial on the tithes, in hopes of depriving the clergy of the greatest part of their sustenance.[1] This confidence from the premier chief sufficiently denotes the sentiments of those men to whom he sent his plans for execution.

Mr. Amelot.

Duke de Praslin.

A minister whose assiduity in corresponding with Voltaire indicates more clearly their perfect coincidence with each other, was the *Marquis d'Argenson,* whom we have already noticed tracing the plan for the destruction of the religious orders. It was he who first protected Voltaire at Court and with the Marquise de Pompadour; he was also one of the most impious of his disciples; and to him it is that Voltaire writes constantly, as to one of the adepts with whom he was most intimate. In fact, he appears more resolute in his antireligious opin-

Marquis d'Argenson.

---

1   To Count d'Argental, 20 June, 1764, vol. 58, let. 130, p. 243.

ions than his master; his Philosophism coincided more with that of the King of Prussia's; for he was also convinced that he was not two-fold, and that he had nothing to fear or hope for, when once his body should rest in eternal sleep.[2]

Duke de Choiseul. More zealous for the reign of impiety, and more active than the Marquis d'Argenson, the *Duke de Choiseul* better knew and more powerfully seconded the secrets of Voltaire. We have already seen him extolling this great protector in his quarrels with the Sorbonne; we have already seen why this Duke, adopting and pressing the execution of d'Argenson's plans against the religious orders, began by that of the Jesuits. It would be useless to dwell long on this minister; his impiety is too well authenticated.

Malesherbes before the revolution. Thus did this series of Antichristian ministers partially anticipate the Jacobins in the overthrow of the Altar. It was to the man who was one day to see that very revolution in all its horrors, and at length fall a victim to it, that these impious chiefs pay their greatest homage; it was to him they were chiefly indebted: and this protector of the Conspiracy against his God, was *Malesherbes*. This name, I am aware, will recal to mind many moral virtues, it will recal his benevolence when alleviating the rigor of the prisons, when remedying the abuse of the *Lettres de Cachet*; but France shall, nevertheless, demand of him her temples that have been

---

2   See, in the General Correspondence, the letters of Mr. d'Argenson.

destroyed; for it was he who above all other ministers abused his authority to establish the reign of impiety in France. d'Alembert, who knew him well, always vouches for his reluctantly executing the *superior orders* issued in favor of religion, and for his favoring Philosophism whenever circumstances would permit; and unfortunately he knew but too well how to avail himself of circumstances. By his office he particularly presided over the laws relative to the press; but with a single word he effaced all distinctions in books, whether impious, religious, or seditious; he declared them all the be a *mere object of commerce.*

Let politicians of other nations argue on the liberty of the press in consequence of what experience has taught them in their own countries; but it is an incontrovertible fact, that France owes the misfortunes of the revolution to the great abuse of the press, and to an actual inundation of bad books at first only impious, but latterly both impious and seditious. There were also many causes peculiar to France which rendered the abuse of the press more fatal than elsewhere.

Liberty of the press dangerous in France.

Without pretending to raise the merit of the French writers, it may be observed (and I have often heard foreigners repeat it) that there is a certain clearness, process, and method, peculiar to them, which by putting our French books more within the reach of the generality of readers, makes them in some sort more popular and thence more dangerous when bad.

Our frivolousness may be a failing; but that failing made a book more sought for in France than would the profoundest meditations of an Englishman. Neither truth nor error could please a Frenchman when latent; he likes to see clearly; epigram, sarcasm, and all what may be called wit, is what he delights in. Even blasphemy, elegantly spoken, will not displease a nation unhappily gifted with the talent of laughing on the most serious subjects, and who will pardon every failing in him who can divert them. It was to this unfortunate taste that the impious writings of Voltaire owed their chief success.

Whatever may be the reason, the English also have their books against the Christian religion; they have their Collins, their Hobbes, their Woolstons, and many others, among whom is to be found, in substance, all that our French Sophisters have only repeated after their way, that is to say, with that art which adapts every thing to the most vulgar minds. In England Hobbes and Collins are almost forgotten or unknown. Bolingbroke and other authors of the same class are little read, though of greater merit as literary men, by a people who knows how to occupy itself with other things. In France, from the idle Marquis or Countess to the attorney's clerk, or even to the petty citizen, who had far other occupations, these impious productions, and particularly Voltaire's, were not only read, but each would have his opinion, and criticise every new publication of the sort. The French, in general, were great readers, and every citizen would have his library. Thus in Paris a bookseller was sure of selling as many copies of the most pitiful performance, as are generally sold in London of a work of no small merit.

In France an author was as passionately cried up as a fashion; the Englishman, who deigns to read his work, passes judgment on it and remains unconcerned. Can this arise from good sense or indifference, or may it not be a mixture of both. Notwithstanding all the benefactions received from the English, I will not pronounce; neither flattery nor criticism is within my sphere; but an undoubted fact, and which ought to have taught Malesherbes, is, that in France, still less than elsewhere, a book either impious or seditious never could be looked upon as a mere article of commerce. The greater readers and arguers, and the more volatile the French people were, the more the minister superintending the press should have enforced the laws enacted to repress the licentiousness of it, which, on the contrary, he favored with all his power. His condemnation is recorded in the encomiums of the conspirators; it was he, they said, who *broke the shackles of literature.*[3]

In vain would it be objected, that the minister left the same liberty to the religious writers. In the first place, that was not always true, it was much against his will that he suffered works refuting

---

3   To d'Alembert, 30 Jan. 1764, vol. 68, let. 128, p. 278.

the Sophisters to appear;[4] and what a minister allows with reluctance, he finds abundant means of preventing. Could a minister be innocent, when letting a poison infuse itself throughout the public, under pretext that he did not forbid the sale of the antidote? Moreover, however well written a religious work may be, it has not the passions to second it; much more talent is required to make such a performance palatable. Any fool may attract the people to the theatre, but the eloquence of a Chrysostom is necessary to tear them from it. With equal talent, he who pleads for licence and impiety will carry more weight than the most eloquent orator who vindicates the rights of virtue and morality. The religious apologist requires a serious and an attentive reading, with a stedfast desire of finding the truth, and such a study fatigues; whereas, depravity requires none; in a word, it is far more easy to irritate and throw the people into revolt, than to appease them when once put in motion.

Malesherbes during the revolution.

At length *Malesherbes*, seeing the revolution consummated in the death of Louis XVI. gave signs of a tardy repentance. His zeal in that moment did not hinder men who had deeply felt his fault from exclaiming,

> Officious defender, cease to plead for that king you yourself betrayed; it is too late. Cease to accuse that legion of regicides who demand his

---

4   To d'Alembert, 8 Feb. 1757, vol. 68, let. 24, p. 43.

head; Robespierre is not his first executioner;
it was you that long since prepared his scaffold,
when you suffered those impious works that
called the people to the destruction of the Altar and of the throne to be openly displayed and
sold in the porticos of his palace. That unfortunate prince confided in you; he had imparted
his authority to you to repress the impious and
seditious writers, and you permitted the people
to inhale blasphemy and hatred of kings from
a Raynal, an Helvétius, or a Diderot, and you
pretended only a wish to encourage commerce.
If then, at the present day, this people, in the
frantic crisis of those poisons which you have
circulated in their veins, call aloud for the head
of Louis XVI. it is too late to make a parade of
his defence, or to criminate the Jacobins.

Men of meditation and reflection had long since
foreseen the reproach that history would one day
make to Malesherbes. They never passed the gal-
leries of the Louvre, without exclaiming in the bitterness of their souls. *Unfortunate Louis XVI.! It
is thus that you are sold at the gates of your own
palace!*

Malesherbes at length leaving the ministry,
overpowered by the reclamations of the friends of
religion, his successors undertook or pretended to
undertake, to enforce the former laws. But soon,
under the title of *Fables*, the Sophisters sought to
spread their poison anew; and, charmed with their
success, d'Alembert writes to Voltaire, "The luck of
it is, that these fables, far superior to Æsop's, are

sold here (at Paris) pretty freely. I begin to think the trade (ot bookselling) will have lost nothing by the retreat of Mr. de Malesherbes."[5] It in truth lost so little, that the writers in defence of the Altar and the throne were the only ones thwarted in their publication.[6]

Meanwhile the conspirators carefully calculated their successes with ministry. At the period when Louis XVI. ascended the throne, they were so great, that Voltaire, writing to Frederick, expresses his hopes in the following terms:

> I know not whether our young king will walk in your footsteps; but I know that he has taken *philosophers for his ministers*, all except one, who is unfortunately a bigot . . . . There is Mr. Turgot, who is worthy of your Majesty's

5 From d'Alembert, 8 Dec. 1763, vol. 68, let. 121, Page 259.

6 We know of several excellent works which never could gain admission into France. Such was the case with Feller's PHILOSOPHICAL CATECHISM, because it contains an excellent refutation of the systems of the day. We are acquainted with several authors, and we might cite ourselves, to whom greater severity was shown than the law could countenance, whilst it was openly transgressed in favor of the conspirators. Mr. Lourdet, of the Royal College, the censor of our Helvian letters, needed all his resolution and firmness to maintain his prerogative and ours, by publishing that work which the Sophisters would fain have suppressed, and that before the first volume was half printed. The same censor invoked in vain the power of the laws to stop the publication of Raynal's works. That seditious writer had daringly presented his pretended PHILOSOPHIC HISTORY to the censor, and, instead of the probate, he received the reproaches of just indignation. In spite of censure or laws, however his work appeared the next day, and was exposed for public sale.

conversation. The priests are in despair. THIS IS
THE COMMENCEMENT OF A GREAT REVOLUTION.[7]

Voltaire, in this, is correct to the full extent of the term. I remember, in those days, to have seen venerable ecclesiastics bewailing the death of Louis XV. while all France, and myself among others, were in expectation of better days. They would say, the king we have lost had indeed many failings, but he that succeeds is very young, and has many dangers to encounter. They foresaw that same revolution which Voltaire foretels to Frederick, and in the anguish of their hearts they shed tears over it. But let not the historian blame the young prince for the unhappy choice in which Voltaire so much exults. Louis XVI., to succeed the better in this choice, had done all that diffidence in his own abilities, or that the love of his subjects or of religion, could suggest. This we see by the deference he paid to the last advice he received from his father, from that Dauphin whose virtues had long been the admiration of France, and whose death plunged it into universal mourning. This is again to be seen in the eagerness with which Louis XVI. called to the ministry that man, who, in Voltaire's language, was unfortunately a bigot. This was the *Mareschal de Muy*. When the historian shall discover the throne surrounded by so many perfidious agents of its authority, let him remember to avenge piety and Christian fervor, courage, and fidelity, in

The Mareschal de Muy to be excepted.

---

7   To Frederick, 3 Aug. 1775, vol. 66, let. 94, p. 219.

short, all the virtues of a true citizen, when he shall treat of the memory of this Mareschal. Mr. de Muy had been the companion and bosom friend of the Dauphin, father of Louis XVI., and such a friendship is more than an equivalent for the scurrilous abuse of Voltaire. The Mareschal de Saxe was soliciting, for one whom he protected, the place of companion (*menin*) to the young prince. On being told that it was intended for Mr. de Muy, he replied, *I will not do Mr. Le Dauphin the injury of depriving him of the company of so virtuous a man as the Chevalier de Muy, who may, hereafter, be of great service to France.* Let posterity appreciate such a commendation; and O that the Sophister could but hear and blush!

Mr. de Muy was the man who bore the greatest resemblance to the Dauphin who loved him. In him were to be found the same regularity and amenity of manners, the same beneficence, the same disinterested zeal for religion and the public welfare. It was through his means that the prince, unable to visit the provinces in person, was acquainted with the misfortunes and grievances of the people; he sent him to examine their situations, and they were occupied together in seeking those remedies which the prince's premature death, alas! hindered from being carried into execution. When, during the war, Mr. de Muy was called upon to give proofs of his fidelity in the victorious fields of Crevelt and Warbourg, the Dauphin would daily offer the following prayer for his safety: "My God, may thy sword defend, may thy shield protect the Count Felix de Muy, to the end, that if ever thou makest me bear the heavy burthen of a crown, he may support me by his virtue, his counsels, and his example."

When the God of vengeance inflicted on France with its first scourge, when the hand of death had struck the Dauphin, Mr. de Muy by his bedside, bathed in the tears of friendship, hears the prince, in a voice that might rend the heart asunder, pronounce these last words:

> Do not abandon yourself to sorrow. Preserve yourself, to serve my children. Your knowledge, your virtues will be necessary to them. Be for them, what you would have been to me. Bestow on my memory that mark of kindness; but above all, let not their youth, during which God grant them his protection, keep you at a distance from them.

Louis XVI. ascending the throne, recalled these words to Mr. de Muy, conjuring him to accept of the ministry. Though he had refused it in the preceding reign, he could not withstand the entreaties of the son of his departed friend. To a court universally assaulted by impiety, he taught that the Christian hero would, in no situation, be ashamed of his God.

When he commanded in Flanders he had the honor of receiving the Duke of Gloucester, brother to the King of England, at a time when the Catholic church commands abstinence from meat. True to his duty, he conducted the Duke to his table, saying,

> My religion is strictly observed in my house; had I ever the misfortune to infringe that law, I should more carefully observe it on a day when I have so illustrious a prince, for a witness and censor of my conduct. The English punctually follow their religion; out of respect for your Royal Highness, I will not exhibit the scandal of a loose Catholic, who in your presence could dare to violate his.

If so much religion, in the eyes of Philosophism, is only unfortunately being a bigot, let it look to the thousands of unhappy creatures that religion relieved by the hands of Mr. de Muy. Let it behold the soldiery, rather led by his example than by the laws of courage and discipline. Let it learn, that the province in which he commanded still gratefully remembers and blesses their former governor, in spite of the revolution, which seems to have tinged the human mind with the black hue of ingratitude.[8]

One of the great misfortunes of Louis XVI. was to lose this virtuous minister at an early period. Maurepas. *Maurepas* was by no means the proper person to replace him in the confidence of the young king. His father even, who mentioned him in his will, had been misled by the aversion this former minister had shown to the Marquise de Pompadour,

---

8   See Mr. Le Tourneur de Tressol, on this Mareschal, also Feller's Hist. Diet.

and his long exile had not wrought the change in him which the Dauphin had supposed. The attention, however, which the young prince paid to the counsels of his father shows how ardently he wished to surround himself with ministers who would promote his views for the good of the people. He might have made a better choice, had he known what had misled the Dauphin. Maurepas was now old and decrepid, but had all the vices of youth. Voltaire transforms him into a philosopher, and he coalesced with the Sect through levity and indolence. He believed in nothing; he was without hatred against the Altar, as without affection for the Sophisters. He would with equal indifference wittily lash a bishop or d'Alembert. He found d'Argenson's plan for the destruction of the religious orders, and he followed it. He would have soon set aside the impious minister, had he known him that would conspire against the religion of the state. An enemy to all convulsions, and without any fixed principles of Christianity, he thought it at least impolitic to attempt its destruction. He certainly was not a man capable of stopping a revolution, but he did not forward it. He rather let others do the harm, than did it himself; but unfortunately that harm which he let others do was great. Under his administration philosophism made a terrible progress. Nothing proves it more clearly than the choice of that Turgot, whose nomination is celebrated by Voltaire as the *beginning of a great revolution.*

The philanthropy of this man has been much extolled; but it was that of a hypocrite, as the reader will be convinced by the following letter from d'Alembert to Voltaire:

> You will soon receive another visit, which I announce to you. It is that of *Mr. de Turgot*, a master of Requests, full of Philosophy, a man of great parts and learning, a great friend of mine, and who wishes to pay you a sly visit. I say sly for *propter metum Judæorum* (for fear of the Jews); we must not brag of it too much, nor you neither.[9]

If at first sight the signification of the fear of the Jews is not understood, d'Alembert will explain it in a second portrait of his friend: "This Turgot," he writes, "is a man of wit, of great learning, and very virtuous; in a word, he is a worthy *Cacouac*, but has good reasons for not showing it too much, for I have learned to my cost, that the *Cacouaquery* (Philosophism) is not the road to fortune, and he deserves to make his."[10]

Voltaire had an interview with Turgot, and formed so true a judgment of him, that he answers, "If you have many sages of that stamp in your Sect, I fear for the *wretch, she* is lost to good company."[11]

To every man who understands the encomiums of Voltaire to d'Alembert, this is as much as to say,

---

9   From d'Alembert, 22 Sept. 1760, vol. 68, let. 74, p. 136.

10   From d'Alembert, 18 Oct. 1760, let. 76, p. 141.

11   To d'Alembert, 17 Nov. 1760, vol. 68, let. 77, p. 144.

Turgot is a secret adept, he is an ambitious hypocrite, and will at once be a traitor to his God, his
king, and his country: but by us, he is called virtuous; he is a conspirator of the true stamp, necessary to compass the overthrow of Christianity. Had
Voltaire or d'Alembert spoken of an ecclesiastic,
or a religious writer, who had only the virtues of a
Turgot, what a monster we should have seen arise
from his pen. Let the impartial historian examine
and lay aside these usurped reputations of virtue;
let him say with truth, that Turgot, rich, above the
common rank of citizens, and still aiming at dignities and further fortune, cannot be called a real
Philosopher. Turgot being the adept of the conspiring Sophisters, and a master of requests, is
already perjured. He will be far more so when he
arrives at the ministry. For by the standing laws
of the state, he could only enjoy these dignities by
affirming, both by himself and others, his fidelity
to the king, to religion, and to the state. He had
already betrayed religion and the state, and he will
soon betray his king. He belonged to that Sect of
Œconomists who detested the French monarchy,
and only endured a king, in order to treat him as
did the first rebels of the revolution.

At length advanced to the ministry by the ca-
bals of the Sect, he uses all his power to inspire the
young king with his disgust for the monarchy, and
with his principles on the authority of a throne he
had sworn to maintain as minister. He would willingly have transformed him into a Jacobin king.

He first insinuates those errors which are one day to throw the sceptre into the hands of the people, and overturn the Altar and the throne; if such are the virtues of a minister, they are those of a treacherous one; if errors of the mind, they are those of a madman. Nature had endowed him with the desire of relieving his fellow-creatures. He heard the declamations of the Sophisters against the remains of the feudal system, under which the people still labored; and what with the Sophisters a mere sign of their hatred for kings, he mistook for the cry of compassion. He was blind to what all the world saw, and that particularly on the Corvées. He would not hearken to the voice of history, which told him that the shackles of the feudal system had as yet been only broken by the wisdom and mature deliberation of the monarch, foreseeing the inconveniences and the means of covering the losses of the suppression. But he would be hasty, and he ruined every thing. The Sophisters thought his dismission was too early; but, alas! it was not early enough; for he had already tainted the throne with those revolutionary ideas on the sovereignty of the people; he had then forgotten that this was making all power dependant on their caprice; he pretended to make the people happy by placing arms in their hands, with which they destroyed themselves. He thought to re-establish the laws in all their purity, and he only taught rebellion; he misleads the youthful monarch, too inexperienced to unravel the sophisms of the Sect; and the very goodness of his heart leads him still more astray. In the pretended rights of the people, he only sees his own to be sacrificed; and it is from Turgot that we may trace that fatal error of his insurmountable patience and fatal condescension with that people whose sovereignty led to the scaffold himself, his queen, and his sister.

Turgot is the first minister who shows that revolutionary spirit at once antichristian and antimonarchial. Choiseul and Malesherbes were more impious than Turgot, Choiseul perhaps was even more wicked; but never before had a minister been known seeking to destroy the principles of that authority in the mind of the king which he imparted to him. It was reported, that Turgot had repented on seeing the sovereign mob threatening his person, on seeing them bursting open the magazines of corn, and throwing both corn and bread into the river, and that under pretence of famine. It was then, as reported, that, seeing his errors, he had laid open to Louis XVI. all the plans of the Sophisters, and that these latter ever after sought to destroy the idol they had set up. This anecdote, unfortunately for the honor of Turgot, is unfounded. Before his elevation to the ministry, he was an idol of the conspirators, and such he remained until his death. Condorcet has also been his panegyrist and historian, and he would not have been tolerant on the repentance of an adept.

Scourges have successively fallen on France since the revolution; but prior to it they had succeeded each other in the persons of Louis XVIth's ministers.

Necker appeared after Turgot, and Necker re-appears after Briennes; and his virtues were extolled by the Sophisters nearly as much as he extols them himself. This is another of those reputations which the historian must judge by facts, not for the mere pleasure of detecting the conspiring hypocrite, but because *these unmerited reputations were a means employed* for the consummation of the conspiracy.

Necker.

Necker, when only banker's clerk, was employed by some speculators both as the confidant and agent in a business which was suddenly and greatly to augment their fortunes. They had the secret of an approaching peace, which was considerably to enhance the value of the Canada Bills; one of the conditions of the future peace being, the payment of those bills which had remained in England; they let Necker into the secret, on condition that, for their common emolument, he would write to London to have a number of these bills bought up at the low price to which the war had reduced them. Necker engaged in the association, and, through the credit of his master, the bills were monopolized. His associates returning to know the state of the bargain, he told them that the speculation had appeared so hazardous and bad, that he had desisted from and countermanded the purchase. Peace comes, and Necker is in possession of these bills on his own account alone, and these make near three million Tournois.[12]—Such was the virtue of Necker when a clerk!

Now become rich, he calls the Sophisters to his table; his house becomes a weekly club, and the new Mecænas is well repaid for his good cheer by the encomiums and flattery of his guests. d'Alembert, and the chiefs of the conspirators, punctually attended these assemblies every Friday.[13] Necker hearing of nothing but philosphy, would be a philosopher, as suddenly as he became a lord, and the intrigue and encomiums of the Sect would transform him into a Sully. At length Louis XVI. hearing so much of the talents of this man in finance, called him to the ministry as Comptroller General. Among the many means of the conspirators, the most infallible was to introduce disorder in the finances. Necker succeeded completely in this plan by those exhorbitant loans which nothing could have hidden from the public, but that blind confidence and those encomiums perpetually thrown out by the Sect.—But supposing Necker to have acted from the impulse of the conspirators, like an ignorant minister who knew not whither he was driven, or deliberately hollowed out the abyss, it is not his pretended virtue that is to plead his

---

12 At the time, the livre tournois, was defined as 4.50516 grammes of silver. —Ed.

13 *Vous qui chez la belle Hippatie* (*Mad. Necker*)
Tous les vendredis raisonnez
De virtu, de Philosophic, &c.
To d'Alembert, 21 June 1770, vol. 69, let. 31, p. 59.

defence. Is it not probable that the man who, when recalled for the second time to the ministry, could dare to starve the people in the midst of plenty in order to convulse them into a revolution, might also attempt to ruin the finances to produce the same convulsive state? Such a virtue as his may be classed with nearly the blackest guilt.

At the time when Necker was recalled to replace Briennes in the ministry, at the time when his great generosity to the people was cried up, and that all France was stunned with his great feats; at that very time was he, in concert with Philippe d'Orléans, starving the people into revolt against their king, the nobles, and the clergy. This virtuous man had bought up all the corn, had ordered it to be shut up in store-houses, or sent it in barges from one place to another, forbidding the intendants to allow of the sale of any corn, until they had received his orders. The magazines remained shut. The boats wandered from port to port. The people clamorously called for bread, but in vain! The parliament of Rouen, concerned for the state to which the province of Normandy was reduced, desired its president to write to the minister (Necker) to demand the sale of a great quantity of corn which they knew to be then in the province. His letter was not answered. The first president received a second summons from his body, to remonstrate in the most pressing manner on the wants of the people; at length Necker answers, that he has sent his orders to the Intendant. His orders are executed, but the Intendant is obliged, for his own justification, to lay them before the Parliament; and so far were they from what was expected, that they were barely an instruction to put off the sale, and to invent divers pretexts and excuses to elude the demands of the magistrates, and to rid him of their applications. Meanwhile the vessels laden with corn proceeded from the ports to the ocean, from the ocean to the rivers, or simply to the interior of the provinces. At the period when Necker was driven from the ministry for the second time, the people were destitute of bread. The parliament had then obtained proof that the same boats, laden with the same corn, had been from Rouen to Paris, and from Paris back again; then embarked at Rouen for the Havre, and thence returned again half rotten.— The *Attorney General* profited of this second dismission to send circular orders to stop these proceedings, and to give the people the liberty of buying this corn. At the expulsion of this minister, the populace of Paris, stupidly sovereign, ran to arms, and demanded their Necker, carrying his bust through the streets with that of Philippe d'Orléans; and never were two assassins better coupled in their triumph. The populace would have its executioner, which it stupidly stiled its father; and Necker, on his return, starves it anew. Scarce had he heard of the orders which the *Attorney General* of the Parliament of Normandy had given, when the revolutionary agents are sent from Paris, the people are stirred up against the magistrate, his mansion is forced and pillaged, and a price is put upon his head!—Such were the virtues of the adept Necker, when minister and protector of the conspirators.

For the authenticity of these facts the historian will appeal to the chief magistrates of the parliament of Rouen. If, to shew the chief agent of such horrid deeds, I have been obliged to anticipate on the second part of this work; it is because Necker had conspired against the throne, equally as against the Altar. It was through him that the Sophisters were to draw the Calvinists into their party, but though pretending to the faith of Geneva, he was really a Deist. Had not the Calvinists been blind to conviction, they could have seen it in his writings or in his universal connections with the impious; for this empty and vain man aimed at every thing. From a Clerk he became Comptroller-General; next a protecting Sophister, and thence imagined himself a divine. He published is ideas on Religious Opinions; and this work was nothing less than Deism; nor in saying this do I judge severely a work which does not look upon the existence of God as proved; for what can the religion of that man be who doubts of the existence of a God? This work obtained for its author an academic crown, as being the best production of the day; that is to say, that which could insinuate the most impiety in the most perfect disguise.

Briennes.   After what has been said of the minister *Briennes*, the intimate friend of d'Alembert, after the

248

wickedness of this man has been made so public, I should not mention him, had I not to discover a plot, a parallel to which history would blush to show, and none but the annals of the modern Sophisters could produce. Under the name of Œconomists, the conspirators held secret meetings (which we shall hereafer lay open to the public), and impatiently waited the death of Mr. de Beaumont, Archbishop of Paris, to give him a successor, who, entering into their views, and under the pretext of humanity, kindness, and toleration, was as patiently to endure with Philosophism, Jansenism, and all other Sects, as Mr. de Beaumont had strenously opposed them. He was to be particularly indulgent as to the discipline of the parish clergy, even so much so as to let it decay in a few years. On tenets he was to be equally relaxed. He was to repress the zeal of those who appeared too active, to interdict and even to displace them as men too ardent or even turbulent. He was carefully to receive all accusations of this sort, and replace the over-zealous by men whom the Sophisters had prepared and would recommend, particularly for dignitaries.—By this plan the parish churches, hitherto administered by a most edifying clergy, were soon to be overrun by the most scandalous. Sermons and catechistical lectures becoming daily less frequent, all instructions running in the philosophic strain, and bad books daily multiplying, the people seeing in their parishes none but a clergy scandalous in their morals, and little zealous in their doctrine, were naturally inclined to abandon the churches and their religion. The apostacy of the capital was to carry with it that of the most essential diocese; and hence the evil was to spread far around. Thus without violence, *without being perceived*, but solely by the connivance of its chief pastor, religion was to be crashed in the capital; not but that Briennes might have given some exterior signs of zeal, had the circumstances required.[14]

Nothing but the ambition of a Briennes, and the wickedness of his heart, could have made him accept the archbishopric on such conditions.—The agreement made, the Sophisters put all their agents in motion. The court is beset; an artful man, of the name of Vermon, who had been made reader to the queen by Choiseul on the recommendation of Briennes, seized on this opportunity to make some return to his protector. The queen recommended the protector of Vermon, and she thought she was doing well; the king thought he did still better in nominating the man whose moderation, whose prudence, and whose genius, were so perpetual a topic, to the Archbishopric of Paris: and one day Briennes was actually named. But no sooner was it known at court and in Paris, than every Christian shuddered at the news. The king's aunts, and the Princess de Marsan in particular, immediately foresaw the scandal with which France was threatened; and the king, prevailed upon by their prayers, annulled what he had already done. The

14   See hereafter the declaration of Mr. Le Roy.

archbishopric was given to a man whose modesty, zeal, and impartiality would form the strongest contrast with the vices of Briennes. Unfortunately for France, neither the king nor the queen were sufficiently convinced to lose all confidence in the pretended virtues of this man; nor did the conspirators lay all hopes aside of hereafter raising him to a more exalted station.

As the thunder-bolt hidden in the clouds blackened by the tempest, and waiting the convulsion of the heavens to break forth, so did Briennes, from the dark cloud which threatened France, convulsed during the sitting of the Notables called by Calonne, burst forth prime minister. To show his subserviency to the Sophisters, he began by that famous edict which Voltaire had solicited twenty years before in behalf of the Huguenots, though he had looked upon them as *mad* and *raving mad*;[15] that edict so long wished for by d'Alembert, as a means of *duping* the Protestants and of *crushing* Christianity, without its *even being perceived*.[16] Offspring of the tempest, he is at length overpowered by those billows which carried Necker to the helm, and which Necker holds solely to immerse his king, the nobility, and the clergy into that sea of impious sophistry and frantic rage, which the conspirators had created. Briennes died covered with infamy, but without remorse, or sign of repentance.

15　To Marmontel, 2 Dec. 1767, vol. 60, let. 200, p. 336.

16　From d'Alembert, 4 May, 1762, vol. 68, let. 100, p. 202.

**Lam-
oignon.**

By the same intrigue that had carried Briennes to the prime ministry, *Lamoignon*, whose ancestors had been an ornament to the magistracy, obtained the seals. He was notoriously, like many other courtiers, an unbeliever; but he was also one of the conspirators. His name is to be found in their most secret committees. On his disgrace, which soon followed that of Briennes, he *philosophically* shot himself.—Two such men at the head of the ministry! what means had they not of countenancing and forwarding the Antichristian Conspiracy!

**Why so
many
impious
ministers.**

Posterity will find it difficult to conceive that a monarch so religious as Louis XVI. should have been surrounded by such a set of impious ministers. Their surprise will be much lessened, when they consider that the Conspirators aimed mostly at the higher orders of society, and that they wished to destroy religion in those who approached the person of the monarch.[17] To the passions of this privileged class, let the facility of satisfying them be added; and we shall easily conceived with what facility Voltaire could attack a religion that so much militated against those passions. Without doubt, eminent virtues and the most distinguished piety were to be found among the nobility and grandees of the court: for instance, Madame Elizabeth, sister to the king, Mesdames de France, the king's aunts, the Princesses de Conti, Louise

---

17 To Diderot, 25 Sept. 1762, vol. 57, let. 242, p. 475, et passim, to d'Alembert and Damilaville.

de Condé, de Marsan, the Duc de Penthièvre, the Mareschal de Mouchi, de Broglie, and many other distinguished personages who would have done honor to the brightest ages of Christianity. Among the ministers themselves history will except Mr. de Vergennes and Mr. de Saint-Germain, and perhaps some others who could not be challenged by impiety. Throughout the whole class of the nobility these exceptions may be more frequent than might be supposed; but, nevertheless, it is unfortunately true to say, that Voltaire had made surprising progress among the great, and that will easily account for the unhappy choices Louis XVI. had made. Virtue seeks obscurity and is little jealous of elevation. None but the ambitious were foremost on the ranks, and the Sophisters would stun the ill-fated monarch with the praises of those whom they thought would best second their views, and who had been initiated in their mysteries. Not only the throne, but the public itself was to be overpowered by the praises which they lavished on the adept whom they wished to elevate to the ministry. Their intrigues were more secret, and surpassed the art of courtiers themselves; besides, acting under the influence of public opinion, in what way could they not direct the choice of a young prince whose greatest failing was diffidence in his own judgment. By such arts were the Turgots, the Neckers, the Lamoignons, the Briennes successively forced into the councils of Louis XVI.; passing over in silence those subaltern ministers and first clerks, importantly great, whose services the conspiring Sophisters carefully secured.

Thus protected, impiety soared above the laws now almost silenced. It was in vain for the clergy to reclaim the hand of power, for it connived at the Conspirators; their writings were circulated, and their persons secure. Voltaire even writes to d'Alembert, "Thanks to a priest about the court, I should have been undone had it not been for *the Chancellor*, who at all times has shown me the greatest kindness."[18] This shows how little any reclamations of the clergy could avail against the chief of the Conspirators. This letter discovers a new protector of the Sophisters in the person of *Mr. de Meaupou*; his ambition, and his connection with the chief of the Conspirators, had always been hidden under the mask of religion.

In a letter written also to d'Alembert, we see of what immense use such protections were, not only to Voltaire but also to the other adepts. He speaks thus of Choiseul: "I am under the greatest obligations to him. It is to him alone that I owe all the privileges I have on my estate.—Every favor that I have asked *for my friends* he has granted."[19]

Some of these protectors also aimed at being authors, and without Voltaire's talents sought to inspire the people with the same principles. Of this umber was the *Duke d'Ufez*,[20] who, to verify

18   To d'Alembert, 28 Sept. 1774, vol. 69, let. 133, p. 223.

19   To d'Alembert, 1 Nov. 1762, vol. 68, let. 110, p. 228.

20   The author appears to be referring to Charles-Emmanuel de

the expression of Voltaire, that he was stronger in mind than in body, had undertaken a work in favor of Equality and Liberty applied to our belief in matters of faith, without consulting either church or pastor. Voltaire only wished to see it finished to declare the work as useful to society as it was to the Duke himself.[21] This work never appeared; we know not, therefore, how to class the genius of the noble divine.

In Voltaire's letters we find many other great personages, that swell the list of adepts and protectors, and many names already famous in history; such was the descendant of a *Crillon* or a *Prince of Salm*, both worthy of better days, according to Voltaire; but let not the reader mistake them for the age of the Bayards and of those bold knights of former times; no, it is of an age worthy of *their modesty and their philosophic science.*—We see Voltaire placing all his hopes in the Prince of Ligne for the propagation of his sophisticated science throughout Brabant; and the *Duke of Braganza* is as much extolled for the similarity of his sentiments.

Other great personages.

Among the Marquisses, Counts, and Chevaliers, we find the *Marquis d'Argens de Dirac,*[22] a brigadier-general, zealous in the destruction of Christianity in the province of Angoumois, and modern-

---

Crussol, 8e duc d'Uzès, with whom Voltaire maintained correspondence between 1750 and 1761. —Ed.

21 To the Duke d'Usez, 19 Nov. 1760, vol. 56, let. 226, p. 450.

22 See Appendix to Part 3 (The Antisocial Conspiracy). —Ed.

izing his fellow-countrymen with his philosophic ideas; the *Marquis de Rochefort*, colonel of a regiment, who through his Philosophism had gained the friendship of Voltaire and d'Alembert; the *Chevalier Chatellux*, bold but more adroit in the war against Christianity. In fine, were we to credit Voltaire, nearly all those whom he was acquainted with in this class were what (in a letter to Helvétius in 1763) he styles honest men.—"Believe me," he writes, "Europe is full of men of reason, who are opening their eyes to the light. Truly the number is prodigious.—I have not seen for these ten years past a *single honest man*, of whatever country or religion he may have been, *but who absolutely thought as you do.*"[23] It is probable, and it is to be hoped, that Voltaire greatly exaggerated his success. It would be impossible to conceive, that of the numbers of the nobility who went to contemplate the Grand Lama of the Sophisters at Ferney, the greatest part were not attracted by curiosity, rather than impiety. The surest rule by which we may distinguish the true adepts is by the confidence he placed in them, or whether he sent them the productions of his own pen or those of other conspirators; and at that rate the list would greatly extend. Many Duchesses and Marchionesses would be found, as philosophic as Sister Guillemetta. But let them be forgotten, those adepts more dupes than wicked; more unfortunate are they still, if they are above being pitied.

---

23   March, 1763, vol. 58, let. 50, p. 100.

Of these protectors, the *Count d'Argental*, Honorary Counsellor of the Parliament, is to be particularly distinguished. Nearly of the same age as Voltaire, he always had been his bosom friend. All that Mr. de La Harpe says of the amiability of this Count may be true; but however amiable he might be, it will also be true to say, that both the Count and Countess d'Argental were the dupes of their admiration and friendship for Voltaire. He corresponds as regularly with these two adepts as he did with d'Alembert, and as confidently exhorts them to crush *the wretch*. He styles them his two angels. He employed the Count as general agent for all higher protections that he might stand in need of; and few agents were more devoted or more faithful; that is to say, more impious.[24]

A name of greater importance, that is not to be overlooked among the protecting adepts, is the *Duc de La Rochefoucault*. To him who knows how much the Duke must have been mistaken in his own wit, it will be matter of little surprise to see him so seldom mentioned in Voltaire's correspondence; but facts supply the place of written proofs. The Duke had been weak enough to be persuaded, that impiety and Philosophism could alone give him a reputation. He protected the Sophisters, and even pensioned Condorcet. It would have been happy for him had he not waited for the murderers sent by Condorcet himself, to learn what were the real principles of this Philosophism.

Count d'Argental.

Duc de La Rochefoucault.

---

24 See General Correspondence.

In foreign courts, many great personages thought to soar above the vulgar by this same Sophistry. Voltaire could not sufficiendy admire the zeal of *Prince Gallitzin*, in dedicating the most impious of Helvétius's works to the Empress of all the Russias.[25] He was still more delighted with *Count Schouwallow*, the powerful protector of the Sophisters at that Court; and with all those, by whose intrigues d'Alembert had been nominated for the education of the heir to the Imperial diadem.

In Sweden, whence the *Chamberlain Jennings*, under the auspices of the King and Queen, had gone to announce to the patriarch of Ferney the great progress of Philosophism in that country,[26] an adept was to be found far more extolled by the Conspirators. This was the *Count de Creutz*, ambassador in France, and afterwards in Spain. He had so well blended his embassy with the apostleship of impiety, that Voltaire, enraptured, was inconsolable at his departure from Paris.—He writes to Madame Geoffrin,

> Had there been an Emperor Julian on earth, the *Count de Creutz* should have been sent on embassy to him, and not to a country where Auto-da-fes are made. The senate of Sweden must be gone mad, not to have left such a man in France; he would have been of use there, and it is impossible that he should do any good in Spain.[27]

25 To d'Alembert, 2 Aug. 1778, vol. 69, let. 118, p. 199.

26 To d'Alembert, 19 Jan. 1769, vol. 69, let. 3, p. 7.

27 To Mad. Geofiin, 21 May, 1764, vol. 58, let. 193, p. 355.

But this Spain, so much despised by Voltaire, could produce a *d'Aranda*, whom he styles the *Favorite of Philosophy*, and who daily went to stimulate his zeal, in the company of d'Alembert, Marmontel, and Mademoiselle d'Espinase, whose club nearly equalled the French Academy.

Other Dukes and Grandees were to be found in Spain equally admiring the French Sophistry. In particular the *Marquis de Mora* and the *Duke of Villa Hermosa*,[28] In this same country, so much despised by the Sophisters, we find d'Alembert distinguishing the *Duke of Alba*. It is of him that he writes to Voltaire,

> One of the first Grandees of Spain, a man of great wit, and the same person who was ambassador in France, under the name of Duke of Huéscar, has just sent me twenty guineas towards your statue . . . . Condemned, he says, secretly to cultivate my reason, I joyfully seize this opportunity of publicly testifying my gratitude to the great man who first pointed out the road to me.[29]

It was at the sight of so numerous a list of disciples, that Voltaire exclaimed, "Victory declares for us on all sides; I do assure you, that in a little time nothing but the rabble will follow the standard of our enemies."[30] He did not sufficiently dive into fu-

28 To Marq. de Villevielle, 1 May 1768, vol. 60, let. 268, p. 469.
29 From d'Alembert, 13 May, 1773, vol. 69, let. 108, p. 182.
30 To Damilaville, 25 Sept. 1762, vol. 57, let. 242, p. 475.

turity, or he would have seen that rabble misled one day by the same principles, and sacrificing its masters on the very Altar they had raised to impiety.

As to d'Alembert, he could not contain himself when informed of the numerous admirers that flocked to Ferney. "What the devil!" would he write, "forty guests at table, of whom two Masters of Requests and a Counsellor of the Grand Chamber, without counting the *Duke of Villars* and company!"[31] Dining at Voltaire's, to be sure, is not an absolute proof of the Philosophism of the guests, but it generally shows men who admired the Chief of that impiety which was one day to be their ruin.

It was not by chance that d'Alembert mentioned the Counsellor of the Grand Chamber. He was fully aware of what importance it was for the Conspirators to have protectors, or even admirers, in the higher orders of the magistracy. Voltaire was of the same opinion when he writes, "Luckily, during these ten years past that parliament (of Toulouse) has been recruited by young men of great wit, who have read, and who think like you."[32] This letter alone denotes how much the tribunals were relaxed for many years preceding the revolution. They were vested with all the authority necessary for stopping the circulation of these impious and seditious works, and of taking cognizance of their authors; but they had so much neglected it, that in the latter times a decree of the parliament was

---

31 From d'Alembert, 18 Oct. 1760, vol. 68, let. 76. p. 141.
32 To d'Alembert, 4 Sept. 1769, vol. 69, let. 11, p. 22.

a means of enhancing the price and extending the circulation of a work.

Voltaire, notwithstanding the numerous conquests made in these temples of justice, often complains of some of those respectable corps, as still containing magistrates who loved religion. But in return he extols the philosophic zeal of those of the South. "There (he writes to d'Alembert) you go from a *Mr. Duché* to a *Mr. de Castillon*, and Grenoble can boast of a *Mr. Servan*. It is impossible that reason and toleration should not make the greatest progress under such masters."[33] This hope was the better founded, as these three magistrates here named by Voltaire are precisely those who, by their functions of attorney or solicitor generals, were obliged to oppose the progress of that reason, synonimous with impiety in the mouth of Voltaire; and to uphold the power of the law against those daily productions and their authors.

Mr. de La Chalotais is of all others the solicitor general who seems to have been in the closest intimacy with Voltaire. It is in their correspondence that we see how much the conspirators were indebted and how grateful they were to him, on account of his zeal against the Jesuits, and how much the destruction of that order was blended with that of all other religious, in their plans for the total overthrow of all ecclesiastical authority.[34]

---

33   To d'Alembert, 5 Nov. 1770, vol. 69, let. 46, p. 81.

34   See their Correspondence, particularly Voltaire's letter to Mr. Chalotaix, 17 May, 1762, vol. 57, let. 192, p. 393.

But in spite of all this Philosophism, which had crept into the body of the magistracy, we meet with venerable men, whose virtues were the ornament of the highest tribunals. The grand chamber of the parliament of Paris, in particular, appeared so opposite to his impiety, that he despaired of ever philosophizing it. He even does it the honor of ranking it with that *populace* and *those assemblies of the clergy* that he despaired of ever rendering *reasonable*, or rather impious.[35]

There even was a time when he expresses his indignation to Helvétius in the following terms:

> I believe that the French are descended from the centaurs, who were half men and *half pack-horses*. These two halves have been separated, and there remained *men like you and some others*; and also horses, *who have bought the offices of counsellor* (in parliament), or who have made themselves doctors of the Sorbonne.[36]

It is an agreeable duty that I fulfil, when I show proof of this spite of the Sophisters against the first corps of the French magistracy. It is certain, that at the time of the revolution many magistrates were yet to be found, who, better informed of the intrigues of the Sophisters, would willingly have given greater vigour to the laws for the support of religion. But impiety had intruded even into the grand

---

35   To d'Alembert, 13 Dec. 1763, vol. 68, let. 122, p. 264.
36   To Helvétius, 22 July, 1761, vol. 57, let. 86, p. 178.

chamber. Terray, well known as a wicked minister, is not sufficiently so as a Sophister.

Whatever may be the turpitude of many facts mentioned in these memoirs, few are of a deeper hue than the following one:

Trait of the Abbé Terray.

The bookseller Le Jay was publicly selling one of those works, the impiety of which sometimes commanded the attention of the parliament. That fold by Le Jay was ordered to be publicly burnt, and the author and sellers to be prosecuted. Terray offered himself to make the necessary investigations, and was to report to parliament. He ordered Le Jay before him, and I will lay before the reader the very words I heard the bookseller use when he gave an account of what had passed on the occasion. As to the title of the work, I am not quite certain whether he mentioned it or not; but I perfectly remember what follows:—

> Ordered before Mr. Terray, counsellor in parliament; I waited on him. He received me with an air of gravity, sat down on a sofa, and questioned me as follows:—Is it you that sell this work condemned by a decree of the parliament? I answered. Yes, my Lord. How can you sell such dangerous works? As many others are sold.—Have you sold many of them? Yes, my Lord.—Have you many left? About six hundred copies.—Do you know the author of this infamous work? Yes, my Lord.—Who is it? Yourself, my Lord!—How dare you say so; how do you know that? I know it, my Lord, from the person of whom I bought your man-

uscript.—Since you know it, all is over; go, but be prudent.

It may be easily conceived that this interrogatory was not reported to the parliament, and the reader will readily comprehend what progress the Antichristian Conspiracy made in a country where its adepts were seated in the very sanctuary of the laws.

CHAPTER XV.

The Class of Men of Letters.

Their passions, and the facility of gratifying them, the yoke of religion once thrown off, had given the conspirators great power among the higher classes of society; and the empty hopes of a reputation brought over to their standards all those who pretended to literary fame. The great talents of Voltaire, and a success perhaps superior to his talents, proclaimed his sway absolute over the class of men of letters. Humbly those men followed his triumphant car who, above all others, will proudly flatter themselves with the perfection of their own ideas. It was only necessary for him to give the fashion. Like those frivolous nations where the high-flown courtezans, by their sole example, can introduce the most wanton fashions in attire, just so does the premier chief. Scarce had he shown his bias towards impiety, when the men of letters would all be impious.

Rousseau. From that cloud of writers and adepts a man shone forth who might have disputed with him the palm of genius; and who, for celebrity, needed not to resort to impiety. This was *Jean-Jacques Rousseau.* That famous citizen of Geneva, sublime when he pleases in his prose, rivalling Milton and Corneille in his poetry, could have rivalled Bossuet under the banners of Christianity. Unfortunately for his glory, he was known to d'Alembert, Diderot, and Voltaire; and for a time he leagued with them, and sought like them the means of crushing Christ and his religion. In this synagogue of impiety, as in that of the Jews, testimonies did not agree; divisions ensued, but, though separated, their attacks were all bent against Christianity. This is to be seen in a letter from Voltaire to d'Alembert, where he says, "What a pity it is that Jean-Jacques, Diderot, Helvétius and you, *cum aliis ejusdem farince hominibus,* (with other men of your stamp,) should not have been unanimous in your attacks on the wretch. My greatest grief is, to see the impostors united, and the friends of truth divided."[1]

When Rousseau seceded from the Sophisters, he did not at the same time forsake either his own

---

1   To d'Alembert, 5 Feb. 1765, vol. 68, let. 156. p. 143.

or their errors; but separately carried on the war. The admiration of the adepts was divided. In either school impiety had only varied its weapons, nor were opinions more constant or less impious.

Voltaire was the most active, but vigor was given to Jean-Jacques. With the strength of Hercules he also partook of his delirium. Voltaire laughed at contradiction, and his pen flew with every wind. Jean-Jacques would insist on the paradoxes fostered in his brain, and, brandishing his club on high, would equally strike at truth or falsehood. The former was the vane of opinion, the latter the Proteus of Sophistry. Both equally distant from the schools of wisdom, both wished to lay the foundations and first principles of philosophy.

The *pro* and *con* was equally adopted by them, and both found themselves condemned to the most humiliating inconstancy. Voltaire, uncertain as to the existence of a God or of a future state, applies to Sophisters bewildered like himself, and remains perplexed. Jean-Jacques, while yet a mere youth, says to himself, "I am going to throw this stone against that tree opposite to me: If I hit, let it be a sign of salvation; if I miss, a sign of damnation." Jean-Jacques hits, and heaven is his lot. This proof sufficed for the philosopher long after his youthful days; and he was far advanced in years when he said, "After that, I never doubted of my salvation."[2]

Voltaire one day believed he could demonstrate the existence of the *Author of the Universe*; he then

---

2   His *Confessions*, book 6th.

believed in an all-powerful God, who remunerated virtue.[3] The day after, the whole of this demonstration is dwindled into probabilities and doubts, which it would be ridiculus to pretend to solve.[4]

The same truth is one day evident to Jean-Jacques, nor does he doubt of it after having demonstrated it himself. He beheld the Deity all around him, with him, and throughout nature, on that day when he exclaimed, "I am certain that God exists of himself."[5] But the day following the demonstration is forgotten, and he writes to Voltaire, "Frankly I confess that neither the pro nor con (on the existence of God) appears to me demonstrated." With Jean-Jacques, as with Voltaire, *Theism and Atheism* could only found their doctrine on *probabilities*.[6] And they both believed in one only principle or *sole Mover*.[7] But at another time they could not deny but that there were two principles or two causes.[8]

Voltaire, after having written that Atheism would people the earth with robbers, villains, and monsters,[9] would pardon Atheism in Spinoza, and

---

3   Voltaire on Atheism.

4   Voltaire on Atheism; and on the Soul by Suranus.

5   The Emile and let. to the Archbishop of Paris.

6   Letter to Voltaire, vol. 12. Quarto edit, of Geneva.

7   Voltaire on the Principle of Action.—-JeanJaques in the Emile, vol. 3, page 115, and Letter to the Archbishop of Paris.

8   Voltaire, Quest. Encyclop. vol. 9.—-JeanJaques, Emile, vol. 3, page. 61, and let. to the Archbishop of Paris.

9   On Atheism.

even allow of it in a Philosopher;[10] and he professes it himself when he writes to d'Alembert, "I know of none but Spinoza who has argued well."[11] That is to say, I know of no true Philosopher but he to whom all matter and this world is the sole God; and after having tried every Sect, he ends by pressing d'Alembert to unite all parties in the war against Christ. Jean-Jacques had written that the Atheists deserved punishment; that they were *disturbers of the public peace*, and as such guilty of death.[12] Then, thinking he had fulfilled Voltaire's wish, writes to the minister Vernier, "I declare that my sole object in the New Eloisa was to unite the two opposite parties (the Deists and Atheists) by a reciprocal esteem for each other, and to teach the philosophers that one may believe in God without being a hypocrite, or deny him without being a rascal."[13] And this same man writes to Voltaire, that an Atheist cannot be guilty before God. That should the law find the Atheist guilty of death, it was the denounciator who should be burned as such.[14]

Voltaire would blaspheme the law of Christ, retract, receive the sacrament, and press the conspirators to crush the wretch! Jean-Jacques would lay aside Christianity, or resume it again, and with

---

10 Axiom 3.

11 To d'Alembert, 16 June, 1773, vol. 69, let. 113, p. 193.

12 Emile, vol. 4, page 68. Social Contract, Chap. 8.

13 Letter to Mr. Vernier.

14 Letters to Voltaire, vol. 12, and New Eloisa.

THE ANTI-CHRISTIAN CONSPIRACY

Calvin partake of the Last Supper.[15] He will write the most sublime encomiums on Christ that human eloquence could devise, and then finish by blaspheming that same Christ as a fanatic.[16] If the Antichristian Revolution was one day to carry Voltaire triumphantly to the Pantheon, Rousseau had the same rights to the inauguration of the Sophisters of Impiety. We shall see him gain far other claims on the Sophisters of Rebellion. If the former secretly solicits kings to subscribe to his statue, the latter openly writes that at Sparta one would have been erected to him.

With so singular a conduct each of these chiefs had his distinctive characteristics. Voltaire hated the God of the Christians; Jean-Jacques admired, but blasphemed him; pride wrought in the latter all that jealousy and hatred produced in the former; and it will long be a doubt which has been most injurious to Christianity, the one by his atrocious sarcasms and impious satire, or the other by his sophistry under the cloak of reason.

---

15   D'Alembert writes to Voltaire, in speaking of Rousseau, "I pity him; and if his happiness depends on his approaching the Holy Table, and in calling holy a religion which he has so much vilified, I own that my esteem is greatly diminished." (25 Sept. 1762, vol. 68, let. 105, p. 217.) He might have said as much of Voltaire's communions, but he never dared. He even seeks to give him a plea for his hypocrisy, when he says, "Perhaps I am in the wrong; for certainly you are better acquainted than I am with the reasons that determined you." He does not mention his esteem being diminished; on the contrary, Voltaire is always his dear and illustrious master ! 31 May 1768, vol. 68, let. 232. p. 482.

16   His Confessions and Professions of the Savoyard Vicar.

After their separation, Voltaire hated Jean-Jacques, scoffed at him, and would have him chained as a madman.[17] But he could not hide his joy, when he Profession of Faith of the Savoyard Vicar, written by this madman, was the book out of which youth were taught to read.[18] Jean-Jacques would at the same time detest the chiefs of the conspirators, expose them and be hated by them: he would preserve their principles, court their friendship and esteem anew, and that of the premier chief in particular.[19]

If to define the Sophister of Ferney be a difficult task, is it not equally so, to paint the citizen of Geneva? Jean-Jacques loved the sciences, and was crowned by those who reviled them; he wrote against the theatre, and composed operas; he sought friends, and is famous for his breaches of friendship. He extols the charms of virtue, and he bends the knee before the prostitute de Varens. He declares himself the most virtuous of men, and, under the modest title of his *Confessions*, he retraces in his old age the dissolute scenes of his youth. To tender mothers he gives the most pathetic advice in nature; and, smothering in himself the cries of that same nature, he banishes his children to that hospital where, from the shame of its birth, the unfortunate babe is condemned to

---

17 To Damilaville, 8 May 1761, vol. 57, let. 52, p. 108, and War of Geneva.

18 To the Count d'Argental, 26 Sept. 1766, vol. 57, let. 270, p. 478.

19 See his letters, and the Life of Seneca by Diderot.

the perpetual ignorance of its parents. The fear of seeing them makes him inexorable to the entreaties of those who would have provided for their education.[20] A prodigy of inconsistency even to his last moments; he wrote against suicide, and perhaps it is treating him too favorably not to assert that he himself had prepared the poison which caused his death.[21]

However inconsistent, error is inculcated by the Sophister of Geneva with all the powers of genius; and many have lost their faith by his works, who would have resisted all other attacks. To be cradled in one's passions gave empire to Voltaire; but to resist Jean-Jacques the acutest sophisms were to be penetrated: youth was led away by the former, while those who were advanced in age fell a victim to the latter, and a prodigious number of adepts owed their fall to these two writers.

Buffon.

Indignantly would the manes of *Buffon* see his name classed after that of Jean-Jacques among the conspiring adepts; and impossible is it for the historian, when speaking of those who have adopted the fashion set by Voltaire, not to sigh at pronouncing the name of the French Pliny. He certainly was rather the victim than the associate

---

20 See his *Confessions*.

21 See his life by the Count Barruel de Beauvert. [Antoine Joseph Barruel-Beauvert (1756 - 1817) was a great admirer of Rousseau and his was the first biography of the subject. The latter was published in 1789 and its author would later take part in the events of the French Revolution. —Ed.]

of the conspirators. But who can erase Philosophism from his writings? Nature had lent her genius, and why would he not content himself with
what she had placed before him? No; he would
ascend higher, he would explain those mysteries
reserved to revelation alone; and, soaring above
his sphere, he often shows himself the disciple of
Maillet and Boulanger. In giving the history of nature, he destroys that of religion. He was the hero
of those men whom d'Alembert had sent to split
mountains, and seek from the depths of the earth
arguments to belie Moses and the first pages of
holy writ. In the praises of the Sophisters he consoles himself for the censures of the Sorbonne; but
the punishment attached to the fault itself, as he
only belied his own reputation for a knowledge of
the laws of nature. They appeared to be null when
he treated of the earth formed by the waters, or
by fire, and of his endless epochs. And to falsify
the scriptures, he makes nature as inconsistent as
his own systems. His style, elegant and sublime,
has always been admired, but found insufficient to
save his works from the smile of the real philosopher; and his glory, like his comet, vanished in
his dreams of incredulity. Happy, if in retracting
his errors he had been able to destroy that spirit
of research in the adepts who only studied nature
through the medium of Voltaire.[22]

---

22 D'Alembert and Voltaire ridiculed all those vain systems of
    Bailly and Buffon on the antiquity of the world and of its in-

Fréret.

After these two men, so justly distinguished by the grandeur of their style, the remaining adepts chiefly owe their celebrity to their impiety; nevertheless, two might have done honor to science by their learning. The first, *Fréret*, had by his immense memory nearly learned Bayle's Dictionary by heart. But his letters to Thrasybulus, the offspring of his Atheism, shows that his vast memory was more than outweighed by his want of judgment.

Boulanger.

The second was *Boulanger*, whose brain, overburdened with Latin, Greek, Hebrew, Syriac and Arabic, had also adopted all the extravagancies of Atheism; but who retracted in the latter part of his life, execrating the Sect that had misled him. We shall soon see that all the posthumous works attributed to these writers were not written by them.

Marquis
d'Argence
de Dirac.

Fain would the *Marquis d'Argence de Dirac*[23] have figured among the learned Sophisters; but his *Chinese and Cabalistic Letters*, and his *Philosophy of Good Sense*, only prove, that to Bayle's Dictionary he was indebted for his pretended reputation. He was a long while a friend of Frederick's, and his

---

habitants. They would call these systems, Nonsense, Follies, an Excuse for the want of Genius, Shallow Ideas, Vain and ridiculous Quackery (From d'Alembert, 6 March 1777, vol. 69, let. 178, p. 296); but d'Alembert took care to keep his opinions secret on this subject. By discrediting these systems he feared lest he should discourage those adepts whom he and sent to forge new ones in the Appenines, in order to give the lie to Moses and the sacred writ.

23   Jean-Baptiste de Boyer, Marquis d'Argens (1704 - 1771). —Ed.

impiety entitled him to that friendship. From his brother, the President d'Éguille, we have learned, that after several discussions on religion, with persons better versed in that science than Frederick, he submitted to the light of the Gospel, and ardently wished to atone for his past infidelity.

As to *La Métherie* the doctor, if he appeared to rave, it was only from the sincerity of his heart. His man-machine, or his *man-plant*, only caused the Sect to blush from the open manner in which he had said what many of them wished to insinuate. *[margin: La Métherie.]*

Even in the first days of the revolution, the Sophisters conspiring against their God thought they could glory in the talents and co-operation of *Marmontel.* But let us not add to the sorrows of the man who needed only the first days of the revolution to shrink with horror from those conspiracies which had given it birth. Of all the Sophisters who have outlived Voltaire, Mr. de Marmontel is the one who most wished to hide his former intimacy with the Antichristian chiefs. But alas, it is to those connections that he owes his celebrity, far more than to his *Incas*, his *Bélisaire*, or his *Tales*,[24] intermingled with Philosophism. We could wish to hide it, but Voltaire's own letters convict the repenting adept of having acted, and that during a long time, a very different part among the conspirators. Voltaire was so well convinced of Mr. de Marmontel's zeal, that, thinking himself on the point of death, he *[margin: Marmontel.]*

---

24 *Les Incas, ou la destruction de l'empire du Perou* (1777), *Bélisaire* (1767), *Contes moraux* (1755 - 1759). —Ed.

bequeathed La Harpe to him. His last will is worded thus, "I recommend La Harpe to you, when I am no more; *he will be one of the pillars of our church.* You must have him received of the academy. After having gained so many prizes, it is but just that he should bestow them in his turn."[25]

La Harpe.

With a taste for literature, and some talents, which in spite of his critics distinguish him above the common rank of the writers of the day, *Mr. de la Harpe* might have rendered his works useful, had he not, from his youth, been the spoilt child of Voltaire. At that age it is easy to believe one's self a Philosopher, when one disbelieves one's catechism; and the young La Harpe blindly followed the instructions of his master. If he never was the pillar, he might be correctly styled the trumpeter of the new church, by means of the *Mercure*, a famous French journal, by which its encomiums or its weekly criticisms nearly decided the fate of all literary productions.[26]

The encomiums which Voltaire lavished on that journal after La Harpe had undertaken the direc-

---

25 To Marmontel, 21 Aug. 1767, vol. 60, let. 159, p. 272.

26 We learn, by the public newspapers, that Mr. de la Harpe was converted, when in prison, by the Bishop of Saint-Brieux. I should be little surprised at it. The examples of this prelate, with the fruits of Philosophism in this revolution, must strongly impress the man who, with a sound judgment, can compare them with the lessons and promises of his former masters. If the news of this conversion be true, I shall have shown him consecrating his talents to error; and nobody will applaud him more than myself, for consecrating them in future to truth alone.

tion of it show how little governments are aware of the influence of such journals over the public opinion. Above ten thousand people subscribed, and many more perused the *Mercure*; and, influenced by its suggestions, they by degrees became as philosophic, or rather impious, as the hebdomadary Sophister himself. The Conspirators saw what advantage could be reaped from this literary dominion. La Harpe ruled the sceptre during many years; then Marmontel jointly with Champfort; as Remi, who was little better, had held it before them. I one day asked the latter, how it was possible that he had inserted in his journal one of the most false and wicked accounts possible of a work purely literary, and of which I had heard him speak in the highest terms. He answered me, that the article alluded to had been written by a friend of d'Alembert's, and that he owed his journal and even his fortune to d'Alembert's protection. The injured author wished to publish his defence in the same journal, but it was all in vain.—Let the reader judge from this how powerfully the periodical papers contributed to the designs of the conspirators; in fact, it was by them that the public mind was chiefly directed to their desired object.

This Sect disposed of reputations by their praises or their censures, as best suited them.—By these journals they reaped the two-fold advantage of pointing out to those writers who hungered after glory or bread[27] what subjects they were to investigate, and of calling, by means of their literary trump, the attention of the public only to those works, which the Sect wished to circulate, or from which they had nothing to fear.

By such artifices the La Harpes of the day forwarded the conspiracy as much, if not more than the most active of the Sophisters, or their most impious writers. The sophistical author would mingle or condense his poison in his productions, whilst the journalist adept would proclaim it, and infuse it throughout the capital, or into all parts of the empire. The man who would have remained ignorant of the very existence of an impious or a seditious work, the man who would neither have spent his time nor his money on such productions, imbibed the whole of their poison from the insidious extracts made by the sophistical journalist.

Condorcet.

Above all the adepts, far more than even Voltaire himself, did a fiend called *Condorcet* hate the son of his God. At the very name of the Deity the monster raged; and it appeared as if he wished to revenge on heaven the heart it had given

---

27 The Sophisters were so well acquainted with the powers of a journal, that they mustered up their highest protections against the religious authors who would dispute one with them. When Voltaire was informed that Mr. Clement was to succeed to Mr. Fréron, whose pen had long been consecrated to the vindication of truth, he did not blush at sending d'Alembert to the chancellor in hopes of hindering Mr. Clement from continuing Fréron's journal. (To d'Alembert, 12 Feb. 1773, vol. 69, let. 97, p. 163.).

him. Cruel and ungrateful, the cool assassion of friendship and of his benefactors, he would willingly have directed the dagger against his God, as he did against La Rochefoucault. Atheism was but folly in La Métherie and madness in Diderot; but in Condorcet it was the phrenzy of hatred and the offspring of pride. It was impossible to convince Condorcet, that any thing but a fool could believe in God. Voltaire, who had seen him when a youth, little foresaw what services he was to render to the conspiracy, even when he wrote, "My great consolation in dying is, that you support the honor of our poor Velches, in which you will be well assisted by the Marquis de Condorcet!"[28]

It could not have been on the talents of this man that the premier rested his hopes. Condorcet had learned as much geometry as d'Alembert could teach him; but as to the Belles Lettres, he was not even of the second class.—His style was that of a man who did not know his own language; and his writings, like his sophisms, required much study to be understood.—But hatred did for him what nature has done for others. Perpetually plodding at his blasphemies, he at last succeeded in expressing them more clearly; for the amazing difference which is observable between his former and his latter works can only thus be accounted for. It is more remarkable in his posthumous work on the human mind, where his pen can hardly be traced, excepting in a few passages, though his genius

---

28   To d'Alembert, 2 March, 1773, vol. 69, let. 101, p. 170.

haunts every page. There he is to be seen, as during his life time, in his studies, in his writings or conversation, directing every thing towards Atheism, seeking no other object in this work than to inspire his readers with his own frantic hatred against his God. Long had he looked for the downfal of the Altar, as the only sight his heart could enjoy. He beheld it, but was soon to fall himself. His end was that of the impious man, a vagabond and wanderer, sinking under pain, misery, and the dread of Robespierre, without acknowledging the hand of God, that struck him by that of the ferocious dictator. Alas, if he died as he lived, will not the first moments of his conviction and repentance be those, when he shall hear that God, whom he blasphemed and denied, confessed by the mouths of those awful victims of eternal vengeance!!

During his lifetime, so great was his hatred, that adopting error, in order to rid men of that fear of an immortal God in heaven, he did not stop short of imagining that his Philosophism would one day render men immortal upon earth. To belie Moses and the prophets, he became himself the prophet of madness. Moses had shown the days of man decreasing unto the age at which God had fixed them, and the royal prophet had declared the days of man to extend from sixty fo seventy, and at the most to eighty years, after which all was trouble and pain. And to the oracles of the Holy Ghost, Condorcet would oppose his! When he calculates his philosophic revolution, which begins by

Conduct of the Clergy towards the Antichristian Conspirators.

hile apostacy bore sway in the palaces of the great, and in the schools of science; and while all the higher classes of citizens were led away from the worship of their religion, some by example, others by the artful Sophisms of the Conspirators; the duties of the clergy could not be doubtful. It was their part to oppose a bank to the fetid torrent of impiety, and save the multitude from being swept away by its waters. Far more than its honour or its interest, its very name called on the clergy, by the most sacred ties of duty and of conscience, to guard the Altar against the attacks of the Conspirators. The least backwardness in the combat would have added treason to apostacy. Let the historian who dared speak the truth on kings be true on the merits of his own body; whether it redounds to the honour or disgrace of his brethren, let him speak the truth. Hence the future clergy will learn from what has been done the line of conduct they ought to follow. The Conspiracy against Christ is not extinct, though it may be hidden; but should it burst forth anew, must not the pastor know how far his conduct may influence or retard its progress?

If under the name of Clergy were comprehended all those who in France wore the half-livery of the church, all that class of men who in Paris, and some of the great towns, styled themselves Abbés, history might reproach the clergy with traitors and apostates from the first dawn of the Conspiracy.

We find the Abbé de Prades the first apostate, and happily first to repent; the Abbé Morellet, whose disgrace is recorded in the repeated praises of Voltaire[1] and d'Alembert;[2] the Abbé Condillac, who was to sophisticate the morals of his royal pupil; and above all, that Abbé Raynal, whose name alone is tantamount to twenty demoniacs of the Sect.

Paris swarmed with those Abbés; we still say, the Abbé Barthélemy, the Abbé Beaudeau, again the Abbé Noël, and the Abbé Sieyès. But the peo-

---

1   Voltaire referred to Morellet as "L'Abbé Mords-les" ("Father Bite-them") on account of the latter's sharp wit. —Ed.

2   To d'Alembert, 16 June, 1760, vol. 68, let. 65, p. 115. To Thiriot, 26 Jan. 1762, vol. 57, let. 157, p. 320.

ple, on the whole, did not confound them with the clergy. They knew them to be the offspring of avarice, seeking the livings but laying aside the duties of the church; or through economy adopting the dress, while by their profligacy and irreligious writings they dishonored it. The numbers of these amphibious animals, and particularly in the metropolis, may be one of the severest reproaches against the clergy. However great the distinctions made between these and the latter may have been, the repeated scandals of the former powerfully helped the Conspiracy, by laying themselves open to satire, which retorted upon the whole body, and affected the real ministers of the Altar. Many of these Abbés, who did not believe in God, had obtained livings through the means of the Sophisters, who by soliciting dignities for their adepts sought to introduce their principles, and dishonour the clergy by their immorality. It was the plague that they spread in the enemy's camp; and not daring to face them in the field, they sought to poison their springs.

If under the title of Clergy we only comprehend those who really served at the Altar, the Conspirators never prevailed against them. I have searched their records; I have examined whether among the bishops and functionary clergy any of these adepts were to be found, who could be classed with the conspiring Sophisters. Antecedent to the Périgords and d'Autuns, or the apostacy of the Gobels,[3]

Conduct of the true clergy, and what may be objected against them.

---

3   The original French has Gobet, but the only constitutionalist I

Grégoires, and other constitutionalists, I only meet with the name of Briennes, and one Judas seated in the College of the Aposdes during the space of thirty years is quite sufficient; or rather, is one too many.[4] Meslier, rector of Étrépigny in Champagne, might be added, were it certain that his impious *Last Will and Testament*, was not a forgery of the Sophisters attributed to him after his death.

At the time when the revolution drew near, Philosophism attached itself to the covenants of men,

---

was able to find with a similar name was Jean-Baptiste-Joseph Gobel (1727 - 1794), Bishop of Paris. —Ed.

4   It is true that Voltaire in his correspondence, sometimes flatters himself with the protection of the Cardinal de Bernis, who was then but the youthful favourite of the Marquise de Pompadour, or the slender poet of the Graces. The mistakes of a young man are not sufficient to prove his concert with conspirators, whom he never supported unless in the expulsion of the Jesuits. But could not what d'Alembert said of the parliaments apply to him, "Forgive them, Lord, for they know not what they do, nor whose commands they obey." D'Alembert writes in a quite another style, when he speaks of Briennes; he shows him acting the most resolute part of a traitor, in support of the Conspiracy, and simply hiding his game from the clergy. (From d'Alembert, 4 and 21 Dec. 1770, vol. 69, let. 48 and 53, p. 85 and 91.)

    I found some few letters also, mentioning the Prince Lewis de Rohan, seconding their intrigues on the reception of Marmontel at the Academy, condescending, as d'Alembert says, from Coadjutor of a Catholic Church, to become the Coadjutor of Philosophy. (From d'Alembert, 8 Dec. 1763, vol. 68, let. 121, Page 260.) If such an error in a prince, naturally noble and generous, proves that he was mistaken in thinking that he barely protected literature in the person of an adept, it does not necessarily follow that he musdt have been initiated into the secrets of those who abused his protection, and ended by sporting with his person.

and soon produced Dom Gerles and his confederates, but these belonged to a different class of conspirators, which will be a future object of our Memoirs. At all times the body of the clergy preserved the purity of its faith; a distinction might have been made between the zealous edifying ecclesiastics, and the lax (not to say scandalous) ones; but that of believing and unbelieving could never stand. Never could the Conspirators exult in this latter distinction. Would they not have availed themselves of their decreasing faith, as they did of the incredulity of the ministers of Geneva?[5] On the contrary, the most scurrilous abuse is uttered against the clergy for their zeal in support of Christianity, and the satire of the Sophisters redounds to their immortal honor.

The purity of faith alone was not sufficient in the clergy; examples far more powerful than lessons were necessary to oppose the torrent of impiety. It is true that in the greater part of their pastors the people beheld it in an eminent degree; but the majority will not suffice. Those who are acquainted with the powers of impression know but too well, that one bad ecclesiastic does more harm than a hundred of the most virtuous can do good. All should have been zealous, but many were lax. There were among those who served the altars men unworthy of the sanctuary. These were ambitious men, who, while they ought to have been giv-

---

5   See the Encyclopedia, article Geneva; and letter of Voltaire to Mr. Vernes.

ing good example to their dioceses, preferred the intrigues and pomp of the capital. It is true, such a conduct could not have constituted vice in the worldling, but what may be venial in the world, is often monstrous in the church. The Sophisters in particular, with their morals, were not authorised to reprobate those of the delinquent clergy. Where is the wonder that some few unworthy members should have intruded on the sanctuary, when the enemies of the church had possessed themselves of its avenues, in order to prevent the preferment of those whose virtues or learning they dreaded? How could it be otherwise, when the bishops wishing to repel an unworthy member, Choiseul answered, "Such are the men we want and will have:" or when the irreligious nobleman only beheld in the riches of the church, the inheritance of a son not less vicious than his father?

The clergy might certainly have thus replied to their enemies. And true it is, that if any thing could astonish us, it is not that with all these intrigues and ambition some few bad pastors had been obtruded on the church, but ather that so many good ones, worthy of their titles, yet remained. But the crimes of the first instigators do not excuse those pastors who gave room for the scandal. Let the future clergy find this avowal recorded; let those men be acquainted with whatever influenced the progress of the Antichristian Revolution, whose duty essentially militates against that progress, and renders the least pretext given criminal in them.

History, however, must also declare, that if the remissness of some few may have furnished a pretext to the conspirators, the majority made a noble stand against them; and though some few spots could be found, the body was nevertheless splendent with the light of its virtues, which shone forth with redoubled lustre, when impiety at length, strengthened in its progress, threw off the mask. Then rising above its powers, the clergy were not to be intimidated by death, or the rigors of a long exile; and the Sophister unwillingly blushed at the calumnies he had spread, when he represented those men as more attached to the riches than to the faith of the church. Those riches remained in the hands of the banditti, while that faith crowns the archbishops, bishops and ecclesiastics butchered at the Carmes, or consoles those who have found in foreign countries a refuge from the armies and bloody decrees of the Jacobins: every where poor, and living on the beneficence of those countries, but powerfully rich in the purity of their faith and testimony of their conscience.

But the Clergy had not waited these awful days to oppose the principles of the Conspirators.— From the first dawn of the Conspiracy we can trace their opposition. Scarcely had impiety raised its voice, when the clergy sought to confound it: the Encyclopedia was not half printed when it was proscribed in their assemblies; nor has a single convocation been held for these fifty years past, which

They oppose the progress of impiety.

295

has not warned the throne and the magistracy of the progress of Philosophism.[6]

At the head of the prelates who opposed it, we find *Mr. de Beaumont*, archbishop of Paris, whose name history could not silently pass over without injustice. Generous as an Ambrose, he was fired with the same zeal, and equally stedfast against the enemies of the faith. The Jansenists obtained his exile, and the Antichristians would willingly have sent him to the scaffold; but there he would have braved their poignards, as he did the Jansenists; when he returned from his exile, he might be said to have acquired new vigor to oppose them both.

Many other bishops following his example, to the most unblemished manners added their pastoral instructions. *Mr. de Pompignan*, then Bishop of Puy refuted the errors of Voltaire and Jean-Jacques; the *Cardinal de Luynes* warned his flock against the *System of Nature*; the Bishops of Boulogne, Amiens, Auch and many others, more powerfully edified their dioceses by their example than even by their writings; nor did there pass a single year, without some bishop combating the increasing progress of the impious Conspirators.

If the Sophistry of the Sect continued its ravages, it was not the fault of the Bishops or the religious writers. The Sorbonne exposed it in their censures. The *Abbé Bergier* victoriously pursues Deism in its very last intrenchments, and makes it blush at its own contradictions. To the sophisticated learn-

---

6   See the acts of the clergy since the year 1750.

ing of the Conspirators, he opposed a more loyal application and a truer knowledge of antiquity and of the weapons it furnished to religion.[7] The *Abbé Guénée*, with all that urbanity and attic salt of which he was master, obliges Voltaire to humble himself at the sight of his own ignorance and false criticism of sacred writ.[8] The *Abbé Gérard* had found a method of sanctifying novels themselves. Under the most engaging forms, he reclaims youth from vice and its tortuous ways, and restores history to its primitive truth. The *Abbé Pey* had searched all the records of the church to reinstate it in its real rights, and under the simple form of a catechism, we see the *Abbé Feller*, or *Flexier Dureval*,[9] uniting every thing that reason, truth, or science can oppose against the Sophisters.

Prior to all these champions of the faith, the *Abbé Duguet* had victoriously vindicated the principles of Christianity, and the *Abbé Houteville* had demonstrated the truth of it from history. From the first dawn of the Conspiracy, the *Père Berthier* and his associates had, in the Journal de Trevoux, particularly exposed the errors of the Encyclopedists. We see, therefore, that if the Celsi and Porphirii were numerous, religion had not lost its Justins or its Origens. In these latter times, as in the primitive days of Christianity, he who sincerely

---

7   His Deism refuted, and his Answer to Fréret.

8   Letters to some Portuguese Jews.

9   Feller's vast oeuvre included works published under the assumed name of Flexier de Reval. —Ed.

sought after truth must have found it in the victorious arguments of the religious authors, opposed to the Sophisms of the Conspirators. And it may be truly said, that many points of religion had been placed by these modern apologists in clearer light than they had been seen in before.

The Christian orators ably assisted the efforts of their bishops, and incessantly invoked the attention of the people to their danger. The refutation of Philosophism was become the object of their public discourses. The *Père Neuville,* and after him *Mr. de Senez,* and the *Père Beauregard* in particular, seem to have been fired by that holy zeal. That sudden inspiration with which he appeared to be seized in the Cathedral Church of Paris is not yet forgotten; when thirteen years before the revolution, expounding the different maxims and exposing the plans of modern Philosophism, he made the vaults of the temple resound with words too shamefully verified by the revolution, and exclaims in a prophetic strain:

> Yes it is at the King—at the King and at religion that the Philosophers aim their blows. They have grasped the hatchet and the hammer, they only wait the favorable moment to overturn the Altar and the throne.—Yes, my God! thy temples will be plundered and destroyed; thy festivals abolished; they sacred name blasphemed; thy worship proscribed.—But what sounds, Great God, do I hear! what do I behold!—to the sacred canticles which caused the vaults of this temple to resound to thy praises, succeed wan-

ton and prophane songs! And thou infamous Deity of Paganism, impure Venus, thou durst advance hither, and audaciously, in the place of the living God, seat thyself on the throne of the Holy of Holies, and there receive the guilty incense of thy new adorers.

This discourse was heard by a numerous audience, collected by their own piety or attracted by the eloquence of the orator; by adepts themselves, who attended in hopes of carping at his expressions; by doctors of the laws with whom we were acquainted, and who often repeated them to us, long before we had seen them printed in various publications. The adepts cried out, Sedition and Fanaticism. The doctors of the law only retracted the severity of their censures after they had seen the prediction completely accomplished.

Such strong cautions from the clergy, and the means they opposed, retarded indeed the progress of the Sophisters; but could not triumph over the conspiracy. It was too deep, the black arts of seduction had been too well planned in the hidden dens of the conspirators. I have still to unfold some of their dark mysteries; and when light shall have shone upon them, with surprise shall the reader ask, not how was it possible, (with so much zeal on the part of the clergy) that the Altar should be overthrown, but how the fall of the temple could have been so long delayed?

CHAPTER XVII.

New and More Subtle Means of the Conspirators to Seduce even the Lowest Classes of the People.

hen Voltaire swore to annihilate Christianity, he did not flatter himself with the hope of drawing the generality of nations into his apostacy. His pride seems often satisfied with the progress that Philosophism had made among those *who governed, or were made to govern, and among men of letters;*[1] for a long time he does not appear to envy Christianity the inferior classes of society, which he does not comprehend under the appellation of the *better sort*. The facts we are about to lay before the reader will show to what new ex-

---

1   To d'Alembert, 13 Dec. 1763, vol. 68, let. 122, p. 264.

tent the conspirators sought to carry their impious zeal, and by what artifices Christ was to be deprived of all worship even from the lowest populace.

Origin of the Œconomists.

A doctor known in France by the name of Duquesnai[2] had so well insinuated himself into the favor of Louis XV. that the king used to call him his thinker. He really appeared to have deeply meditated on the happiness of the subject, and he may have sincerely wished it; nevertheless he was but a system-maker, and the founder of that Sect of Sophisters called Œconomists, because the œconomy and order to be introduced into the finances, and other means of alleviating the distresses of the people, were perpetually in their mouths. If some few of these Œconomists sought nothing further in their speculations, it is certain, that their writers took no pains to conceal their hatred for the Christian religion. Their works abound in passages which at least show their wish of substituting natural religion to the Christian religion and revelation.[3] Their affectation of solely speaking of agriculture, administration, and œconomy, render them less liable to suspicion, than those conspirators who are perpetually intruding their impiety.

Their plan for free schools.

Duquesnai and his adepts had more especially undertaken to persuade heir readers, that the country people, and mechanics in towns, were en-

2 François Quesnay (1694 - 1774), author of *Tableau économique*. —Ed.

3 See the analysis of those works, by Mr. Le Gros, Prevost of St. Louis du Louvre.

tirely destitute of that kind of instruction necessary
for their professions; that men of this class, unable to acquire knowledge by reading, pined away
in an ignorance equally fatal to themselves and
to the state; that it was necessary to establish free
schools, and particularly throughout the country,
where children might be brought up to different
trades, and instructed in the principles of agriculture. D'Alembert, and the Voltairian adepts, soon
perceived what advantages they could reap from
these establishments. In union with the Œconomists, they presented various memorials to Louis
XV. in which not only the temporal but even the
spiritual advantages of such establishments for
the people are strongly urged. The king, who really loved the people, embraced the project with
warmth. He opened his mind on the subject to Mr.
Bertin, whom he honored with his confidence, and
had entrusted with his privy purse. It was from
frequent conversations with this minister, that the
memorial from which we extract the following account was drawn up. It is Mr. Bertin himself who
speaks:

"Louis XV." says that minister,

> having entrusted me with the care of his privy
> purse, it was natural that he should mention
> to me an establishment of which his Majes-
> ty was to defray the expence. I had long since
> closely observed the different Sects of our phi-
> losophers; and though I had much to reproach
> myself with as to the practice, I had at least pre-

Seconded
by the
Sophisters.

M. Bertin
unde-
ceives
Louis
XV.,

served the principles of my religion. I had little doubt of the efforts of the Philosophers to destroy it. I was sensible that they wished to have the direction of these schools themselves, and by that means seize on the education of the people, under pretence that the bishops and ecclesiastics, who had hitherto superintended them and their teachers, could not be competent judges in subjects so little suited to clergymen. I apprehended that their object was not so much to give lessons on agriculture to the children of husbandmen and trades-people, as to withdraw them from their habitual instructions on their catechism or on their religion.

I did not hesitate to declare to the king, that the intentions of the Philosophers were very different from his. I know those conspirators, I said; and beware, Sire, of giving them your aid. Your kingdom is not deficient in free schools, or schools nearly free; they are to be found in every little town, and almost in every village, and perhaps they are already but too numerous. It is not books that form mechanics and plowmen. The books and masters sent by these Philosophers, will rather infuse system than industry into the country people. I tremble lest they render them idle, vain, and jealous; in a short time discontended and seditious, and at length rebellious. I fear, lest the whole fruit of the expence they seek to put your Majesty to, should be gradually to obliterate from the hearts of the people the love of their religion and their sovereign.

To these arguments I added whatever my mind could suggest to dissuade his Majesty. I advised him, in place of sending and paying

those masters whom the Phiosophers had chosen, to employ the same sums for multiplying
the catechists, and in sesarching for good and
patient men, whom his Majesty, in concert with
the bishops, should support, in order to teach
the poor peasantry the principles of religion,
and to teach it them by rote, as the rectors and
curates do to those children who do not know
how to read.

Louis XV. seemed to relish my arguments;
but the Philosophers renewed their attacks.
They had people about his person who never
ceased to urge him, and the king could not persuade himself that his *thinker*, Duquesnai, and
the other Philosophers, were capable of such
detestable views. He was so constantly beset by
those men, that during the last twenty years of
his reign, in the daily conversations with which
he honored me, I was perpetually employed in
combating the false ideas he had imbibed respecting the Œconomists and their associates.

At length, determined to give the king positive proof that they imposed upon him, I sought
to gain the confidence of those pedlars who
travel throughout the country, and expose their
goods to sale in the villages, and at the gates of
country seats. I suspected those in particular
who dealt in books to be nothing less than the
agents of Philosophism with the good country
folks. In my excursions into the country I above
all fixed my attention on the latter. When they
offered me a book to buy, I questioned them
what might be the books they had? Probably
Catechisms or Prayer-books? Few others are
read in the villages? At these words I have seen
many smile. No, they answered, those are not

*and dis-
covers the
means of
the con-
spirators.*

our works; we make much more money of Voltaire, Diderot, or other philosophic writings.
What! said I, the country people buy Voltaire
and Diderot? Where do they find the money
for such dear works? Their constant answer
was, We have them at a much cheaper rate than
Prayer-books; we can sell them at ten sols (5d.)
a volume, and have a pretty profit into the bargain. Questioning some of them still farther,
many of them owned that those books cost
them nothing; that they received whole bales of
them without knowing whence they came, but
being simply desired to sell them in their jour-
neys at the lowest price.

Such was the account given by Mr. Bertin, and
particularly during his retreat at Aix la Chapelle.
All that he said of those pedlars perfectly coincides
with what I have heard many rectors of small towns
and villages complain of. They looked upon these
hawking booksellers as the pests of their parishes,
and as the agents of the pretended philosophers in
the circulation of their impiety.

Louis XV. warned by the discovery made by his
minister, at length was satisfied that the establishment of these schools so much urged by the conspirators, would only be a new instrument of seduction in their hands. He abandoned the plan; but,
perpetually harrassed by the protecting Sophisters,
he did not strike at the root of the evil, and but fee-
bly impeded its progress. The pedlars continued to
promote the measures of the conspirators; but this
was but one of the inferior means employed to sup-

ply the want of their free schools, as a new discovery brought to light one far more fatal.

Many years prior to the French Revolution, a rector of the diocese of Embrun had had frequent contests with the school-master of the village, charging him with corrupting the morals of his pupils, and with distributing most irreligious books among them. The lord of the village, one of the protecting adepts, supported the school-master; the good rector applied to his archbishop. Mr. Salabert d'Anguin, Vicar-general, desired to see the library of the master. It was filled with these sort of works; but the delinquent, so far from denying the use he made of them, with a pretended simplicity, said he had always heard those works spoken of in the highest terms; and, like the hawkers, declared that he was not at the trouble of buying them, as they were sent to him free of all costs.

Country school-masters corrupted.

At about a league from Liège, and in the adjacent villages, masters still more perfidious carried their means of corruption to a far greater extent. These would assemble on certain days, at particulr hours, a number of trades-people and poor country fellows, who had not learned to read. In these meetings one of the pupils of the professor would read in an audible voice a chapter in some work with which he himself had already been perverted; for example, one of Voltaire's romances, then the *Sermon of the Fifty*, the pretended *Good Sense*, or other works of the Sect furnished by the master. Those that abounded in calumny and abuse against the clergy were read with particular emphasis. These meetings, the fore-runners of the Liège revolution, were only discovered by an honest and religious carpenter, who, working for a canon of that cathedral, declared the sorrow he had felt at finding his two sons in one of these meetings reading such lectures to about a dozen of country fellows. On this discovery, a proper search was made in the adjacent country; many school-masters were found guilty of the same perfidy; and, shocking to say, by the exterior practice of their religion, these men had done away all suspicion of such infernal dealings. The inquiry was carried still further, and the plots were traced up to d'Alembert. The following was the result of this new discovery; and it was the very person to whom the honest carpenter opened his mind, and who made the necessary inquiries on this important object, who gave me the information.

D'Alembert's committee of education.

In seeking what men had been the prompters of these corrupters of youth, they were found to be men whose connexions with the Sophisters of the day were no secret. At length they were traced to d'Alembert himself, and his office for tutors. It was to this office that all those heretofore mentioned addressed themselves, who wanted the recommendation of the Sophisters to obtain a place of preceptor or tutor in the houses of the great or wealthy. But at this period private education was not the sole object of d'Alembert. He now had established a correspondence throughout the provinces and beyond the kingdom. Not a place of professor in a college, nor of a simple school-master in a village, became vacant, but he or his coadjutors were immediately informed of it by his agents; as also of the persons who petitioned for these places, of those who should be accepted or rejected, and of the means necessary to be employed, or persons to be applied to, to obtain the nomination of an adept competitor, or of those who were to be sent from Paris; in short, of the proper instructions to be given to the elected with regard to local circumstances, or the greater or less progress that Philosophism had made around them. Hence the impudence of the school-master in the diocese of Embrun, and that hypocrisy in those of the principality of Liège, where a government totally ecclesiastical was to be feared, and where infidelity had not yet made the same ravages it had in France.

It is thus that d'Alembert, faithful to the mission Voltaire had given him, *to enlighten youth as much as lay in his power*,[4] had extended his means of seducing them. Voltaire no longer regretted the colony of Cleves. That manufacture of impiety, which was to have been its chief object, the philosophic *confraternity*, like *that of the Freemasons*, the SECRET ACADEMY, more zealous in crushing Christ and his religion, than any other ever had been in the propagation of science or learning, was now established in Paris. And it was in the capital of the Most Christian empire that these asso-

---

4   To d'Alembert, 15 Sept. 1762, vol. 68, let. 104, p. 214.

ciations were held, the parents of the revolution that was to bring devastation on France, and destruction on Christianity throughout the world. This was the last *mystery of Mytra*; this was the deepest intrigue of the conspirators; nor do I know that it has been hitherto laid open by any writer. In the correspondence of the Sophisters no trace can be discovered of this intrigue, at least in what the adepts have published. They had their reasons for suppressing such letters; for even in the first days of the revolution the people would have been indignant at hearing of such means to wrest their religion from them; and never would such a mystery of iniquity have emerged from the darkness in which it had been conceived, if Providence had not ordained that the unfortunate adept of whom we are about to speak, stung with remorse, should make an avowal of it.

The Secret Academy discovered by the Secretary.

Before we publish his declaration, it is incumbent on us to say by what means we became acquainted with it, and what precautions we have taken to ascertain its authenticity. The honor and probity of the person who gave us the account placed its veracity beyond all doubt; nevertheless we requested to have it under his signature. Still further, seeing that a great nobleman was mentioned as a witness, and even as the second actor in the scene, we did not hesitate in applying directly to him. This nobleman, of distinguished honor, virtue, and courage, bears the first distinction of French knighthood, and is in London at this time. We attended to the recital he was pleased to make, and found it perfectly consonant with the signed memorial we had carried with us. If his name is omitted, it is only because he was loath to see it appear in a fact that criminates the memory of a friend, whose error was rather owing to the seduction of the Sophisters than to his own heart, and whose repentance in some sort atoned for the crime of which he had been guilty. The following is the fact, which will complete the proofs, as yet only drawn from the letters of the conspirators themselves.

About the middle of the month of September 1789, little more than a fortnight antecedent to the atrocious 5th and 6th of October, at a time when the conduct of the National Assembly, having thrown the people into all the horrors of a revolution, indicated that they would set no bounds to their pretensions, Mr. *Le Roy*, Lieutenant of the King's Hunt, and an Academician, being at the house of Mr. D'Angevilliers, Intendant of the Buildings of his Majesty, the conversation turned on the disasters of the revolution, and on those that were too clearly to be foreseen. Dinner over, the nobleman above-mentioned, a friend of Le Roy, hurt at having seen him so great an admirer of the Sophisters, reproached him with it in the following expressive words: *Well, this, then, is the work of* PHILOSOPHY! Thunderstruck at these words,—Alas! cried the Academician, *to whom do you say so? I know it but too well, and I shall die of grief and remorse!*

At the word remorse, the same nobleman questioned him whether he had so greatly contributed towards the revolution as to upbraid himself with it in that violent manner? "Yes," answered he,

> I have contributed to it, and far more than I was aware of. I was secretary to the committee to which you are indebted for it; but I call heaven to witness, that I never thought it would go to such lengths. You have seen me in the king's service, and you know that I love his person. I little thought of bringing his subjects to this pitch, *and I shall die of grief and remorse!*

Pressed to explain what he meant by this committee, this secret society, entirely new to the whole company, the Academician resumed:

> This society was a sort of club that we Philosophers had formed among us, and only admitted into it persons on whom we could perfectly rely. Our sittings were regularly held at the Baron d'Holbach's. Lest our object should be surmised, we called ourselves Œconomists. We created Voltaire, though absent, our honorary and perpetual president. Our principal members were d'Alembert, Turgot, Condorcet, Diderot, La Harpe and that Lamoignon, Keeper of the Seals, who, on his dismission, shot himself in his park.

The whole of this declaration was accompanied with tears and sighs, when the adept, deeply penitent, continued: "The following were our occupations; the most of those works which have

Its object and means.

appeared for this long time past against religion, morals, and government, were ours, or those of authors devoted to us. They were all composed by the members or by the orders of the society. Before they were sent to the press, they were delivered in at our office. There we revised and corrected them; added to or curtailed them according as circumstances required. When our philosphy was too glaring for the times, or for the object of the work, we brought it to a lower tint; and when we thought that we might be more daring than the author, we spoke more openly. In a word, we made our writers say exactly what we pleased. Then the work was published under the title or name we had chosen, the better to hide the hand whence it came. Many supposed to have been posthumous works, such as *Christianity Unmasked*, and divers others, *attributed to Fréret and Boulanger* after their deaths,[5] were issued from our society.

> When we had approved of those works, we began by printing them on fine or ordinary paper, in sufficient number to pay our expences, and then an immense number on the commonest paper. These latter we sent to hawkers and booksellers free of cost, or nearly so, who were to circulate them among the people at the lowest rate. These were the means used to pervert

---

5   The book, first published in London in 1766 under the pseudonym Feu M. Boulanger, came later to be attributed to Baron d'Holbach. A stylistic analysis by Rudolf Besthom later supplied clear confirmation. —Ed.

the people and bring them to the state you now see them in. I shall not see them long, *for I shall die of grief and remorse!*

This recital had made the company shudder; nevertheless, they could not but be struck at the remorse and horrid situation in which they beheld the speaker. Their indignation for Philosophism was carried still further when Le Roy explained the meaning of ECR. L'INF. (*ecrasez l'infame, crush the wretch*), with which Voltaire concludes so many of his letters. The reader will perceive, that in the whole of these Memoirs we had uniformly given the same explanation; and indeed the context of the letters makes the sense evident; but he revealed what we should not have dared assert on our own authority, that all those to whom Voltaire wrote under that horrid formula were members or initiated into the mysteries of this secret committee. He also declared what we have already said on the plan of elevating Briennes to the archbishopric of Paris; and many other particulars which he related would have been precious to history, but have escaped the memory of those present. None of them could give me any information as to the exact time when this secret academy was formed; but it appears from the discovery made by Mr. Bertins, that it must have existed long before the death of Louis XV.

I think it necessary, on this occasion, to lay before my reader a letter of March 1763, which Voltaire writes to Helvétius. "Why," says he to his zealous brother,

> do the worshippers of reason live in silence and fear? They are not sufficiently acquainted with their own strength. *What should hinder them from having a little press of their own,* and from publishing small works, short *and useful, and which should only be confided to their friends.* This was the method followed by those who printed the Last Will of the good and honest curate (Meslier); his testimony is certainly of great weight. It is further *certain, that you and your friends could, with the greatest facility, pen the best works possible, and throw them into circulation without exposing yourselves in the least.*[6]

There also exists another letter, in which Voltaire, under the name of *Jean Patourel,* heretofore a Jesuit, and in his ironical style seeming to felicitate Helvétius on his pretended conversion, describes the method employed for the circulation of those works among the lower classes.

> In opposition to the *Christian Pedagogue,* and the *Think well on it,* books formerly so much famed for the conversions they had wrought, pretty little philosophic works are *cleverly* circulated; these little books rapidly succeed each other. *They are not sold, they are given to people who can be relied on, who in their turn distribute them to women and young peo-*

---

6   Vol. 58, let. 50. p. 99.

ple. At one time it is the *Sermon of the Fifty*, attributed to the King of Prussia; at another an *Extract from the Will* of the unfortunate curate Jean Meslier, who, on his death-bed, implored forgiveness of his God for having taught Christianity; or, lastly, the *Catechism of the Honest Man*, written by a certain Abbé Durand, (that is, Voltaire himself).[7]

These two letters may throw great light on the subject. First, we see Voltaire giving the plan of a secret society, which perfectly coincides with the one described by Le Roy; secondly, we find that one of a similar nature existed at Ferney; thirdly, that it had not taken place at the period when these letters were written, as he presses the establishment of it. But on the other side, the pretended posthumous works of Fréret and Boulanger, which the adept Le Roy declares to have been issued from this secret academy holding its sittings at the Baron d'Holbach's, were published in 1756 and 1757.[8] It therefore appears

When established.

that this secret committee was established at Paris between the years 1763 and 1766. That is to say, that for three and twenty years preceding the Revolution they had been incessantly endeavouring to seduce the people by those artifices and intrigues, the shame of which, drew the above avowal from its repenting secretary. Such would have been the manufacture of Voltaire's colony!

---

7   To Helvétius, 25 Aug. 1763, vol. 58, let. 91, p. 179.

8   See *L'Antiquité devoilée*, Amsterdam, anno 1766, and *L'Examen des Apologistes du Christianisme*, anno 1767.

It was with truth that this unhappy adept repeated, *I shall die of grief and remorse*; for he did not survive his avowal three months. When he mentioned the principal members, he added that all those to whom Voltaire wrote under the abominable formula of *Crush the Wretch*, were either members, or initiated into the mysteries of this secret academy. It's principal adepts.

According to this clue the first of these adepts will certainly be Damilaville, who exulted so much on hearing that none but the rabble were left to worship Christ; for it is to him in particular that Voltaire always ends his letters by, *crush the wretch*. This man was himself very little above that rabble whom he so much despised. He had made a small fortune by being one of the clerks in the office for the tax called the Vingtiemes, and had a salary of about 18ol. per ann. His philosophy had not taught him to endure poverty, as we see Voltaire excusing himself on his not having been able to procure him a more lucrative employment.[9] Damilaville.

The distinctive character which Voltaire gives him in one of these letters is that of *hating God*. Could that have given rise to their great intimacy? It was through his means that he transmitted his most impious productions or particular secrets to the conspirators. We should have remained in the dark as to his literary talents, had it not been for a letter from Voltaire to the Marquis de Villevielle, which so perfectly describes the meanness of the

9   To Damilaville, 14 Dec. 1767, vol. 60, let. 211, p. 356.

Sophisters, and how distant they were from the true Philospher, ready to sacrifice every thing in the cause of truth. "No, my dear friend (says Voltaire to the Marquis), the modern Socrates will not drink hemlock. The Athenian Socrates, with respect to us, was a very imprudent man, an eternal quibbler, and who foolishly set his judges at defiance.

> The philosophers of our days are wiser than that. They are not possessed with that foolish vanity of putting their names to their works. They are invisible hands, who, from one end of Europe to the other, pierce fanaticism with the shafts of truth. Damilaville is just dead; he *was the author of Christianity Unmasked* (which he had published as a posthumous work of Boulanger's) and of many other writings. *It was never known, and his friends kept his secret with a fidelity worthy of Philosophy.*[10]

Such then is the author of that famous work which the Sophisters had given us as flowing from the pen of one of their most learned adepts. Damilaville, under the name of Boulanger, from his public-office, sallies forth the phœnix of modern Philosophism, and with the courage of a Sophister shrinks from his own works, lest they cost him dearly if ever called upon to support his principles before the tribunals. He also would have shrank from the hemlock potion, under the infamy and eternal shame with which such abominable calum-

10   20 Dec. 1768, vol. 60, let. 331, p. 592.

nies as he had vomited forth against Christianity must have overpowered him.

This adept, so worthy of Voltaire's and d'Alembert's friendship, died a bankrupt clerk in office, and had been parted from his wife for the last twelve years. Voltaire is his panegyrist when he says, "I shall always regret Damilaville; I loved the intrepidity of his soul; he was enthusiastic like Saul Paul; he was a necessary man."[11] Decency forbids us to quote the remainder of the panegyric.

Next to this Sophister, whose chief merits appear to have been his enthusiastic Atheism, we find the Count d'Argental. I have already spoken of his intimacy with Voltaire, and now only mention him as one of those initiated in the secret mysteries of the secret academy; being one of those correspondents to whom Voltaire expresses himself in the most unreserved manner on his plan of crushing Christ.[12]

Count d'Argental.

On the same claim a sort of scribbler called Thiriot is to be enumerated among the members of the academy. No more elevated than Damilaville in rank or fortune, he for a longer time subsisted on the benefactions of Voltaire, who first made him his disciple and then his agent. Brother Thiriot added ingratitude to his impiety, and Voltaire complained bitterly of him. But Thiriot, notwithstanding his ingratitude, always remained

Thiriot.

11   To d'Alembert, 23 Dec. 1768, vol. 68, let. 243, p. 500, and 13 Jan. 1769, vol. 69, let. 2, p. 6.

12   See numbers of letters in the *General Correspondence*.

Saurin.

impious, which reconciled Voltaire to him, and preserved him within the fraternal embrace of the conspirators.[13]

It is with concern that Mr. Saurin is found to have been a member of this academy. Certainly it is not his literary works that raise this sentiment; for were it not for his Tragedy of Spartacus, both his prose and verse would equally be forgotten; but we are told that it was rather his want of fortune, than to his disposition, that he owed his connexions with the Sophisters. He is even said to have been a man of great probity; but that he was drawn into that society for the consideration of a pension of a thousand crowns which Helvétius paid him. What an excuse! And where is the probity of the man who will sacrifice his religion to his interest, and for a pension coalesce with those who conspire against his God? We see Voltaire writing to Saurin himself, and placing him on the same line with Helvétius and the initiated Brethren, entrusting him with the same secrets, and exhorting him to the same warfare against Christ. As we have never seen him disclaim the connexion, the shame of it must attach to him.[14]

Grimm.

A Swiss Baron of the name of Grimm must also necessarily find his place here. He was the worthy

---

13 See *Correspondence* and Letters to d'Alembert, and letters from the Marchioness of Chatellet to the King of Prussia.

14 To Saurin, 2 Feb. 1761, vol. 57, let. 23, p. 52, and to Damilaville, 28 Nov. 1762, let. 259, p. 506.

friend and co-operator of Diderot; like him travelling to Petersbourg to form adepts, then returning to Paris, he also joins in his absurdities, repeats after him, that *between a man and his dog there is no other difference than their dress*, and exults in being able to apprize Voltaire that the Emperor Joseph II. was initiated into his mysteries.

We will terminate our list by the German Baron d'Holbach, who, destitute of abilities, lends his house. He had acquired at Paris the reputation of a lover and protector of the arts, nor did the Sophisters contribute a little to it. This was a cloak to their meetings at his house. Unable to vie with the poet, he wishes to be the Mecenas. Nor is he the only person who has owed his reputation to his purse, and to his having disposed of it in favor of the Sophisters. In spite of these pretences, used for coloring the frequent meetings of the adepts, the public repute of those who resorted to his house had thrown such an odium on him, as to cause it to be openly said, that to gain admittance at his house it was necessary, as in Japan, to trample on the cross.

Such then were the members of this famous academy, whose sole object was to corrupt the minds of the people and prepare the way to universal apostacy, under the pretext of public happiness, public œconomy, or the love and advancement of the arts. We have mentioned fifteen of its members, Voltaire, d'Alembert, Diderot, Helvétius, Turgot, Condorcet, La Harpe, the keeper of the

Baron d'Hobach.

seals Lamoignon, Damilaville, Thiriot, Saurin, the Count d'Argental, Grimm, the Baron d'Holbach, and the unfortunate Le Roi, who died consumed with grief and remorse for having been the secretary to so monstrous an academy.

If we now revert to the real founder of this academy, and to Voltaire's letter to Helvétius, already quoted, the following one to d'Alembert should be added:

> Let the Philosophers unite in *a brotherhood like the Freemasons*, let them assemble and support each other; let them be faithful to the association. Then I would suffer myself to be burnt for them. This Secret Academy will be far superior to that of Athens, and to all those of Paris. But every one thinks only for himself, and forgets that his most sacred duty is to *annihilate the wretch*.

This letter is dated 20th April 1761.[15] Confronting it with the declaration of Le Roi, we see how faithfully the Parisian adepts had followed the plans of the premier chief. Often did he lament his inability of presiding over their labours but at a distance; and it was difficult to persuade him, that the capital of the most Christian empire was a proper seat for so licentious an establishment. It is for that reason that we see him pursuing his favorite plan of the philosphic colony, even after the establishment of the secret academy. But the time

---

15   Vol. 68, let. 85, p. 163.

came when the direful success of the latter more than compensated the loss of the former. Triumphant in Paris, and surrounded by the adepts, he was one day to reap the fruits of such unrelenting constancy in the warfare which during the last half century he waged against his God.

CHAPTER XVIII.

Of the Progress of the Conspiracy throughout Europe.—Triumph and Death of the Chiefs.

s the conspirators advanced in their arts of seduction, their hopes were daily heightened by some new success. Already was that success so great, that a few years after the Encyclopedia had first appeared we find d'Alembert confidently writing to Voltaire, "Let Philosophy alone, and in twenty years the Sorbonne, however much Sorbonne it may be, will outstrip Lausanne itself;" that is to say, that in twenty years time (and this was written 21st July, 1757),[1] the Sorbonne would be as incredulous and Antichristian as a cer-

Hopes of the conspirators.

---

1   Vol. 68, let. 30, p. 51.

tain minister of Lausanne (Voltaire himself), who furnished the most impious articles that are to be found in the Encyclopedia.

Soon after Voltaire, improving on d'Alembert, says, "Twenty years more, *and God will be in a pretty plight!*[2] That is to say, twenty years more, and not an altar of the God of the Christians shall remain.

Their progress.

Every thing indeed seemed to forbode the universal reign of impiety throughout Europe. The district in particular which had fallen to Voltaire was making such an awful progress, that eight years after he writes, *not a single Christian is to be found from Geneva to Berne.*[3] Every where else, to use his expressions, the *world was acquiring wit apace*; and even so fast, *that a general revolution in ideas threatened all around.* Germany in particular gave him great hopes.[4] Frederick, who as carefully watched it as Voltaire did Switzerland, writes, that "philosphy was beginning to penetrate even into superstitious Bohemia, and into Austria, the former abode of superstition."[5]

In Switzerland.

In Germany.

Russia.

In Russia the adepts gave still greater hopes. This protection of the *Scythians* is what consoles Voltaire for the persecutions which befel the Sect elsewhere.[6] He could not contain himself for

2   To d'Alembert, 25 Feb. 1758, vol. 68, let. 44, p. 79.

3   To d'Alembert, 8 Feb. 1766, vol. 69, let. 151, p. 257.

4   To d'Alembert, 5 Apr. 1765, vol. 68, let. 162, p. 352.

5   From Frederick, 8 Jan. 1766, vol. 65, let. 143, p. 344.

6   To Diderot, 25 Dec. 1762, vol. 57, let. 242, p. 475.

joy when he wrote to d'Alembert how much the brethren were protected at Petersburg, and informed him, that during a journey made by that court the Scythian protectors had each one, for his amusement, undertaken to translate a chapter of Belisarius into their language: that the Empress had undertaken one herself, and had even been at the trouble of revising the translation of this work, which in France had been censured by the Sorbonne.[7]

D'Alembert wrote, that in Spain Philosophism was *undermining* the Inquisition;[8] and according to Voltaire, a great *revolution was operating in ideas there, as well as in Italy.*[9] A few years later we find that this Italy swarmed with men thinking like Voltaire and d'Alembert, and that their interest only prevented them from openly declaring for impiety.[10] *In Spain. In Italy.*

As to England, they made but little doubt of its falling an easy prey. According to them, it was overrun with Socinians who scoffed at and hated Christ, as Julian the apostate hated and despised him, and who only differed in name from the philosophers.[11] *In England.*

Finally, according to their calculations, Bavaria and Austria alone (this was during the lifetime

---

7   To d'Alembert, July, 1767, vol. 68, let. 212, p. 445.

8   From d'Alembert, 13 May, 1773, vol. 69, let. 108, p. 182, and 5 April 1768, vol. 68, let. 226, p. 473.

9   To Riche, 1 March, 1768, vol. 60, let. 254, p. 434.

10   To d'Alembert, 16 June 1773, vol. 69, let. 113, p. 194.

11   To Frederick, 8 Nov. 1773, vol. 66, let. 46. p. 112.

of the Empress Queen) continued to support the divines and defenders of religion. The Empress of Russia *was driving them on gloriously*; and they were at *their last gasp in Poland,* thanks to the King Poniatowski. They were already *overthrown in Prussia,* through the care of Frederick; and *in the north of Germany* the Sect daily gained ground, thanks to the Landgraves, Margraves, Dukes and Princes, adepts and protectors.[12]

In France.   Far otherwise did matters stand in France. We often see the two chiefs complaining of the obstacles they had to encounter in that country, the favorite object of their conspiracy.

The perpetual appeals of the clergy, the decrees of the parliaments, the very acts of authority which the ministers, though friendly to the conspirators, were obliged to exert in order to hide their predilection, were not entirely ineffectual. The bulk of the nation still remained attached to its faith. That numerous class called the people, in spite of all the intrigues of the secret academy, still flocked to the Altar on days of solemnity. In the higher classes, numerous were the exceptions to be made of those who still loved religion. Indignant at so many obstacles, Voltaire would perpetually stimulate his countrymen, whom he contemptuously calls his *poor Velches.* Sometimes however he was better pleased with them, and would write to his dear Marquis Villevieille,

---

12   To d'Alembert, 4 Sept. 1767, vol. 68, let. 219, p. 459.

*The people are mighty foolish; Philosophism
nevertheless makes its way down to them.* Be
well assured, for instance, that there are not
twenty people in Geneva who would not abjure
Calvin as soon as they would the Pope; and that
many philosphers are to be found in Paris behind the counter.[13]

But, generally speaking, his complaints about
France predominate in his correspondence with
the conspirators; sometimes he would despair of
ever seeing Philosophy triumph there. D'Alembert,
on the spot, judged of matters very differently; and
though every thing did not answer his wishes, he
nevertheless thought himself authorised to flatter
Voltaire, that though *philosophy might receive a
temporary check, it never could be subdued.*[14]

About the period when d'Alembert wrote this,
it was but too true that Philosophism could flatter
itself with the hopes of triumphing over the attachment of the French nation to their religion. During the last ten or twelve years impiety had made
a dreadful progress; the colleges had sent forth a
new generation educated by new masters; they
were nearly void of all knowledge, and particularly
destitute of religion or piety. It perfectly coincided with Condorcet's expression, that Philosophism *had descended from the thrones of the North
into the very universities.*[15] The religious gener-

---

13   20 Dec. 1768, vol. 60, let. 331, Page 593.

14   From d'Alembert, 5 Nov. 1776, vol. 69, let. 49, p. 282.

15   See his Preface to his edition of Pascal's *Thoughts*.

ation was nearly extinct, and the revealed truths were obliged to give place to the empty sounds of reason, philosophy, prejudices, and such terms. In the higher classes impiety made large strides, whether at court or in the tribunals. From the capital it gained the provinces, and the master set the example to the servant. Every one would be a Philosopher, whether minister or magistrate, soldier or author. He that wished to adhere to his religion was exposed to all the sarcastic irony of the Sophisters, and that particularly among the great, where it required as much courage to profess one's religion after the conspiracy, as it did audacity and rashness to declare one's self an Atheist before.

Voltaire's triumph.

Voltaire was at that time in his eighty-fourth year. After so long an absence, and always under the power and lash of the law, he could only have appeared publicly in Paris to controvert those impieties which had brought the animadversion of the parliament on him. D'Alembert and his academy resolved to overcome that obstacle. In spite of religion they easily succeed, and ministers, chiefly adepts, abusing the clemency of Louis XVI. obtain the recal of this premier chief, under pretence that this aged man had been sufficiently punished by his long exile; and that in consideration of his literary trophies, his failings might be over-looked. It was agreed that the laws should be silent with regard to him on his approach to Paris; the magistrates seemed to have forgotten the decree they had passed against him. This was all that the conspirators wished. Voltaire arrives in Paris, he receives the homage of the Sect, and his arrival constitutes their triumphal day. This man, bending under the weight of years spent in an unrelenting warfare, whether public or private, against Christianity, is received in the capital of his Most Christian Majesty, amidst those exclamations which were wont to announce the arrival of the favorite child of victory returning from the arduous toils of war.

Whithersoever Voltaire bent his steps, a croud of adepts and the gazing multitude flocked to meet him. All the academies celebrate his arrival, and they celebrate it in the Louvre, in the palace of the kings, where Louis XVI. is one day to be a prisoner and victim to the occult and deep conspiracies of he Sophisters. The theatres decree their crowns to the impious chief; entertainments in his honor rapidly succeed each other. Intoxicated through pride with the incense of the adepts, he fears to sink under it. In the midst of these coronations and acclamations he exclaimed, *You wish then to make me expire with glory!*—Religion alone His death. mourned at this sight, and vengeance hung over his head. The impious man had feared to die of glory; but rage and despair was to forward his last hour still more than his great age. In the midst of his triumphs a violent hemorrhage raised apprehensions for his life. D'Alembert, Diderot, and Marmontel, hastened to support his resolution in his last moments; but were only witnesses to their own ignominy as well as to his.

Here let not the historian fear exaggeration. Rage, remorse, reproach, and blasphemy, all accompany and characterize the long agony of the dying Atheist. This death, the most terrible that is ever recorded to have stricken the impious man, will not be denied by his companions in impiety; their silence, however much they may wish to deny it, is the least of those corroborative proofs which could be adduced. Not one of the Sophisters has ever dared to mention any sign given of resolution or tranquillity by the premier chief uring the space of three months, which elapsed from the time he was crowned at the theatre until his decease. Such a silence expresses how great their humiliation was in his death.

On his return from the theatre, and in the midst of the toils he was resuming in order to acquire fresh applause, Voltaire was warned, that the long areer of his impiety was drawing to an end.

In spite of all the Sophisters flocking around him, in the first days of his illness he gave signs of wishing to return to the God he had so often blasphemed. He calls for the priests who ministered to *Him* who he had sworn to crush, under the appellation of *the wretch*. His danger increasing, he wrote the following note to the Abbé Gaultier. "You had promised me, Sir, to come and hear me. I intreat you would take the trouble of calling as soon as possible, *signed,* VOLTAIRE. Paris, the 26th Feb. 1778."

A few days after he wrote the following declaration, in presence of the same Abbé Gaultier, the

CHAPTER XVIII

Abbé Mignot, and the Marquis de Villevieille, copied from the minutes deposited with Mr. Momet,
Notary at Paris.

> I, the underwritten, declare, that for these four
> days, having been afflected with a vomiting of
> blood at the age of eighty-four, and not having
> been able to drag myself to the church, the Rev.
> the Rector of Saint-Sulpice having been pleased
> to add to his good works that of sending to me
> the Abbé Gaultier, a priest, I confessed to him;
> and if it pleases God to dispose of me, I die in
> the *Holy Catholic Church* in which I was born;
> hoping that the divine mercy will deign to par-
> don all my faults: if ever I have scandalized the
> Church, I ask pardon of God and of the Church.
> 2d March 1778. *Signed*, VOLTAIRE: in presence
> of the Abbé Mignot, my nephew, and the Mar-
> quis de Villeveille, my friend.

After the two witnesses had signed this declaration, Voltaire added these words, copied from the
same minutes:

> The Abbé Gaultier, my confessor, having ap-
> prized me, that it was said among a certain set
> of people, that I should protest against every
> thing I did at my death; I declare I never made
> such a speech, and that it is an old jest attribut-
> ed long since to many of the learned more en-
> lightened than I am.

Was this declaration a fresh instance of his former hypocrisy? Unfortunately, after the explana-

tions we have seen him give of his exterior acts of religion, might there not be room for doubt? Be that as it may, this is a public homage paid to that religion in which he declared he meant to die, notwithstanding his having perpetually conspired against it during his life. This declaration is also signed by that same friend and adept the Marquis de Villevielle, to whom eleven years before Voltaire was wont to write, *"Conceal your march from the enemy* in your endeavours to crush the wretch."[16]

Voltaire had permitted this declaration to be carried to the rector of Saint-Sulpice, and to the Archbishop of Paris, to know whether it would be sufficient. When the Abbé Gaultier returned with the answer, it was impossible for him to gain admittance to the patient. The conspirators had strained every nerve to hinder the chief from consummating his recantation, and every avenue was shut to the priest which Voltaire himself had sent for. The demons haunted every access; rage succeeds to fury, and fury again to rage during the remainder of his life. Then it was that d'Alembert, Diderot, and about twenty others of the conspirators who had beset his apartment, never approached him, but to witness their own ignominy; and often he would curse them and exclaim,—"Retire; it is you that have brought me to my present state; begone, I could have done without you all; but you could not exist without me; and what a wretched glory have you procured me!"

16   27 April 1767, vol. 60, let. 102, p. 180.

Then would succeed the horrid remembrance of his conspiracy. They could hear him, the prey of anguish and dread, alternately supplicating and blaspheming that God against whom he had conspired; and in plaintive accents he would cry out, Oh Christ! Oh Jesus Christ! And then complain that he was abandoned by God and man. The hand which had traced in ancient writ the sentence of an impious revelling king, seemed to trace before his eyes CRUSH THEN, DO CRUSH THE WRETCH. In vain he turned away his head; the time was coming apace when he was to appear before the tribunal of him he had blasphemed; and his physicians (particularly Mr. Tronchin), calling in to administer relief, retire thunderstruck, declaring the death of the impious man to be terrible indeed. The pride of the conspirators would willingly have suppressed these declarations; but it was in vain: the Mareschal de Richlieu flies from the bedside declaring it to be a sight too terrible to be sustained; and Mr. Tronchin says, that the ravings of Orestes could give but a faint idea of those of Voltaire.

Thus died on the 30th of May, 1778, rather worn out by his own fury than by the weight of years, the most unrelenting Conspirator against Christianity that had been seen since the time of the Apostles. His persecution, longer and more perfidious than those of Nero or Diocletian, had yet only produced apostates; but they were more numerous than the martyrs made in the former persecutions. (*See the note at the end of the chapter.*)

D'Alembert succeeds as chief,

The conspirators, in losing Voltaire, had lost every thing with respect to talents; but his arms of impiety they had remaining in his numerous writings. The art and cunning of d'Alembert proved more than a succedaneum to the genius of their deceased founder, and he was proclaimed chief. The secret committee of education in Paris, the country conventicles, and the correspondence with the village school-masters, owed their origin to him. He continued to direct the works of the secret academy in the propagation of impiety, until called upon to appear before that same God who had already judged Voltaire. He died five years after his patron, that is in November 1783.—Lest remorse should compel him to similar recantations to those which had so much humbled the Sect, Condorcet undertook to render him inaccessible, if not to repentance and remorse, at least to all who might have availed themselves of any homage that he might do to religion.

and dies.

When the Rector ot Saint-Germain's, in quality of pastor, presented himselt, Condorcet, like a devil watching over his prey, ran to the door and barred his entrance! Scarcely had the breath left his body when the pride of Condorcet betrays his secret. D'Alembert really had felt that remorse which must have been common to him with Voltaire; he was on the eve of sending, as the only method of reconciliation, for a minister of that same Christ against whom he had also conspired; but Condorcet ferociously combated these last signs of repentance in the dying Sophister, and he gloried in having forced him to expire in final impenitence. The whole of this odious conflict is comprized in one horrid sentence. When Condorcet announced the decease of d'Alembert, and was relating the circumstances, he did not blush to add—*Had I not been there, he would have flinched also.*[17]

Frederick alone had succeeded, or pretended to have succeeded, in persuading himself that death was but an eternal sleep.[18] And he alone appears to have been an exception from among the chiefs of the conspiracy, with whom the approach of death had substituted, in lieu of their pretended hatred for the *wretch*, the fear of his judgments. *Frederick.*

Diderot, that hero of Atheism, that conspirator who long since had carried to insanity his audacity against his Christ and his God, Diderot, I say, was he who was nearest to a true reconciliation. This is another of those mysteries of iniquity carefully hidden by the Antichristian conspirators. *Diderot.*

---

17 *Historical Dictionary,* Article d'Alembert. It is true that Condorcet, sorry for having inadvertendy revealed the secret of his associate's remorse, sought to destroy the effect of it. It is true, that questioned another time on the circumstances of d'Alembert's death, he answered in his philosophic jargon, that he did not like a coward. In his first letter to the King of Prussia, dated the 22d Nov. 1783, he represents d'Alembert as dying with a tranquil courage, and with his usual strength and presence of mind. But it was too late to lead Frederick into error on that subject, as the adept Grimm had already written. That sickness had greatly weakened d'Alembert's mind in his last moments (11th of November 1783).

18 *Vide supra.*

When the Empress of Russia purchased Diderot's library she left him the use of it during his life. Her munificence had enabled him to have near his person, in quality of librarian, a young man who was far from partaking in his impiety. Diderot liked him much, and he had particularly endeared himself by the attentions he had shown Diderot during his last illness. It was he who generally dressed the wounds in his legs. Terrified at the symptoms he perceived, the young man runs to acquaint a worthy ecclesiastic, the Abbé Lemoine, then resident at the house called the Foreign Missions, Rue du Bac, Fauxbourg Saint-Germain. By his advice the young man prays for half an hour in a church, begging of Almighy God that he would direct him in what he should say or do to ensure the salvation of one who, though he detested his impieties, he could never forget was his benefactor. Rising from his prayers he returns to Diderot, and the same day, while dressing his wounds, he spoke as follows:

> Mr. Diderot, you see me this day more anxious than ever as to your fate. Do not be surprised; I am aware how much I am indebted to you; it is by your kindness that I subsist; you have deigned to put greater confidence in me than I had reason to expect. I cannot prove ungrateful; I should for ever accuse myself of ingratitude were I to hide from you the danger which your wounds declare you to be in. Mr. Diderot, you may have dispositions to make; and above all you have preparations to make for the world

you are about to enter. I am but a young man,
I know; but are you certain that your Philosphy
has not left you a soul to save? I have no doubt
of it; and it is impossible for me to reflect on it,
and not warn my benefactor to avoid the eternal
misery which may await him. Sir, you have still
sufficient time left; and excuse an advice which
gratitude and your friendship forces from me.

Diderot heard the young man with attention,
and even melted into tears. He thanked him for
his frankness, and for the concern he had shown
for him. He promised to consider and to reflect
what line of conduct he should adopt in a situation
which he owned to be of the greatest importance.

The young man waited his decision with the
greatest impatience, and the first signs were con-
formable to his wishes. He ran to inform the Abbé
Lemoine that Diderot asked to see a clergyman,
and the Abbé directed him to Mr. de Tersac, Rector of Saint-Sulpice. Mr. de Tersac waited on Diderot, and had several conferences with him.—He
was preparing a public recantation of his past errors; but, unfortunately, he was watched by the
conspirators. The visit of a priest to Diderot had
given the alarm to the Sophisters, who thought
themselves dishonored by the dereliction of so
important a chief. They surround him;—they persuade him that he is imposed upon; that his health
is not in so bad a state, but that a little country air
would immediately recover him.—Diderot was for
a long time deaf to all the arguments Philosoph-

ism could invent, but at length consented at least to try the country air. His eparture was kept secret, and the wretches who carried him away knew that his last hour was fast approaching. The Sophisters who were in the plot pretended to think him still in Paris, and the whole town was misled by daily reports; while those jailors who had seized on his person watched him till they had seen him expire; then, continuing their horrid duplicity, they bring back the lifeless corpse to Paris, and spread the report that he had died suddenly at table. He expired the 2d of July 1784, and was represented as having died calm in all his Atheism, without giving any signs of remorse. The public are again misled, and thus many are confirmed in their impiety, who might have followed the example of this chief, had he not by the most unheard-of cruelty been deprived of all spiritual relief in his last moments.

Thus in the whole of this conspiracy, from its origin to the death of its first promoters, we have seen but one continued chain of cunning, art, and seduction; of the blackest, falsest, and most disgusting means employed in the tremendous art of seducing the people. It was on these horrid arts that Voltaire, d'Alembert, and Diderot had built all their hopes of working universal apostacy; and in their last moments they are a prey to those very arts. In that awful moment when glory vanishes, and the empty name he has acquired by their deceit is no more, the disciple of seduction lords it over his master. When reason calls on them to make use of that liberty, (so much cried up when opposed to their God) to reconcile themselves with him they had blasphemed, even their very remorse is sacrificed to the vanity of their school: when it calls on them to use that courage they had shown when blaspheming, it fails them in their repentance, and they show none but the slavish symptoms of weakness and fear. Under the subjection of their adepts they expire fettered in those chains which they themselves had forged, and consumed by that impiety which their hearts now abhor.

At the time of their death, hatred to Christianity and the Conspiracy against the Altar was not the only object of their school. Voltaire had been the father of the Sophisters of Impiety, and he lived to be the premier chief of the Sophisters of Rebellion. He had said to his first adepts, "Let us crush the Altar, let the temples be destroyed, and let not a single worshipper be left to the God of the Christians;" and his school soon re-echoed with the cry of, "Let us break the sceptres, let the thrones be destroyed, and let not a single subject be left to the kings of the earth." It is from their mutual success, that the combined revolution is to be generated, which, grasping the hatchet, shall in France overthrow the Altar and the throne, murder the pontiffs, strike off the head of the monarch, and proudly menace the kings of the earth and all Christian altars with a similar fate.—We have now given the history of the plots and of the means of the ANTICHRISTIAN CONSPIRACY, or of the *Sophisters of Impiety*. Before we begin that of the ANTIMONARCHIAL CONSPIRACY, or of the *Sophisters of Rebellion*, let us reflect on the extraordinary illusion which Philosophism has thrown over all nations, and which may be considered as having been one of the most powerful agents of the Sect.

***

Note to CHAPTER XVIII.

Some person, on perusing the first edition of this work, thought proper to send a flat denial of the above account of Voltaire's death to the authors of the British Critic, under the initials D. J. They gave him no degree of credit; but it is to his anonynmous assertion that we are indebted for the following letter from Mr. De Luc, a name that needs no observation to enhance the value of his testimony.

Letter from M. DE LUC on the *Death of Voltaire*.

Sir,

Your *Memoirs illustrating the History of Jacobinism* having been the other day the subject of conversation, it was objected, that the description of Voltaire (so prominent a feature in our Work) was so very dissimilar to that given by the other historians of his life, that persons at a distance from the source of information were at a loss what judgment to form. The difference between your account of his death, and that which appeared in a *Life of Voltaire* translated from the French by Mr. Monke, and published in London 1787, was particularly noticed, and incited me to consult that work. The

Translator describes himself as *a young naval officer, who, while at Paris, wished to employ his recess from professional duty, both to his improvement and advantage.* Nothing but the youth of Mr. Monke, and his want of experience, can excuse his undertaking; for, to let his countrymen benefit by the proficiency he was making at Paris, he diffused among them, through the medium of this translation, all that poison which was then so industriously emitted, to produce an effect now but too well known, and which I hope he does not this day contemplate without horror.

I will make no observations on this *Life of Voltaire*; you know from what source it came,[19] and how little capable it was of seducing any but heedless youths who, without any knowledge of the age they lived in, were still susceptible of a sort of admiration for every thing that was great, though in vice and villany. As one of the artifices of impiety is to represent its champions calmly breathing their last in the bed of honour, I feel it incumbent on me to confirm what you have said on one of those circumstances of the death of Voltaire which is closely connected with all the rest.

Being at Paris in 1781, I was often in company with one of those persons whose testimony you invoke on public reports, I mean Mr. Tronchin. He was an old acquaintance of Voltaire's at Geneva, when he came to Paris in quality of first physician to the father of the late Duke of Orléans.—He was called in during Voltaire's

19   I have seen this life of Voltaire. Mr. de Villette was the author of it; and Mr. Monke might just as well have exercised his talents in translating Condorcet.

last sickness; and I have heard him repeat all those circumstances on which Paris and the whole world were at that time full of conversation, respecting the horrid state of this impious man's soul at the approach of death. Mr. Tronchin (even as physician) did every thing in his power to calm him; for the agitation he was in was so violent, that no remedies could take effect. But he could not succeed; and, unable to endure the horror he felt at the peculiar nature of his frantic rage, he abandoned him.

So violent a state in an exhausted frame could not be of long duration. Stupor, the forerunner of dissolution, must naturally succeed, as it generally does after any violent agitations generated by pain; and it is this latter state which in Voltaire has been decorated by the appellation of calm. Mr. Tronchin wished to discredit this error; and with that laudable view, as an eye witness, he immediately published in all companies the real facts, and precisely as you have stated them. This he did to furnish a dreadful lesson to those who calculate on being able in a death-bed to investigate the dispositions most proper to appear in before the judgment-seat of the Almighty. At that period, not only the state of the body, but the condition of the soul, may frustrate their hopes of making so awful an investigation. For justice and sanctity as well as goodness are attributes of God; and he sometimes, as a wholesome admonition to mankind, permits the punishments denounced against the impious man to begin even in this life by the tortures of remorse.

But this inaccuracy respecting the death of Voltaire is not the only one with which the aforenamed author might be upbraided. He has suppressed many well known circumstances relating to his first disposition to return to the church, and his consequent declarations, which you have given on well-authenticated records, all anterior to that anguish of mind which his co-operators have wished to suppress, and of which they themselves were too probably the cause. They surrounded him, and thus cut him off from that which alone could restore tranquility to his soul, by employing the few moments he still had to live in making what reparation he could for the evil he had done. But this artifice could not deceive those who were better acquainted with Voltaire's character; for, not to notice the acts of hypocrisy which earthly considerations frequently made him commit, those of which the sudden fear of a future state have made him guilty are also known. I will give you an example of one, which was related to me at Gottinguen in December 1776, by Mr. Dieze, second librarian of that university; and you may. Sir, make what use of it you please.

During Voltaire's residence in Saxony, where Mr. Dieze served him as a secretary, he fell dangerously ill. As soon as he was apprized of his situation he sent for a priest, confessed to him, and begged to receive the sacrament, which he actually did receive, showing all the exterior signs of repentance, which lasted as long as his danger; but as soon as that was over, he affected to laugh at what he called his *littleness*, and, turning to Mr. Dieze, "My friend (said he) you have seen the *weakness of the man.*"

It is also to human weakness that sectaries of his impiety have attributed the paroxisms of fear in him and some of his accomplices. Sickness, say they, weakens the mind as well as the body, and often produces pusillanimity. These symptoms of conversion in the wicked at the approach of death are, undoubtedly, signs of a great weakness; but to what is it to be attributed? Is it to their understanding? Certainly not; for it is in that awful moment that every thing vanishes which had clouded it during their life. That weakness, therefore, is to be wholly attributed to their *internal conviction* that they have sinned.

Led away by vanity, or some other vicious passion, those men aspire at creating a Sect: Ignorance and the passions of other men second their undertaking. Inebriated with their triumph, they persuade themselves that they are capable of giving laws to the whole world: They boldly make the attempt, and the hoodwinked crowd become their followers.—Having attained the zenith of happiness for the proud and vain glorious soul, they abandon themselves to all the wantonness of imagination and desire. The world then, in their eyes, becomes a vast field of new enjoyments, the legitimacy of which has no other standard but their own inclinations; and the fumes of an incense lavished on them by those whom they have taught to scoff like themselves at every law, perpetuates their delirium. But when the sickness has dispersed the flattering cohort, has blasted their pleasures, and all hopes of new triumphs; when they feel themselves advancing, abandoned and naked, toward that awful *Eternity* on which they have taken upon themselves to decide, not only for themselves but for all those who have been led away in the whirlwind of their fictions- If in this terrible moment, when pride has lost its support, they come to reflect on the arguments on which they grounded their attack against the universal belief of a *Revelation* which was to serve man as a positive and universal rule in matters of faith.—The weakness then of their arguments (which they dare no longer attire in the garb of sophistry, stares them in the face; and nothing but the total extinction of their feelings can quell the terrors of a conscience which tells them that they are about to appear before the tribunal of the author of that same *Revelation.*

It is to point out this real *weakness* of the Antichristian chiefs that we must labor throughout their whole history, for the benefit of those who, without any further examination (and persuaded that these opinions are grounded on deep research) become their dupes and disciples: It is, I say, incumbent on us to show that those men had not, any more than their sectaries, any real conviction, and that their obstinacy in their opinions solely proceeded from the narcotic fumes of the incense of their admirers. For this purpose it is my intention shortly to give to the public, in confirmation of what you have said of Voltaire, all that my former acquaintance with him has brought to my knowledge. The times in which we live makes it the duty of every man who has had a nearer view of the plots laid by the Sect against Revelation to unfold the circumstances of them, which are as shameful from their voluntary ignorance, as from their atrocity; and it is this sentiment, Sir, which makes me partake in common with all true friends to humanity, of that admiration and gratitude which are due to you for your generous exertions in this charitable career.

I remain, Sir, your's, See. Sec.

DE LUC.

Windsor, the 23d of October, 1797.

After such a testimony, let people talk of Voltaire dying with the calmness of a hero.

Of the great Delusion which Rendered the Conspiracy against the Altar so successful.

I n the first part of these Memoirs on Jacobinism, our object was to demonstrate the existence, to unmask the chiefs, and deduce the means and progress of a conspiracy, planned and executed by men, known by the name of Philosophers, against the Christian religion, without distinction of Protestant or Catholic, without even excepting those numerous Sects which had sprung up in England or Germany, or in any other part of the universal world, provided they did but adore the God of Christians. To unfold this mystery of impiety, we had promised to adduce our proofs solely from their own records, that is from their letters, writings or avowals, and we flatter ourselves with having given real historical demonstration of it, sufficient to convince a reader, the most difficult of conviction. Let us for a moment examine what pretensions its authors could have had to be styled PHILOSOPHERS, a name which gave them so much weight in their conspiracy.

The generality of men attending rather to words than things, this affectation of dominion over wisdom and reason proved a very successful weapon in their hands. Had they called themselves unbelievers, or the declared enemies of Christianity, Voltaire and d'Alembert would have been the execration of all Europe; while only calling themselves Philosophers, they are mistaken for such. Is not their school to this day venerated by many as that of Philosophy, notwithstanding the numerous massacres and all the horrid disasters which we have seen naturally flowing from their conspiracy? And every man who will adopt their way of thinking on religion styles himself a Philosopher!—This is a delusion of more consequence than can be imagined, and has carried the number of adepts perhaps farther than any other of their artifices. As long as their school shall be mistaken for that of reason, numberless will be the thoughtless persons who, pretending to depth of thought, will adopt the sentiments of a Voltaire or a Diderot, of a d'Alembert or a Condorcet, and conspire like them, against the Altar; and that disastrous blast will once more spread around the throne, and over all the orders

Delusion on the word Phi-losophy.

of society. Their oaths, their wishes and their plots have been laid open; where then are their pretensions to wisdom? Is it not the historian's duty to tear off that mask of hypocrisy, which has misled such numbers of adepts, who, miserably seeking to soar above the vulgar, have only sunk into impiety, gazing after this pretended Philosophy. The empty sounds of Reason, Philosophy, and Wisdom, have made them believe themselves inspired, when, like Voltaire, they hated or despised the religion of Christ. But it is time they should know that they have only been the dupes of designing men. Let them hearken; the numerous proofs we have adduced give us a right to be heard when we tell them, "that at the school of the conspirators they have mistaken the lessons of hatred and phrenzy, for those of reason; they have been the dupes of folly and madness, under the cloak of wisdom; of ignorance, under the pretence of science; of vice and depravity, under the mask of virtue; and their zeal for Philosophy still makes them err through all the tortuous windings of wickedness and impiety." We do not pretend, in holding such language, to dispute the talents of the premier chief. That his poetic genius should enjoy itself in fictions, on the banks of Parnassus, or on the heights of Pindus, is much to be admired; but is he to be allowed to substitute those fictions for truths? The greater his genius, the less we are astonished to see him entangled when he has once adopted error. If stupidity can never attain to genius, the genius that dares to soar above reason is not the less within the regions of delirium. In a raging fever, your strength will be redoubled; but is there a more humiliating sight for man! Where then is the excuse of genius or of talents in the Sophister conspiring against his God? Can the adepts, who believe their master to be a hilosopher even to his last moments admire that frantic rage in which he expired? But first let them tell us what other titles he may have to the empire of reason.

What Philosophy can there be in that extraordinary *hatred* which Voltaire had sworn against the God of Christianity? That a Nero should have sworn to crush the Christians and their God may be explained, because the idea could only have been that of a cruel monster. That a Dioclesian should have sworn it may be understood, because the idolatrous tyrant thought to appease the anger of his gods and avenge their glory. That a Julian, mad enough to restore the worship of idols, should have sworn it, appears only to have been a consequence of his former delirium. But that a pretended sage, who neither believes in the God of the Christians nor in the Gods of the Pagans, and who knows not in what God to believe, should vent all his rage and fury precisely against Christ, is one of those phænomena of modern Philosophism which can be considered but as the delirium of the impious man.

I do not pretend by this to exclude from the school of reason every one who is not fortunate enough to be within the pale of Christianity; let that man rank with an Epictetus or a Seneca, or before the Christian era with a Socrates or a Plato, who has been unfortunate enough not to have known the proofs of Christianity. But this real Philosophy of reason sought what Voltaire has conspired to destroy. The greatest of Socrates's disciples pants for the coming of that just man who shall dissipate the darkness and the doubts of the sage. I hear him exclaim, "Let him come; let that man come who will teach us our duties toward the Gods, and our duty towards man. Let him come instantly; I am ready to obey whatever he may ordain, and I hope he will make me a better man."[1] Such is the language of the Philosophy of reason. I think I behold him again, when in the bitterness of his heart he foresees that should this just man appear upon earth, he would be scoffed at by the wicked, buffeted, and scourged, in a word treated as the outcast of men.[2] That man has appeared, so much sought for by the Pagan Philosopher; and the conspiring Sophisters, a d'Alembert or a Voltaire, seek to crush him, and yet pretend to the Philosophy of reason. Let their disciples answer for them. If in the son of Mary they will not acknowledge the Son of the Eternal Father, let them confess him to be at least that just man sought for by Plato. What then are their pretensions to the Philosophy of reason in conspiring against him? If the awful testi-

---

1   Plato in his *Second Alcibiades*.

2   *Ibid.*

mony of the sun being darkened, the dead rising from their graves, the veil of the temple being rent, cannot convince them; let them at least admire the most holy, the justest of men, the prodigy of goodness and meekness, the apostle of every virtue, the wonder of oppressed innocence praying for his executioners. Where is their Philosophy when they conspire against the Son of Man? Yes, Philosophy they had; but it was that of the Jews, that of the synagogue, whence issued those blasphemous cries of, "Crucify him, crucify him!" *or crush the wretch!* Judas himself confesses him to be the just man; and shall he approach to perfection when compared to their school of modern Philosophy? Oh, what a Philosophy! that after seventeen centuries repeats the blasphemous cries which resounded in the courts of Pilate or Herod against the Holy of Holies!—In vain shall the disciple deny the hatred of Voltaire against the *person* of CHRIST; does he not particularly distinguish Damilaville for that hatred, does he not sign himself *Christ-moque* (Christ-scoffer), just as he terminates his letters by *crush the wretch*, or talks of the *Christicole* superstition. Yet while the Sophister denies the power of Christ, he cannot refuse acknowledging his wisdom, his goodness, and his virtue.

But they may object, that it is not so much at the person as at the *religion* of Christ they aim their blows. Where then is the Philosophy in attacking a religion whose essence is to enforce every virtue, and condemn every vice. Has there ever appeared, either before or since Christ, a Philosopher, who has even formed the idea of a virtue of which this religion does not give the precept or set the example? Is there a crime or a vice which it does not condemn and reprobate? Has the world ever seen a sage impressing such divine doctrines with more powerful motives? Did there ever exist, either before or since Christ, laws more conducive to the interior happiness of families, or to that of empires; laws that better teach men the reciprocal ties of affection; laws, in short, that more peremptorily command us to afford each other mutual assistance? Let the Philosopher appear who pretends to perfect this religion; let him be heard and judged. But should he, like Voltaire and his adepts, only seek to destroy it, let him be comprised in the common epithet of madman and of enemy to humanity.

But it is said to be only at the altars, at the *mysteries* of that religion, and not at the morality of it, that they aim their blows.—In the first place that is not true, as we have already seen and shall see again. Their attack was common on the morality of the Gospel, as well as on the mysteries or the altars of Christianity.—But had it been true, what is there to be found in these mysteries sufficient to render the Christian religion so hateful in the eyes of the Philosopher? Do any of them favor the crimes and faults of men? Do any of them counteract his affection for his neighbour, or render him less attentive to his own duties, less faithful to friendship or gratitude, or less attached to his country? Is there a single mystery which does not elevate the Christian, stimulate his admiration for his God, or spur him on to his own happiness and to the love of his neighbours? The son of God expiring on a cross to open the gates of heaven to man, to teach him what he has to dread, should he, by his crimes, be unfortunate enough to close them again; the bread of angels, given only to those who have purified themselves from the dross of sin; those words pronounced on the man repenting of his crimes, and firmly purposing rather to die than to fall into them anew; the awful sight of a God who comes to judge the living and the dead, to call to him those who have loved, cloathed, and fed their brethren, while he casts into eternal flames the ambitious man, the traitor and the tyrant, the hard-hearted rich, the bad servant, the violator of the nuptial tie; and lastly, all persons who have not loved and helped their neighbour: are all these, I say, mysteries against which the Philosopher should direct his hatred; or can reason, on such a plea, authorise his conspiracy against the religion of the Christians?

Should Voltaire and his disciples refuse to believe these *mysteries*, does it import to them that other people should not equally disbelieve them? Is the Christian more dangerous to them, because he that forbids me to injure my brother is the same God before whom we are both one day to appear in judgment? Is that God less tremendous to the wicked, or less favorable to the just, because on his word we believe him to be one in essence, though three in persons? This hatred of Voltaire must be a phrenzy which the very infidels themselves could not ground on such pretexts. What frantic rage must it be that blinds the Sophisters, when, in contradiction with themselves, they applaud the toleration of the ancient Philosophers, who, though disbelieving the mysteries of Paganism, never attempted to rob the people of their religion; while, on the other hand, they incessantly conspire against Christianity under pretence that it contains mysteries.

Another objection no less extravagant, is that against *Revelation* itself. It is God, they say, whom the Christians declare to have spoken; hence there can be no further liberty of opinion in man on matters of faith; the Sophister of Equaliy and Liberty is then authorised to rise in arms against Christianity and its mysteries. Such are their arguments. But to what lengths does their phrenzy carry them? Voltaire, d'Alembert, and Diderot, conspire to overthrow every Altar, Roman or Lutheran, Calvinist or Anglican, and that in order to avenge the rights of liberty and toleration in matters of faith. What a bedlamite idea is this? Can reason be traced through plots and conspiracies, of which the sole tendency is the overthrow of the universal religion of Europe, under pretence of liberty of worship? We have heard Voltaire invoking Bellerophon and Hercules to his aid, to crush the God of the Christians, and d'Alembert, expressing the frantic wish of seeing a whole nation annihilated for its attachment to that God and his worship. Have we not seen them for half a century past meanly conspiring and using all the artifice of cunning intrigue to rob the world of its religion? And because they utter the empty sounds of EQUALITY, LIBERTY, and TOLERATION, we must mistake their voice for that of Philosophy!—Far be from us the idea of such Philosophy. Terms themselves must have been changed, for this must be extravagance and absurdity; and is not such REASON madness and phrenzy? Such must be the explanation of these words to expound the REASON and PHILOSOPHY of a Voltaire or a d'Alembert conspiring to crush the religion of Christ.

I wished not to have had to mention Frederick again. I reflect that he was a king; but, alas! he is also the royal Sophister. Let us then examine how far philosophy misled him, and whether his wisdom extended beyond the genius of the meanest adept.

Frederick wrote; but why? It is a problem. Was it to impose on the public, or to delude himself? Decide it who can. Probably for both, and he seems to have succeeded. Frederick would sometimes write in favor of toleration, and he was believed to be tolerant. In the *Monthly Review*, October 1794, page 154, we see him cried up as a model of toleration, and the following passage of his works is quoted:

I never will constrain opinions on matters of religion. I dread religious wars above all others. I have been so fortunate, that none of the Sects who reside in my states have ever disturbed civil order. We must leave to the people the objects of their belief, the form of their devotion, their opinions, and *even their prejudices*. It is for this reason that I have tolerated priests and monks, IN SPITE *of Voltaire and d'Alembert, who have* QUARRELLED WITH ME ON THIS HEAD. I have the greatest veneration for all our modern Philosophers; but I am indeed compelled to acknowledge that a general toleration is not the *predominant virtue in these gentlemen.*

From this the editors draw many excellent conclusions, by objecting the wisdom of Frederick's doctrine to the atrocious persecutions and ferocious intoleration of the French Sophisters; but the reader who has seen him stimulate these same Philosophers to overthrow the Altar, *to crush the wretch*; who has seen him trace the plan so much admired by Voltaire as that of a *Great Captain* for the destruction of the priests and monks, in order to attack the bishops, and to compass the overthrow of religion; who has heard him decide that the Antichristian Revolution, which he so *much longed to see*, could only be accomplished *by a superior force*, and that *the sentence* which was definitively *to crush religion was to issue from government*; will that reader, I ask, recognize the toleration of the sophistical monarch! No, he will pass the same judgment on the Sophister which the editors have passed on the disciples of that school. "When such men tell us their object *is to carry into practice all the perfection of theory,* we know not which it ought principally to excite, *our* DISGUST *or* INDIGNATION." But let us revere the Monarch; let us vent our indignation against that frantic Philosophism which involves in darkness the royal adept on his throne, as it did his masters in their sanhedrims and secret academies, eradicating from man every symptom of reason.

If any thing could paint the folly of the masters in stronger colors, it would be that empty pride of the adepts at the period when they look upon the grand object of their conspiracy as accomplished. Religion was mourning over her altars overthrown, her temples profaned when Concorcet exalting the triumph of Voltaire, exclaims:

> Here at length it is permitted openly to proclaim the right, so long disused, of reducing all opinions to the standard of *our own reason*; that is to say, to employ, in order to arrive at the truth, the only *implement* that has been given us to recognize it. Man learns with a certain pride, that he is not designed by nature to believe on the affirmation of others; and the superstitions of antiquity, the degradation of reason in the phrenzy of a supernatural faith, are vanished from society as they were from Philosophy.[3]

---

3 *Sketch on the Progress of Mind,* epoch 9.

Condorcet, when writing these words, no doubt meant to describe the triumph of reason over revelation and over the whole Christian religion. The adepts applaud, and, like him, believe in the pretended triumph of reason. But it had not less cause than religion to mourn over such triumphs. Was it then to reinstate man in his right of bringing his opinions to the test *of reason*, that the Sophisters had with unrelenting fury conspired against the religion of Christ? What could they have intended by this test? Was it to exercise the right of only believing what their reason, when convinced, invited them to believe? If so, where the necessity of conspiring? Does the religion of Christ command man to believe what his enlightened reason does not induce him to believe? Is it not to convince our reason that Christianity surrounded itself with incontestable proofs; that Christ and his Apostles wrought numberless miracles; that religion has preserved its records, and that her pastors invite the Christian to the spirit of research, that he may know what has been proved and what he ought to believe; that her apostles formally declare, that *his faith, his submission should be reasonable* (*rationabile obsequium vestrum*)? And can the Sophister hence infer, that conspiracies and the darkest plots are necessary to vindicate the rights of reason believing in religion? a religion whose God is the God of reason; whose tenets are the tenets of reason; whose rights are the rights of reason rejecting Sophistry and false prejudices; but whose duty is to believe, from the numerous proofs of the power, of the sanctity, of the wisdom and sublimity of the God who speaks, and on the authenticity of his word.

If by the rights of reason the Sophister means the right of only believing what his reason can conceive, and that ceases to be myterious, then these rights of reason must truly border on phrensy. The Sophister is no longer to believe in the light of the day nor the darkness of the night, till fight and its action on man shall cease to be a mystery; no longer shall he believe in the oak towering over the forest, raised from an acorn; nor in the humble flower glowing in the brightest colors; no longer shall he believe in man, succeeding from generation to generation; nature shall be denied, and his own existence remain a doubt, until all is clearly conceived by his reason, and the veil of mystery spread over these various objects shall be rent asunder.—Thus to attain the honors of infidelity, he submits to the garb of folly.

How different is the language of the real sage! His reason declares that objects once proved are to be believed, however mysterious they may be, under the penalty of absurdity; for then they are believed to exist because their existence is demonstrated, and not, as the Sophister would pretend, because their nature is inconceivable.

But another right, equally inconceivable and triumphantly inculcated by Condorcet, is that of being reduced *in order to arrive at truth, to the only implement that has been given us to distinguish it!* If then nature has left me in the dark on objects of the greatest importance, on my future state, on the means of avoiding a destiny I dread, or of obtaining the lot I desire, the man who shall dissipate the mist with which I am surrounded, will have robbed me of my rights? Why did he not say that the right of the blind man is also to keep to the only instrument nature had given him, and that it would be encroaching on his rights if he that has eyes should attempt to lead him? Why did he not conclude that the blind man had also learned with a *sort of pride* that nature had never designed that he should believe in light on the assertion of another.—What philosophic pride is that of the Sophister! His reason is degraded by a *supernatural faith!*—Christianity, he thinks, has debased his reason by raising it above the sphere of this world; he thinks that the God of the Christians has vilified man by explaining to him his eternal destiny, and leaving him the memory of his miracles as a proof of his word.—Such a pretense was the grand plea for the Antichristian Conspiracy, and dared they invoke the name of reason? Were they believed to be Philosophers? And do many yet labor under this error?—But let us return to their masters, to Voltaire, d'Alembert and Diderot; let us show to the adepts the unfortunate dupes of ignorance also decorated with the title of Philosophers.—To accomplish this, it will only be necessary to point out the most formal avowals and mutual confidences of these pretended Philosophers.

Does God exist, or does he not?—Have I a soul to save, or have I not?—Is this life to be entirely spent for my present interest?—Am I to believe in a future state?—Is this God, this soul, and this future state what I am told; or am I to believe quite another thing?—Such certainly are the elementary questions of true science, of Philosophy the most apposite to the happiness of man both in itself and in its consequences. On questions of such importance, what do these assuming sages reply, what are their mutual answers to each other, at the very time they are conspiring against Christ? Has not the reader seen their letters, and their own expressions? Did not these men, who pretended to the empire of knowledge, formally and repeatedly declare that they were unable even to form an opinion on any of these questions? Voltaire, consulted by the citizen or by the prince, consults d'Alembert in his turn, whether there is a God, whether he has a soul; and a *non liquet* (I do not know), is the answer he receives—These must be strange Philosophers indeed, uncertain on the very principles of Philosophy. How can they assume the title of rulers of reason, who are ignorant of that science on which the morals, principles and basis of society rest; on which the duties of man, of the father of a family and of the citizen, of the prince and of the subject, on which, in short, their conduct and happiness entirely depend? What can be their science on man if they are perfectly ignorant of his nature? What can be their doctrine on his duties, on his grand concerns, if they are ignorant of his future destiny? What is that Philosophy which barely tells me that I am ever to be in the dark with regard to those objects which most concern me and those with whom I am to live?

We have seen d'Alembert, in order to conceal his ignorance, absurdly excusing it by answering, that it could be of little concern to man, not to be able to solve these questions on the soul, on God, or on a future state. We have seen Voltaire declaring that nothing was known of these first principles, yet owning that uncertainty was a disagreeable state, but pleading this uncertainty itself, he adds, that certainty is a ridiculous state and that of a quack. Thus because the former is ignorant on these questions, it can little import man to know whether his concerns extend no further than this mortal life, or whether a happy or an unhappy eternity is to be his fate. Because the latter is equally ignorant, though more unhappy in his ignorance, man is to despise whoever shall pretend to dispel his doubts; Christ and his Apostles are to be treated with ridicule, and certainty shall be the doctrine of a Quack!—This cannot be ignorance alone; it must be pride and folly. What! Man is to be buried in darkness, because the jealous eye of the Sophister is dazzled with the light.

Hatred, jealousy, and destruction, contain the whole science of these pretended sages. Hate the of depravity mistaken for virtue.

Gospel, calumniate its author, overthrow his altars, and your science will be that of the modern Philosopher. Profess yourself a Deist, an Atheist, a Sceptic, a Spinosist, in short, whatever you please; deny or affirm, set up a doctrine or a worship in opposition to the religion of Christ, or set up none, that is not what either the Sect or Voltaire himself requires to constitute a modern Philospher. When asked what doctrine he wished to substitute to that of Christ, did he not think himself authorised to answer, I have delivered them from the physicians (he called the clergy physicians), what farther service do they require? Require! have you not infected them with the plague? Have you not unbridled every passion? And what remedies have you left them? In vain were it for us to challenge Voltaire and his panegyrist Condorcet, they will not answer.—No; follow their example; declare all religious truths to be erroneous, false, or popular prejudices, to be superstition and fanaticism; glory in destruction, little troubling yourself with substituting science for ignorance, or truth for error. To have destroyed will suffice; and for that you shall be entitled to the high-sounding name of a modern Philosopher.

At this rate, the reader's surprise at the numerous tribe of Philosophers to be found in every rank, of all ages and sexes, must cease. But at such a rate can an honest man pride himself in the title of Philosopher: such a science is, alas! but too easily acquired. It is as yet a problem why Voltaire, on

his outset, seemed to confine his views to the higher classes, to kings, nobles and the rich, why he
should have excluded *beggars and the rabble.* On
seeing the guests smile at the blasphemies uttered
at table, will not the footman soon equal his master in the Philosophic science, will he not also learn
to scoff at the pontiff and the pastor, at the altar
and the gospel? Will not the butchering Marseil-
lais, like Condorcet, glory in having cast off those
vulgar prejudices, when in the bloody murders
of September he overthrows the altar and stains
its steps with the blood of its priests and pontiffs.
Like Voltaire, will he not style this the Age of Reason, and of enlightened Philosophy: harangue the
vilest of the populace; tell them that the priests
are imposing on them, that hell is of their invention; that the time is come to throw off the yoke
of fanaticism and superstition, and to assert the
liberty of their reason; and in a few minutes, the
ignorant plough-boy will rival, in Philosophic science, the most learned of the adepts. The language
may vary, but the science will be the same. They
will hate with the adept, and will destroy what he
wished to crush. The more ignorant and ferocious
they are, the more easily shall they adopt your hatred, which constitutes the whole of this sophisticated science.

If adepts are sought for in another line, it is easy
to increase their numbers, but without adding to
the science of the Sect. Thus let the daughter of
Necker but find some impertinent sarcasm of hers

against the Gospel taken for wit by d'Alembert, and she immediately becomes as Philosophic as he and as void of religious prejudices as sister Guillemetta. It had astonished many to see the numbers of young fops who were already styled Philosophers, at so early an age they scarcely had had time to read any thing except a few impious pamphlets. But this age of enlightened Philosophy can no longer be a subject of surprise.

What! shall every wanton coquette partake of this Philosophy; shall every husband or wife who scoffs at conjugal fidelity; shall every son who throws aside all sentiments of duty, and denies the authority of a parent; shall they all be styled Philosophers? The courtier destitute of morals, or the man who is a slave to, and imprudently quits all control over his passions, these also will glory in the name of Philosophers! Voltaire, in spite of all their vices, rejects none of these from his school, provided they have the necessary requisites of scoffing at the mysteries, of insulting the priesthood, and hating the God of the gospel. Certainly these cannot be simply the dupes of ignorance mistaken for science. No; these must be the children of corruption substituted for the school of virtue. That folly, that frantic rage which consumes Voltaire, conspiring against his God, or setting heaven at defiance, when he writes to d'Alembert, *Twenty years more, and God will be in a pretty plight*; or when he repeatedly writes to Damilaville, *Crush, crush the wretch*; that, I say, may be more worthy of pity than of blame. Yes, Voltaire in the phrensy of his rage is to be pitied. That multitude of adepts, of noblemen, ministers, and citizens, are to be excused, who, without having the least idea of Philosophy, have believed themselves Philosophers, misled by those impious Sophisters. I will not even ask them since when could the bare title of Philosopher, assumed by Frederick and Voltaire, suffice to constitute them masters in a science of which they openly professed their ignorance and contempt: I will not tell them, that if Frederick, consummate in the art of war, could form warriors; that if Voltaire, rivalling Corneille, could give lessons to the poet, they were nevertheless both equally ignorant in point of religion. I will not say to them, that this latter is a science, like all others, requiring great application and study in order to excel; that it was absurd to look for masters and teachers in men who blasphemed what they neither understood nor sought to understand; in men who, often stammering out a petty sophism which they deemed unanswerable, resembled the child, who dashes the watch on the ground because the spring is hidden from him. Such would be the reflexions of common sense, which should have rendered the school of the Sophisters at least suspected, if not absurd and ridiculous to its adepts; when Frederick combats the Sorbonne, or Voltaire St. Thomas; when d'Alembert attacks St. Augustin, or Sister Guillemetta St. Paul.

It is possible, that all these great Sophisters, debating on divinity, religion, and tenets, may have been mistaken by the ignorant adepts for learned doctors. But when the whole school, treating of morality and virtue, pretend to direct them solely by the rules of natural religion, the very shadow of a pretext for their delusion disappears. Casting an eye on the Sect, could they perceive a single adept who, under the direction of Voltaire or d'Alembert, had quitted his religion to become a better father or a better son, a better husband or a better man; in short more virtuous! Would not the simple reflexion have sufficed, that this pretended Philosphy of virtue had regularly been the refuge of all those men who were publicly known to scoff at every duty, at all morality: that when the friends to religion reproached them with the dissoluteness of their morals, as constantly answered with a sort of sneer, "Such reproaches may do for men who have not as yet shaken off the prejudices of the Gospel; but we are Philosphers, and we know what to believe!!"

It would be impossible to dissemble that every vice was cloaked under such a Philosophy; the faithless wife; the profligate youth; the man practising every art, whether just or unjust, to attain his ends; even to the loose women, whose characters were openly disparaged; all decorated themselves with the high-sounding name of Modern Philosophers. None would have dared to justify their criminal conduct by answering,—I am a Christian,—I believe in the Gospel.—Let not the chiefs charge the error and ignorance on the disciples. The adept knew but too well that nothing but the name of virtue remained in the school of the Sophisters; that the greater progress he made in their science, the more he adopted their principles, by setting at defiance the reproach of the virtuous man, and by smothering the cries of his own conscience. It is true, they had not barefacedly blasphemed the morality of the Gospel; but they had erased from their code all those virtues *which religion maintains to be descended from heaven.* He had seen the long list of those which they called *sterile and imaginary virtues, or virtues of prejudice*; he had seen erased from their code all the list of real virtues, such as modesty and continence, conjugal fidelity and filial piety, gratitude, and forgiveness of injuries, disinterestedness, even probity itself.[4] To these virtues they had substituted ambition, pride, vain glory, the pleasures, and the passions. Their morality acknowledged no other virtue than that *which is advantageous*; nor vice but that *which is hurtful* in this world; and virtue is declared to be but an *idle dream* if the virtuous man is unhappy. Personal interest is laid down as the sole principle of all Philosophic virtues; they sometimes indeed name *beneficence* as one; but that is merely as an excuse to dispense them from the practice of every other virtue. *Friend, do good to us, and we will overlook every thing else,* is the express doctrine

---

4   See the original texts quoted in the *Helvian Letters*, vol. 5.

of Voltaire:[5] but that was not all. It was necesssary to bring the adepts to doubt even of the existence of virtue, to doubt whether in morality there existed a right and wrong, and it was to such a question that Voltaire did not blush to answer, *non liquet* (it is not known).[6] As a further step, they were to decide that all that is called "perfection, imperfection, righteousness, wickedness, goodness, falsehood, wisdom, and folly, only differed from each other by their sensations of pleasure or pain;"[7] that "the more the Philosopher examined the nature of things, the less he dared to assert that it depended any more on man to be pusillanimous, choleric, vicious, or voluptuous, than it did to be squint-eyed, hump-backed or lame."[8] Such were the lessons of the conspiring Sophisters; and can it be believed that such lessons could be mistaken for those of virtue and Philosophy?

Had the adept been certain as to the existence of vice and virtue, of what consequence would this distinction have been to him, when his masters teach him, that man is born for happiness, and that the latter consists *in pleasure, or the absence of pain;*[9] when laying aside all solicitude for his soul, he is taught that *the motto of the wise man*

5   Fragments on divers subjects. Art. Virtue.

6   *Philosophical Dictionary*, Art. TOUT EST BIEN.

7   Let. of Thrasybulus.

8   Encyclopedia, Geneva edition, Art, Vice.

9   Encyclopedia, Art. HAPPINESS, and Preface.

ought to be to watch over his body;[10] or that it is by *pleasure* that God *stimulates to virtue.*[11] Such are the lessons taught by Voltaire, Diderot and d'Alembert, the chiefs of the conspirators.

What motives to virtue did these chiefs suggest to their adepts when they declared that a God neither *regards their virtue nor their vices, that the fear of this God is an absolute folly!* or when, wishing to stifle all remorse of conscience, they tell them, that "the man void of fear is above the laws— That a bad action, when useful, can be committed without remorse—That remorse is no other than the fear of men and of their laws;" or again, when (carrying their doctrine beyond all absurdity) they on one side assert the liberty of opinions in order to leave man free to choose the false, while, on the other hand they destroy in him all liberty of action to smother all symptoms of remorse.[12]

Such was the doctrine of the Sophisters. In vain would they attempt to deny it; all their writings are full of it, and particularly those which they most extolled as their principal master-pieces. What could have been the conduct of these great Philosophers had they undertaken to draw up a code of villainy and depravity? What more could be required to demonstrate to the world that this pretended age of Philosophy was no other than that of vice, than that of wickness organized into principles and pre-

---

10   D'Alembert on the Elements of Philosophy, No. 5.

11   Voltaire's *Discourse on Happiness.*

12   See their texts quoted in the *Helvian Letters*, vol. 3.

cepts for the use of the abandoned, to whom they might be advantageous.

The only plea that can be left to the numbers of adepts who styled themselves Philosophers, in alleviation of their criminality, is the amazing constancy and artfulness which it required from the chiefs to propagate their principles, and ensure the success of their conspiracy.

But with these artifices, these intrigues, what was their Philosophy? Let us suppose that during the life-time of Voltaire, of Frederick, or of d'Alembert, and before depravity had attained to such a height, the frequent and repeated orders given to the conspirators of *strike, but hide your hand*, had been known; let us suppose that the people had been acquainted with all the tortuous means secretly used to seduce them; would any one then have traced the actions of the Philosopher in such dark hypocrisy, in such perpetual dissimulation, or in the ambushes which were their only means of success?

At the time when d'Alembert and Condorcet, Diderot, Helvétius and Turgot, held their sittings at the Hotel d'Holbach under the name of Œconomists, and under the pretence of meditating on the happiness of the people, had it been known by that same people, that they were only plotting against the altars of the God whom it adored; had it been known that those teachers, who had been appointed to instruct the rising generation, were only the impious emissaries of d'Alembert, sent to corrupt its morals; that all those hawkers of books sold at so low a rate were the agents of the secret academy, employed to circulate its poisons from towns to villages, and thence to the poorest cottages; would such means, I ask, have entitled the Sect to that respect and veneration which it has usurped? Their wicked plots once detected, could such sages have sufficed to have given to the century they lived in the appellation of the Philosophic Age? No:—without doubt, horror would have succeeded to this admiration; and if the laws had remained silent, public indignation would have avenged Philosophy of the infamous plots carried on under the cloak of its name.

Let then this age of pretended Philosophy cast off the delusion under which it has been led away, a delusion arising perhaps more from its own vices and corruption than from the arts of the conspirators; let it blush and repent. That unpolished multitude, confessing its inexperience in the ways of the Sophisters, whom instinctive virtue so long preserved from the arts of seduction, may be excusable; but let those thousand of adepts, who are to be found in the courts and palaces of the great, in the seats of literature, let them reflect on and scrutinize their past conduct. In adopting impiety they believed themselves Philosphers.—In throwing off the yoke of the Gospel, and laying aside its virtues rather than its mysteries, they mistook the empty sounds of *prejudice* and *superstition*, perpetually repeated by the Sophisters, for profound reasoning. They were ignorant that the word prejudice only signifies an opinion void of proofs; and that they themselves had become slaves to prejudice, by casting off a religion of which they gloried in not having studied the proofs, while they continued to read all the calumnies that its enemies could compile against it. Let them seek still further claims to this Philosophy in their own hearts. Was it not to a lukewarm weariness for the virtues of the Gospel that they were indebted for their admiration of the Conspirators? Was it not for the love of their passions which made them a prey to infidelity, far more than all the intrigues and ambushes of the Sophisters? It is much to be feared, that that man is already wicked who makes himself so happy and glories so much in following the apostles of wickedness; or small indeed must have been his portion of Philosophy, if such duplicity, such meanness, and such conspiracies, could have been mistaken for wisdom or virtue.

Whatever may have been the causes, it was ordained, that an age duped by the intrigues and conspiracies of impiety should glory in styling itself the *Age of Philosophy*. It was ordained that an age, a dupe to the frantic rage of impiety substituted to reason; a dupe to the oaths of hatred and the wish of crushing all religion, mistaken for toleration, for religious Equality and Liberty; to ignorance for science; to depravity for virtue; a dupe, in short, to all the intrigues and plots of the most profound wickedness mistaken for the proceedings and means of wisdom; it was ordained, I say, that this *Age of Philosophy* should also be a dupe to the plots of the rebellious Sophisters, mistaken for the love of society and the basis of public happiness.

The Conspiracy against the Altar, the hatred sworn by the chiefs against their God, were not the only legacies bequeathed by the chiefs to this school of modern Philosophy. Voltaire was the father of the Sophisters of Impiety, and before his death he becomes the chief of the Sophisters of Rebellion. He had said to his first adepts. Let us crush the Altar, and let not a single altar nor a single worshipper be left to the God of Christians; and his school soon resounded with the cry of, *Let us crush the sceptre*, and let not a single throne, nor a single subject, be left to the kings of the earth! It was from the mutual co-operation and success of these two schools, that the revolution was to be generated in France, which, grasping the hatchet, was at the same time to destroy the altar of the living God, and imbue its steps with the blood of its pontiffs; to overturn the throne, and strike off the head of the unfortunate Louis XVI.; menacing all the altars of Christendom, all the kings of the earth, with a similar fate. To the plots contrived under the veil of Equality and Liberty *applied to religion*, and of religious toleration, are to succeed those begotten under the veil of political Equality and Liberty. The mysteries of the second conspiracy of the *Sophisters of Rebellion*, combining with those of Impiety, in order to generate the modern Jacobins, will be the object of the Second Part of these Memoirs.

END OF THE FIRST PART.

Index.

C

W

Y

Z

www.ingramcontent.com/pod-product-compliance
Lightning Source LLC
Chambersburg PA
CBHW030944150426
42812CB00072B/3433/J